THE OSCAR WILDE FILE

OSCAR WILDE AT THE TIME OF THE TRIALS

By Count Henri de Toulouse-Lautrec

(From the portrait in the the collection of Mr. Conrad Lester in
Los Angeles, California, U.S.A.)

THE OSCAR WILDE FILE

Compiled by

JONATHAN GOODMAN

Allison & Busby
Published by W. H. Allen & Co Plc

For Fred and Dor Pemberton

Compiler's Note

Only rarely do the reprints and facsimiles of journal material contained herein consist of the entirety of what was originally printed; the usual reason for excision was to reduce repetition. In some cases, I have transposed items appearing on a single page of a journal.

My special thanks go to Langley Iddins, designer of this book. I am grateful to the following, who have helped in particular ways: Albert Borowitz; Richard Boyd-Carpenter; Sarah Brown, of The National Monuments Record; Mick Etridge, of the Blackall Cooke & Dew photographic studio, Great Portland Street, London; Joe Gaute; Bob Scoales, Reference Librarian, Ealing Central Library; Richard Whittington-Egan; the respective Press Officers of Liberty & Co Ltd and the Savoy Hotel.

Sources of unattributed material:

Page 6: the drawing of the Theatre Royal, Haymarket, by Nick Charlesworth, is taken, by permission, from one of a series of postcards published by the Badger Press, West Wilts Trading Estate, Westbury, Wiltshire. 9: the quotation is from Alison Adburgham's book, *Liberty's: A Biography of a Shop*, Allen & Unwin, London, 1975. 10: the quotation is from Vyvyan Holland's book, *Oscar Wilde and His World*, Thames & Hudson, 1960. 11: the quotation is from Philip Collins's essay, '"Agglomerating Dollars with Prodigious Rapidity": British Pioneers on the American Lecture Circuit', in *Victorian Literature and Society: Essays Presented to*

Richard D. Altick, Ohio State University Press, 1984. 16: the quotation is from *The Life of Lord Carson*, Volume One, by Edward Marjoribanks, Gollancz, London, 1932. 88 and 132: the translation of items in *Le Figaro* are by Lindy Foord. 101: the cover of the catalogue is reproduced by courtesy of John Latimer Smith. 143: the quotation in the second column is from *Selected Letters of Oscar Wilde*, edited by Sir Rupert Hart-Davis, Oxford University Press, 1979. 156/7: the photographs of scenes in *The Trials of Oscar Wilde* are reproduced by courtesy of John Fraser.

An Allison & Busby Book
Published in 1988 by
W. H. Allen & Co Plc
44 Hill Street, London W1X 8LB

British Library Cataloguing in Publication Data

Goodman, Jonathan
 The Oscar Wilde file.
 1. Wilde, Oscar — Biography 2. Authors,
 Irish — 19 century — Biography
 I. Title
 828'.809   PR5823

 ISBN 0-85031-693-6

Typeset by Ann Buchan (Typesetters)
Printed and bound in Great Britain by
Adlard and Son Limited,
Dorking, Surrey, and Letchworth, Hertfordshire

It is 1895; the Spring of that year.

Cartographic publishers are amending maps of the Dark Continent, now that the British South Africa Company has chosen to honour its founder, the itinerant Cecil Rhodes, by calling its territory south of the Zambesi River 'Rhodesia'. How is one meant to pronounce that? Presumably as *Rhodes-ia.* Mr. Rhodes, who is presently premier of the Cape Colony ('dictator of all South Africa', in the opinion of recalcitrant Boers – who, sooner rather than later, we shall, by jingo, need to subjugate), is in England for discussions with, *inter alios*, members of Lord Rosebery's disunited cabinet and, at Windsor, our blessed Queen Victoria (long more than fifty-eight years may She reign over us!), who has admitted him to Her privy council. Seeming to some to be an act of vicarious lèse-majesté, the Travellers' Club has blackballed Mr. Rhodes: but never mind – he has been elected, presumably at his wish, to the Athenaeum.

Another new land, of Ruritania, does not concern cartographers, for, though it has a stronger reality in many persons' minds than does Rhodesia, it is a fictive place: the setting of a remarkably popular tale of derring-do entitled *The Prisoner of Zenda,* ascribed to 'Anthony Hope' but actually a month's work, at the rate of two chapters per diem, of a lawyer of Middle Temple called Anthony Hope Hawkins – a first cousin of Kenneth Grahame, a senior clerk at the Bank of England whose delicate essays about childhood, many originally published in *The Yellow Book*, are relished by the poet of 'The Pines' at Putney, Algernon Charles Swinburne, his (shall we say?) chaperone, Theodore Watts-Dunton, and, diverse from that couple, Theodore

Roosevelt, the newly-appointed president of the board of police commissioners of New York. (Mr. Roosevelt, by the bye, is tipped as a future president of the States of America, said to have been re-United for some thirty years, and now presided over by Grover Cleveland – who, should he expire while in office, will be succeeded by a man with the surely unrepeatable name of Adlai E. Stevenson.) Considering that Joseph Conrad was born in Poland, as Teodor Josef Konrad Korzeniowski, and that he has spent all but the past year of the last twenty as a merchant mariner, his first novel, *Almayer's Folly,* just published by T. Fisher Unwin, is not at all bad; his ability to write English with little trace of an accent may be an inheritance from his father, who, according to literary-gossip columnists, translated the entire works of Shakespeare into Polish. Among new books by native authors are H.G. Wells's *The Time Machine,* the idea of which is quite as incredible as anything from the *plume* of M. Jules Verne; the second of Rudyard Kipling's *Jungle Books*; *Esther Waters* by George Moore. In 1892, Stephen Crane, an American newspaper reporter in the year of his majority, published at his own expense a novel called *Maggie: A Girl of the Streets*; his second novel, *The Red Badge of Courage,* which speaks, seemingly intimately, of his country's civil war, augurs of greatness, so long as he is able to resist the Demon Rum. Last year, *Punch's* cartoonist George du Maurier scored a literary success with *Trilby,* a novel based on the premiss that hypnotism can induce a young girl to sing like Nellie Melba (who, currently appearing at Covent Garden, has had an ice-cream concoction named after her by Auguste Escoffier, the chef at the

◄ St. James's Theatre.

THE CAMBERWELL THEATRE

NEW NATIONAL STANDARD THEATRE SHOREDITCH.

SOLE PROPRIETOR.   MR JOHN DOUGLASS

ACKNOWLEDGED BY THE PRESS TO BE THE LARGEST & MOST ELEGANT THEATRE IN EUROPE

OPEN EVERY EVENING

THEATRE ROYAL HAYMARKET

THEATRE METROPOLE, CAMBERWELL.
J. B. Mulholland, Sole Owner and Manager.

THE NEW THEATRE THEATRE THEATRE THEATRE THEATRE THEATRE METROPOLE. METROPOLE. METROPOLE. METROPOLE. METROPOLE. METROPOLE.

This Beautiful and Luxurious Theatre has repeatedly accommodated an audience of over 2,000 persons.

"This commodious theatre."—*The Times.*

Savoy Hotel, built five years ago by the impresario Richard D'Oyly Carte from the proceeds of Messrs Gilbert & Sullivan's comic operas); now two Viennese physicians, Sigmund Freud and Josef Breuer, have written a book explaining how they use hypnosis in the treatment of hysteria, but neglecting to mention how they treat patients suffering from hypnosis. Though this is a poor period for verse, let alone poetry, Frank Gelett Burgess's purple-cow jingle delights so multitudinously that any attempt to recite it is the cue for a chorus:

> I never saw a Purple Cow,
> I never hope to see one;
> But I can tell you, anyhow,
> I'd rather see than be one.

If any fisherman's tale can be credited, then quite as queer as Mr Burgess's cow is – or rather, was – the cod, said to be over six feet tall and weighing more than 210 pounds, caught off the coast of Massachusetts. One wonders – thinking the while of a study of children in a part of the East End of London which found that, for four out of five, only four meals of the weekly twenty-one consist of more than bread – how many portions dissection of the cod provided. And one wonders – thinking the while of Professor Wilbur Atwater's measurement, based on the common calorie, of the energy provided by different sorts of food – how many of the bread-dependent urchins will have the strength to survive into the twentieth century. And, speaking of a different sort of survival, will Joseph Lyons's teashop at 213 Piccadilly attract sufficient custom to make it pay?

What are the chances for the clever young engineer Frederick Lanchester, who, having only last year started up on his own, is seeking venturesome buyers for his four-wheeled gasoline-propelled automobile, the first of its kind from a British firm? And for Herbert Austin – at twenty-nine, two years older than Lanchester – who has designed a motor-car with an air-cooled engine for the Wolseley Sheep Shearing Machine Company? Apropos of automobiles, we lag behind both the French (Peugot Frères are building a four-horsepower delivery vehicle that will be capable, they reckon, of carrying half a ton at 9½ miles per hour; André and Edouard Michelin have made the first pneumatic tyres for motor-cars) and

the Prussians (a Benz omnibus with a single-cylinder rear engine, spacious enough for eight slim passengers, is in service; Rudolf Diesel has invented an engine that operates on a petroleum fuel less refined, and so cheaper, than gasoline).

At least we can claim that the most popular song of the day is part-British, since its words, starting, 'Casey would waltz with a strawberry blonde / And the band played – on,' were written by the actor Charles Ward, who emigrated to America from these shores. His emigration must reflect on his histrionic talent, for the British theatre is – as it always has been, always will be – supreme. There is widespread jubilation that, at long last, an actor – no, not *an* actor but *the* actor: Henry Irving, 'the guv'nor' of the Lyceum – has been knighted. In the evening of the day when the Birthday Honours were announced, he was playing Don Quixote. The audience tittered when he rasped the line, 'Knighthood sits like a halo round my head,' and cheered and clapped at the Housekeeper's reply: 'But Master, you have never been knighted.'

Among the early West End successes of the year are *The Shop Girl* at the Gaiety, just across Aldwych from the Lyceum, *An Artist's Model* at Daly's, in Leicester Square, and *An Ideal Husband*, which opened at the Haymarket on 3 January, in the presence of His Royal Highness, the Prince of Wales.

Oscar Wilde, author of the last-mentioned play, is all of a sudden astoundingly successful. For consider: a revival of his *Lady Windermere's Fan* – first produced, by George Alexander at the St. James's, in 1892 – is in rehearsal for presentation at the Metropole, a theatre with more than 2,000 seats that has lately opened in the South London district of Camberwell, on 11 February. A revival of his *A Woman of No Importance* – first produced, by Beerbohm Tree at the Haymarket, in 1893, and subsequently played over 700 times by companies touring the provinces – is announced as a forthcoming attraction at the vast Standard, in that eastern part of the capital called Shoreditch. And his 'trivial comedy for serious people', *The Importance of Being Earnest*, will be presented for the first time – by George Alexander at the St. James's – on Saint Valentine's Day, which this years falls upon a Thursday. . . .

8

The caricature by 'Ape' (Carlo Pellegrini) on the facing page is from *Vanity Fair*, 24 May 1884. Under nom-de-plume of 'Jehu Junior', Thomas Gibson Bowles, the founder and editor of the magazine, summarised the subject's antecedents as follows:

Oscar, the younger son of the late Sir William Wilde, archaeologist, traveller, and Queen's Surgeon in Ireland, won the Berkeley Medal for Greek in Trinity College, Dublin, and a Scholarship. Migrating to Magdalene College, Oxford, he took two 'Firsts' and 'the Newdigate' [the chief prize for poetry at the University]. He went wandering in Greece; and, full of a Neo-Hellenic spirit, came back to invade social London. He invented the aesthetic movement. He preached the doctrine of possible culture in external things. He got brilliantly laughed at. . .

. . .MOST OFTEN, IN PUNCH:

"O, I feel just as happy as a bright Sunflower!"
Lays of Christy Minstrelsy.
(Punch's Fancy Portraits No. 37; June, 1881)

Part of a verse about the Grosvenor Gallery (May, 1881):

The haunt of the very aesthetic,
  Here comes the supremely intense,
The long-haired and hyper-poetic,
  Whose sound is mistaken for sense.
And many a maiden will mutter,
  When Oscar looms large on her sight,
'He's quite too consummately utter,
  As well as too utterly quite.'

"O.W."

Alison Adburgham writes:

[In 1881] F.C. Burnand, then editor of *Punch*, wrote a comedy named *The Colonel* – in which the character of Lambert Stryke, played by Beerbohm Tree, satirised Wilde. It was the play in which the principal lady breathes the immortal words: 'There is so much to be learned from a teapot.'

9

While *The Colonel* was still running, Gilbert and Sullivan's *Patience, or Bunthorne's Bride* was produced at the Opéra Comique in London, first performance April 23, 1881. Durward Lely played Bunthorne, the fleshly poet in rivalry with the idyllic poet Archibald Grosvenor for the love of the village milkmaid, Patience... Durward Lely's appearance was that of [the expatriate American artist, James McNeill] Whistler, complete with his monocle. Archibald Grosvenor was unmistakeably Oscar Wilde. . . .

> Though the Philistine may jostle,
>   you will rank as an apostle in
>   the high aesthetic band,
> If you walk down Piccadilly with
>   a poppy or a lily in your
>   mediaeval hand.

Wilde had done just that, attired in a loose shirt with Byron collar and large knotted green tie, velvet knee-breeches, silk stockings and velvet beret. He was taking a madonna lily in homage to the fashionable beauty, Lillie Langtry.

"The Idyllic Poet"
Mr. Barrington

Illustration to the review of *Patience* in the Illustrated Sporting and Dramatic News, April 1881.

THE SIX-MARK TEA-POT
Aesthetic Bridegroom. "IT IS QUITE CONSUMMATE, IS IT NOT?"
Intense Bride. "IT IS, INDEED! OH, ALGERNON, LET US LIVE UP TO IT!"

(By George du Maurier. *Punch,* October, 1880)

Vyvyan Holland writes:

[Early in 1881] at the request of Miss Mary Anderson, the New York actress, he began to write the five-act tragedy which was afterwards to develop into *The Duchess of Padua*. And while negotiations concerning this play were proceeding, he received an offer to go on a lecture tour in America from Colonel F.W. Morse, business manager of Richard D'Oyly Carte, who produced all the Gilbert and Sullivan operettas. . . .

Wilde left England in the *Arizona* on 24th December 1881, and arrived in New York on 2nd

January 1882, declaring that he was 'disappointed in the tame Atlantic'. His ship arrived too late to pass quarantine before sundown, but he was immediately besieged by a group of hostile reporters, anxious to do their worst for 'the poet and apostle of English aestheticism'.

New York Tribune, 3 January 1882

The most striking thing about the poet's appearance is his height, which is several inches over six feet, and the next thing to attract attention is his hair, which is of a dark brown colour, and falls down upon his shoulders. . . . When he laughs his lips part widely and show a shining row of upper teeth, which are superlatively white. The complexion, instead of being of the rosy hue so common in Englishmen, is so utterly devoid of colour that it can only be said to resemble putty. His eyes are blue, or a light grey, and instead of being 'dreamy', as some of his admirers have imagined them to be, they are bright and quick – not at all like those of one given to perpetual musing on the ineffably beautiful and true. Instead of having a small delicate hand, only fit to caress a lily, his fingers are long and when doubled up would form a fist, that would hit a hard knock, should an occasion arise for the owner to descend to that kind of argument. . . . One of the peculiarities of his speech is that he accents almost at regular intervals without regard to the sense, perhaps as a result of an effort to be rhythmic in conversation as well as in verse.

Philip Collins writes:

. . . Oscar Wilde – only twenty-seven when he toured America in 1882 – could gleefully report, within days of his arrival: 'I am torn to bits by Society. Immense receptions, wonderful dinners, crowds wait for my carriage. . . . I have a sort of triumphal progress, live like a young sybarite, travel like a young god.' The entertainment he received, even out in the Far West, was delicious,

An American lampooning pamphlet.

including such exotic items as a banquet down a silver mine. . . . No wonder that on his return home he found Europe cold and hard after these intoxicating adventures – despite his famous quip, on hearing that Rossetti had given some importunate hanger-on enough money to go to America, 'Of course, if one had enough money to go to America, one would not go.' Wilde inevitably had a witticism for, or about, many moments on his tour, beginning with his splendid words to the Customs officer at New York ('I have nothing to declare – except my genius'), and including such unexpected jokes – who would have attributed this chestnut to Oscar? – as the notice found (or so he said) in those silver miners' dancing-saloon: 'Please do not shoot the pianist: he is doing his best.' Though he received, in big Eastern towns, the thousand dollar fee, he spent lavishly and did not bring much money home: but, like many of his compatriots on

From *Frank Leslie's Illustrated Newspaper* (New York),
21 January 1882

anything is better than virtuous obscurity, even one's own name in alternate colours of Albert blue and magenta and six feet high. . . . I feel I have not lived in vain.'

When Oscar Wilde got back to England, he made further money out of his tour by lecturing about the United States. . . .

In August 1883, he returned to New York for the opening of *Vera*, a drama centred around nihilism in Russia which he had written three years before. The production, at the Union Square Theatre, ran for only a week.

NEW YORK HERALD: 'long-drawn dramatic rot'.
NEW YORK TIMES: 'unreal, long-winded and wearisome'.
NEW YORK TRIBUNE: 'foolish'.

Three months later, while lecturing in Dublin, he became engaged to Constance Mary Lloyd, the daughter of the well-known Irish barrister, Horace Lloyd, QC. Constance had first met Wilde in London in 1881. They were married on 29 May 1884 at St. James's Church, Paddington. Following a honeymoon in Paris, they moved into 16 Tite Street, Chelsea, the redecoration of which was paid for from an allowance Constance received from her paternal grandfather. In June 1885, she gave birth to a son, Cyril; a second son, Vyvyan, was born in November 1886.

this trail, he was rewarded too by the excitement and the adulation. It was something, he said, to see one's name placarded in enormous letters: 'printed it is true in those primary colours against which I pass my life protesting, but still it is fame, and

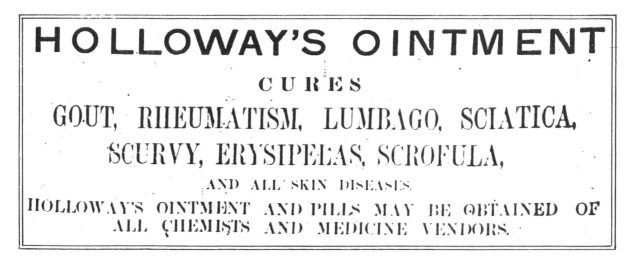

Oscar Wilde, a study in concentration. A drawing by William Speed, 1888

Title-page of the first edition, 1891

Constance Wilde

For two years from 1887, Wilde edited the *Woman's World*. During that time, his book, *The Happy Prince and other Tales*, was published.

His novel, *The Picture of Dorian Gray* – first published in the July 1890 issue of *Lippincott's Monthly Magazine* (New York) – was extensively reviewed. One of the many hostile notices appeared in the *Scots Observer*. Wilde wrote to the editor, W.E. Henley:

. . . Your reviewer, sir, while admitting that the story in question is 'plainly the work of a man of letters,' the work of one who has 'brains, and art, and style,' yet suggests, and apparently in all seriousness, that I have written it in order that it should be read by the most depraved members of the criminal and illiterate classes. Now, sir, I do not

THE PICTVRE OF
DORIAN.GRAY
B.Y
OSCAR
WILDE

WARD LOCK & Co
LONDON NEW YORK
& MELBOURNE

suppose that the criminal and illiterate classes ever read anything except newspapers. They are certainly not likely to be able to understand anything of mine. So let them pass, and on the broad question of why a man of letters writes at all let me say this. The pleasure that one has in creating a work of art is a purely personal pleasure, and it is for the sake of this pleasure that one creates. The artist works with his eye on the object. Nothing else interests him. What people are likely to say does not even occur to him. He is fascinated by what he has in hand. He is indifferent to others. I write because it gives me the greatest possible artistic pleasure to write. If my work pleases the few, I am gratified. If it does not, it causes me no pain. As for the mob, I have no desire to be a popular novelist. It is far too easy. . . .

It was necessary, sir, for the dramatic development of this story to surround Dorian Gray with an atmosphere of moral corruption. Otherwise the story would have had no meaning and the plot no issue. To keep this atmosphere vague and indeterminate and wonderful was the aim of the artist who wrote the story. I claim, sir, that he has succeeded. Each man sees his own sin in Dorian Gray. What Dorian Gray's sins are no one knows. He who finds them has brought them. . . .

Early in 1891, the poet Lionel Johnson, a homosexual, introduced Wilde to Lord Alfred Bruce Douglas, the third son of the Marquis of Queensberry. Wilde was then thirty-six years of age; Lord Alfred – known to his family and friends as Bosie, a contraction of Boysie – was approaching his majority. Educated at Winchester, he was a second-year undergraduate at Magdalen College, Oxford.

Wilde published four books in 1891: in addition to *The Picture Of Dorian Gray*, there was a collection of essays under the title of *Intentions; Lord Arthur Savile's Crime and Other Stories*, and a second collection of fairy tales, called *A House of Pomegranates*. Also, his play *The Duchess of Padua* was staged in New York as *Guido Ferranti*; the production was unsuccessful – as were Wilde's subsequent efforts to persuade Henry Irving to present the play in London.

Top: Lionel Johnson
Above: Oscar Wilde and Lord Alfred Douglas

14

In 1892, shortly after the successful production of *Lady Windermere's Fan*, the Lord Chamberlain refused to license Wilde's play *Salome*, under a rule forbidding the representation of Biblical characters on the stage. Wilde wrote to his friend, the artist Will Rothenstein:

. . .The licenser of plays is nominally the Lord Chamberlain, but really a commonplace official — in the present case a Mr Pigott, who panders to the vulgarity and hypocrisy of the English people, by licensing every low farce and vulgar melodrama. He even allows the stage to be used for the purpose of the caricaturing of the personalities of artists, and at the same moment when he prohibited Salome, *he licensed a burlesque of* Lady Windermere's Fan *in which an actor dressed like me and imitated my voice and manner! ! !*

The 'Captious Critic' of *The Illustrated Sporting and Dramatic News,* 4 June 1892:

"THE POET AND THE PUPPETS"
By Mr. Charles Brookfield

That Mr. Oscar Wilde is open to chaff, those who had to sit out that terribly long talk of his at the Theatrical Fund dinner recently will be the last to dispute. But that any amount of laughing at him is likely to make him better I fear I cannot believe. It appears to me that from the first we have, all of us, gone out of our way to convert Mr. Wilde into a personage, and that he quite appreciates the advantage of the position and does not mean to let us off. For myself I had heard more than enough for one lifetime about Mr. Oscar Wilde long before *The Poet and the Puppets* was produced at the Comedy; and I do not therefore thank Mr. Brookfield for adding to the surfeit. There is too much in the so-called travesty of *Lady Windermere's Fan* which seems to me entirely personal to Mr. Wilde and to those who consider it worth while to be acquainted with lateral opinions, or vagaries of his which do not come into the St. James's piece in any

MR BROOKFIELD
AS
HAMLET BEERBOHM
TREE

Mr NUTCOMBE GOULD

MR S. BANCO

MR PINERO

way. For my own part, for instance, I do not care a fig to be told that Mr. Wilde lives in Tite Street; I am sorry to say that I should not have fretted even if he had never lived at all. . . . Here and there Mr. Brookfield, who certainly writes fluently, has fairly parodied Mr. Wilde's peculiarity in epigram. . . . Mr. Brookfield has written some capital songs for his piece, which Mr. Glover has set to the liveliest and most popular music. These songs, and the excellent imitations by the company of Mr. Wilde and other persons, with which the instructive and controversial portions of the performance are sprinkled, give it a good deal of spirit at intervals and may make it a success. . . . Mr. Brookfield, who undertakes quite a portfolio of portraits on this occasion, is passable as Lord Darlington (Mr. Nutcombe Gould). In the course of the performance he represents also Mr. Tree as

Hamlet, looking the part and bringing out some of its manner – though with more breadth than subtlety. . . . Mr. Charles Hawtrey makes up wonderfully as Mr. Wilde, and I dare say reproduces his manner and attitude very well also; I can say no more than that, for I have not thought Mr. Wilde of sufficient importance to observe him very closely. I fancy that the bulk of our British forty millions are much in the same position. . . . I wonder how Mr. Brookfield himself would like to be taken off; he is very clever – one of the cleverest of our character actors, and one of the most original, but still he affords opportunity – in his unmistakeable voice, for example. . . . The audience – a full one – was enthusiastic on the night we went. If there were points at which it could not fully understand it was nevertheless always sufficiently polite to pretend to do so. . . .

Salome was published in French in February 1893 (two months before the opening in the West End of *A Woman of No Importance*), and was published in English, with decidedly unEnglish illustrations by Aubrey Beardsley, a year later. Wilde's long poem *The Sphinx*, which he appears to have begun while he was at Oxford, was published in the summer of 1894.

Above: 'The Peacock Skirt' one of Aubrey Beardsley's Salome illustrations
Below: A Fashionable Poet

Edward Marjoribanks writes:

There have been, it is true, ugly rumours concerning him for years. But so have there been, and so there will always be, of most men to whom the world gives fame and homage during their lives. Nor do the slanders come from very reputable people; good Society, as a whole, ignores what has not been blazoned in their powerful enemy, the popular Press. Is he not happily married to a charming and devoted wife, the daughter of a distinguished lawyer? Is she not constantly beside him at parties and at first nights, and entertaining his brilliant circle of friends in Tite Street? And, in any event, who can resist Oscar's infectious laugh, that gay, almost ethereal merriment, which redeems the heavy, sensual lines of his great olive-coloured face? When he laughs, the grossness of his features seems to vanish away, and his companions feel that they are in the presence of a rare and gay spirit, obstinately young, and wonderfully brilliant. None of the photographs reveal even a hint of the strange charm which he is able to exercise, and they present an awkward, cumbrous body and the huge, self-indulgent face of a middle-aged man. Yet the smile changes everything. Is there not some affinity between the magical, transfiguring smile and the tale of Dorian Gray?

Among those whose slanders of Oscar Wilde are well known and taken for granted is the Marquis of Queensberry. But his stories are hardly to be taken seriously; the bearer of a great name, he has little else to recommend him. Although he was once a fine boxer, and a fearless and successful horseman, he has been divorced by his first wife, a

cultured, sensitive, and beautiful woman, whom he has treated abominably, and his second marriage has been annulled; he is a confessed atheist, and has lost his seat in the House of Lords, as a Scottish representative peer, for refusing to take the oath. He is a combative, obstinate fellow, who denies God and fears no man. Several of his children have not seen him for years. After a short period of service in the Navy, he has, despite fine natural ability, done little that was useful, and a great deal that was violent, cruel, and eccentric.

Perhaps there is in him a streak of eccentricity which is near both to madness and genius; for he transmitted to his children undeniable talent. His eldest son, Lord Drumlanrig, who died young, was Lord Rosebery's private secretary, and was made a peer of the United Kingdom, as Lord Kelhead, in his own right by Mr. Gladstone, before his promising career was cut short by an early death. The Marquess was furious, for now the son had a seat in the hereditary assembly from which the father was excluded.

More promising even than Lord Drumlanrig is his third son, Lord Alfred Douglas. He is as beautiful as a woman, but he does not show effeminacy; indeed, he has the making of a first-class athlete; he could easily have won his blue on the track. His intellectual promise is even higher; his first published poem in the *Oxford Magazine* was an earnest of great literary talent.

Although Lord Queensberry is the last man who has the right to play the part of a dutiful parent, his vain and combative nature took flame at the ugly rumours coupling the names of Oscar and his son. Alfred Douglas left Oxford without a degree: his father discontinued his allowance until such time as his friendship with Wilde ceased; with the inevitable result, having regard to his son's proud and obstinate nature, that Wilde and Douglas were drawn more closely together. Queensberry was foiled, but he had drawn up the well-known "Queensberry Rules of Boxing," and he did not recognise defeat in the first round. He has sworn vengeance. "I'll do it," he has been heard to boast, "I'll teach the fellow to leave my son alone: I'll not have their names coupled together." No doubt his pride has lashed him into a real sincerity. But his blows are not dextrous: he hits about wildly. . . .

QUEENSBERRY, MARQUESS OF. (Douglas.)

JOHN SHOLTO DOUGLAS, 8th Marquess, and a Baronet: *b.* July 20th, 1844; *s.* 1858; ed. at Magdalene Coll., Camb.; formerly Lieut. R.N., and Lieut.-Col. 1st Dumfriesshire Rifle Vol.; was a Representative Peer for Scotland 1874-80; is a D.L. of Dumfriesshire: *m.* 1866, Sibyl, dau. of Alfred Montgomery, Esq. [see Montgomery, Bart.], and has issue.

Arms.—Quarterly: 1st and 4th argent, a human heart gules, ensigned with an imperial crown or, on a chief azure, three mullets of the field, *Douglas*: 2nd and 3rd azure, a bend between six cross crosslets fitchée or, charged with a double tressure of Scotland. *Mar*: the whole within a bordure or, charged with a double tressure of Scotland. *Crest.*—A human heart gules, ensigned with an imperial crown, and between two wings displayed or. *Supporters.*—Two pegasi argent, wings, tails, manes, and hoofs, or.

Seats.—Kinmount House, near Annan, co. Dumfries; Glen Stuart, Dumfriesshire, N.B. *Clubs.*—Turf, Hurlingham.

SONS LIVING.

FRANCIS ARCHIBALD (*Viscount Drumlanrig*), *b.* Feb. 3rd, 1867; ed. at Roy. Mil. Coll., Sandhurst; is Lieut. 2nd Batn. Coldstream Guards.
Lord Percy, *b.* 1868; is Lieut. 3rd Batn. King's Own Scottish Borderers.
Lord Alfred Bruce, *b.* 1870.　　　　　　*Lord* Sholto George, *b.* 1872.

DAUGHTER LIVING.

Lady Edith Gertrude, *b.* 1874.

BROTHERS LIVING.

Rev. Lord Archibald Edward, *b.* 1850; is in Holy Orders of Church of Rome. *Residence,*—Wellington Street, Annan, N.B.
Lord James Edward Sholto, *b.* 1855; was Lieut. West Kent Militia 1875-6: *m.* 1888, Martha Lucy, widow of — Hennessy, Esq. *Residence,*—16, Kensington Court, W. *Club,*—Boodle's.

SISTERS LIVING.

Lady Gertrude, *b.* 1842: *m.* 1882, Mr. Thomas-Stock. *Residence,*—Maryland, Dumfries, N.B.
Lady Florence Caroline, *b.* 1855 (twin): *m.* 1875, Sir Alexander Beaumont Churchill Dixie, 11th Bart. *Residence,*—The Fishery, Windsor.

AUNT LIVING. (*Daughter of 6th Marquess*).

Lady Georgina, *b.* 1819. *Residence,*—68, South Eaton Place, S.W.

Theatre Royal 👑 Haymarket.

Sole Lessee ... ... Mr. TREE.
Managers ... . Mr. LEWIS WALLER AND Mr. H. H. MORELL.

Mr. TREE begs to announce that during his absence in America his Theatre has been taken for the Spring Season by Mr. LEWIS WALLER and Mr. H. H. MORELL.

EXTENDED RUN.—Arrangements have been made with Mr. Tree whereby the run of " AN IDEAL HUSBAND " at this Theatre will be prolonged until Saturday, April 6th. On Thursday, March 28th, will take place the **100TH** performance of " AN IDEAL HUSBAND."

TO-NIGHT at 8.30, A New and Original Play of Modern Life, entitled

AN IDEAL HUSBAND,

By OSCAR WILDE.

The Earl of Caversham, K.G.	Mr. ALFRED BISHOP
Lord Goring ... (his Son) ...	Mr. CHARLES H. HAWTREY
Sir Robert Chiltern	Mr. LEWIS WALLER
(Under Secretary for Foreign Affairs)	
Vicomte de Nanjac	Mr. COSMO STUART
Mr. Montford	Mr. HENRY STANFORD
Phipps	Mr. CHARLES BROOKFIELD
Mason	Mr. H. DEANE
Footman ... ... (at Lord Goring's) ...	Mr. CHARLES MEYRICK
Footman ... (at Sir Robert Chiltern's) ...	Mr. GOODHART
Lady Chiltern	Miss JULIA NEILSON
Lady Markby	Miss FANNY BROUGH
Lady Basildon	Miss VANE FEATHERSTON
Mrs. Marchmont	Miss HELEN FORSYTH
Miss Mabel Chiltern ... (Sir Robert's Sister)	Miss MAUDE MILLETT
Mrs. Cheveley	Miss FLORENCE WEST

The 'Captious Critic' of *The Illustrated Sporting and Dramatic News*, 26 January 1895:

"AN IDEAL HUSBAND."

When we go to see a piece by Mr. Oscar Wilde we find ourselves at once among the aristocracy. In *An Ideal Husband*, for example, anyone who is anybody has a title, or is related to one, and it is impossible to believe that even the subordinates – valets and others – are not Herschellian J.P.s, or Parish Councillors at least. The fact is, that Mr. Oscar Wilde is a very superior person, and must have around him superior people and things. It will always be a regret to me that the purveyors of novelettes at a halfpenny will insist upon dealing with "society" as well as he. It hurts me to think that in its free use of heroes and heroines from an imaginary Debrett, our fiction for the kitchen should have so much in common with our drama for the exceedingly select. Leaving the playbill for the piece, and coming to these noblemen and noblewomen of Mr. Oscar Wilde as *dramatis personæ* in action, I do not know that we find them particularly more natural in their wise than are the peers and peeresses of the below stairs repertory in theirs. It is not more ridiculous that handsome young lords, with blue eyes and fair moustaches, should desert weeping Lady Gwendolines in order to marry lovely Sarah Janes, than that the nobility and gentry of the neighbourhood of Mr. Oscar Wilde should live a life of asking and solving conundrums, as though "society" were a Christy Minstrel troupe. Mr. Wilde, as before, says some good things and some improved platitudes, in the duologues which go so far to fill out his production to four acts length. But they are tedious occasionally – the more so when they devolve upon members of the company who have not yet fully mastered the acoustic conditions of the theatre. Epigram, or paradox, or cynicism – polished always but not always worth the labour of it, do duty in *An Ideal Husband* for a great deal that is missed of plot and incident. Indeed, the story, which recalls, without improving upon, the *Dora* of Sardou, is scarcely worth considering. I can find no purpose in it whatever. It appears to me to contradict itself as soon as an attempt is made to work it out. The hero has committed a great wrong, and to escape its consequences is ready to commit a greater – an actual crime. But his wife implores, and a friend intervenes, and, because he reluctantly foregoes the second offence, he is graciously forgiven the original one. Sir Robert Chiltern is a man with a past, it will be seen. It is the fashion, I suppose Mr. Wilde would plead, to forgive any gentleman – or lady – who comes to the stage with a past. But it really does seem a little too much to make Sir Robert, who had been but Under Secretary, a Cabinet Minister, because, no thanks to himself, he is dissuaded from a course which would have landed him at the Old Bailey or in Argentina. In his youth this Sir Robert Chiltern has sold a government secret to a Jew financier and his pecuniary reward for the treason has laid the foundation of his fortune. He has entered Parliament, been promoted to office, and married a woman who believes him the incarnation of everything noble and good – "an ideal husband." But now, after twenty years, Mrs. Cheveley, an adventuress, armed with a letter proving his transactions with the Hebrew speculator, insists that he shall suppress a state report exposing a South American bubble – nay, what is more, advocate the fraud in Parliament. At first he refuses, but Mrs. Cheveley threatening to publish the facts of his earlier breach of confidence he ultimately consents to carry out her wishes. His wife, whom he loves so well, and who believes in him so fully, would abandon him if she were to learn of his dishonour. To retain her adoration – and his office – which is he admits a great consideration – he must do this second wrong, which will bring ruin to thousands. Mr. Wilde seems to forget, however, that apart from any moral consideration, Chiltern's promise was a most unwise one, for a fraud so gigantic would have soon made itself evident, and Sir Robert would have been in a worse position than ever. Is he a Conservative or a Radical, this Under Secretary for Foreign Affairs; and is he promoted at the end because he can see so little ahead? Fortunately the influence of Lady Chiltern, and of his friend Lady Goring, induces him to do the right thing – the sensible thing, I should say, were he anything but a Foreign Under Secretary. Instead of helping Mrs. Cheveley's scheme from his place in the House he denounces it in a righteous speech, which fills the country with his name. In the meantime his wife is supposed to be lost to him – her idol is shattered by her discovery of his youthful escapade, and there is the vengeance of Mrs. Cheveley to count with, who has promised to proclaim his sin, and is capable of fulfilling her threat. She does not know, however, that the clever, cool, and apparently careless Lord Goring – the heir of Caversham – has picked up a diamond bracelet which she stole from an aunt of his. He produces the jewel at a critical moment, and, despite her indignant denials, gains a victory *à la Still Waters Run Deep*. The bribe of his silence against hers – the compounding of a felony – enables him to obtain and burn the dangerous letter, and Sir Robert is a free man. The Government offers him a seat in the Cabinet, and his wife offers to forgive him if he will retire into private life. He ought to retire, and agrees to do so, but here also Lord Goring intervenes. Lady Chiltern consents, at his persuasion, to forego the resignation, and Sir Robert is promoted full minister, apparently by an extension of the First Offenders Act. It would not be like Mr. Charles Hawtrey to be in a part in which there were no fibs to tell, and, although Lord Goring is an exceedingly good fellow, he allows himself the weakness of falsehood on one occasion at least. It is when, like all foolish and innocent wives, Lady Chiltern writes a note which might compromise her – all guiltless as she is – and talks of calling on Lord Goring secretly, who might so openly have called on her. To screen her – as he believes – Lord Goring lies. Mrs. Cheveley, who is quite a kleptomaniac, purloins the note and sends it to the husband, who, as it is not addressed to any one in particular, assumes that it is meant for himself, so malice is frustrated and reconciliation furthered. Mr. Haw-

trey is very good as Lord Goring, a part which affords his clever comedy more variety of colour, and more versatility of characterisation, than the somewhat monotonous *rôle* of the calm teller of falsehoods. Miss Florence West, as Mrs. Cheveley, makes an audacious smiling adventuress, about whom no mistake can be made; I mean that her performance does not exercise one unduly by its excess of subtlety. Mr. Waller is the Sir Robert Chiltern, a miserable personage. No one could well make him interesting, and Mr. Waller's Sir Robert is like Mr. Wilde's original, pale, preachy, and a trifle heavy. Such an "ideal husband" as Chiltern naturally has an unsympathetic effect upon the wife who has regarded him as a divinity. Miss Neilson, as Lady Chiltern, is very graceful and very tender, but could not carry me away either in her devotion, her disillusion, or in the final compromise of pity. The central figures of the production are, to my mind, the weakest part of it. Other parts are well played – notably the Earl of Caversham, struggling all the while to overcome the inertia of the *insouciant* Lord Goring. It is amusing to see Mr. Alfred Bishop in the character of the energetic father, striving in vain to move his placid heir to work, or marry, or do something, no matter what, in the world. Mr. Charles Brookfield,

Mr. LEWIS WALLER

MISS FLORENCE WEST.

Above: Lord Goring (Mr Hawtrey)
Right: Lord Goring and Mr Phipps (Mr Brookfield)

There is much oral comment, both in theatrical circles and beyond, at the presence in the cast of Charles Brookfield, author of and player in the Wilde-burlesquing *The Poet and the Puppets*, and Charles Hawtrey, depicter of Wilde in that travestie.

"Remember to what a point your Puritanism in England has brought you. In old days nobody pretended to be a bit better than his neighbours. Nowadays, with our modern mania for morality, every one has to pose as a paragon of purity, incorruptibility, and all the other seven deadly virtues – and what is the result? You all go over like ninepins – one after the other. Not a year passes in England without somebody disappearing. Scandals used to lend charm, or at least interest, to a man – now they crush him. And yours is a very nasty scandal. You couldn't survive it."

An Ideal Husband, Act 1.

in the small part of a servant to Lord Goring, displays his usual individuality. Mr. Cosmo Stuart as the Vicomte de Nanjac, plays a foreigner whose nationality I am not sure about. Miss Fanny Brough, as a bustling elderly woman, Lady Markby, also puzzled me a little; I do not know whether she takes her nobility by marriage or descent, and consequently whether I ought to be disappointed or not by its lack of distinction. Miss Maude Millett, as a frank young girl who very decidedly sets her cap at Lord Goring, is capital, and her scenes with Mr. Hawtrey do much to lighten the play. Miss Vane Featherston and Miss Helen Forsyth have unimportant parts – except from the point of view that they do a fair share of epigram and paradox talking. The piece, I believe, is doing very well indeed.

22

JANUARY 19, 1895.

"AN IDEAL HUSBAND" is doing so well at the Haymarket that Messrs Waller and Morell have announced morning performances every Wednesday and Saturday. We heartily congratulate these clever and enterprising gentlemen on the success of their courageous venture.

"THE RECRUITING PARTY," the "tableaux vivant piece" by the Earl of Kilmorey, which has been produced at the Theatre Royal, Shrewsbury, this week, is not the only dramatic work which was written at the Raven Hotel, Shrewsbury. In the year 1705 George Farquhar penned his well-known comedy, *The Recruiting Officer*, at the same inn.

MISS EDITH COLE, who is appearing as Josephine, in *A Royal Divorce*, in the provinces, told a north-country interviewer the other day, in reference to a pretty basket of flowers handed to her on her first appearance at Darlington, that she wished that some great actress would set the fashion of having gloves or even stockings thrown on to the stage. They would, she thought, be more permanent tokens of respect, for a pair of gloves could be worn a fortnight at least, whereas, she added, the poor flowers thrown on to the stage frequently drooped and died before they were got out of the theatre.

MESSRS WHALLEN AND MARTELL'S American drama *The South Before the War* will be taken on tour in the provinces this spring, with twelve white artists, fifty genuine Negroes, and a piccaninny brass band.

JANUARY 26, 1895.

MR. OSCAR WILDE, in an interview just before his departure for Algiers, emitted some characteristic quips. "The stage is the refuge of the too fascinating." "It is only in the last few years that the dramatic critic has had the opportunity of seeing plays written by anyone who has a mastery of style." "Only mediocrities improve." "When a play that is a work of art is produced on the stage, what is being tested is not the play, but the stage." "In a play dealing with actualities, to write with ease one must write with knowledge." These are quite up to the Wildeian standard of sententious statement. The critiques upon *An Ideal Husband* have evidently "touched" Mr. Wilde "up a little." He is, it must be confessed, rather hard to please. Write a commonplace, matter-of-fact, non-committal report of his work and he sneers "Philistinism;" take him at his own valuation and demand from him the ethical consistency and artistic excellence to which he lays claim, and he strikes your name from his list of capable critics – now reduced, alas! to one.

THE Hotel Vendôme, New York, caught fire on Thursday morning, and before the flames could be extinguished, a large portion of the building had been destroyed. A number of the ladies and gentlemen of Mr. Beerbohm Tree's company were staying at the hotel. Mr. Henry Neville was aroused from sleep just in time in his bedroom on the fourth floor, and escaped uninjured, with the exception of some slight cuts he received from falling glass. Miss Cissy Fitzgerald was knocked down by a stream of water from one of the fire-engines, and was drenched.

FEBRUARY 2, 1895.

Mr Oscar Wilde's new play, *The Advantage of Being Earnest*, which will be produced at the St. James's Theatre on the 14th inst., is a kind three-act farce, its comic complications springing from the adventures of four young people, represented by Mr. George Alexander, Mr. Allan Aynesworth, Miss Evelyn Millard, and Miss Irene Vanbrugh.

People are saying a terrible thing about *The Advantage of Being Earnest*. They declare that this title is merely a common pun – which superior persons consider the lowest of all wit, though Dr. Parr punned admirably when he called it, therefore, "the foundation of all wit." But it is actually maintained that the hero of Mr. Oscar Wilde's new farce is named Ernest, and that therefore – but we need not explain. Yet the high-toned British critic will not fail to assure Mr. Wilde that it is of little use to avoid doors – and their complications in a farcical comedy which descends to word-plays of this ingenuosity. But the author of *Lady Windermere's Fan* is a law to himself, and we must hear even his puns before striking them – or him – off the rolls of the serious drama.

Mr. Beerbohm Tree opened his American tour at Abbey's Theatre, New York, on Monday, appearing to a closely filled house as Demetrius, in *The Red Lamp*, and Gringoire, in *The Ballad Monger*, and making a profound impression in both characters. The American press is eulogistic in praise of Mr. Tree's acting, and his triumph has been shared by Mrs. Tree, who has been very favourably received.

'Carados' (H. Chance Newton) in *The Referee*, 17th February 1895:

It is time to take Oscarissimus seriously now he has written a farce. In "The Importance of Being Earnest," which was given for the first time on Thursday at the St. James's, Mr. Oscar Wilde, descending from the pedestal upon which he has placed himself, makes up to the gallery. If the manual humours of the piece delight the unsophisticated, there are verbal jokes and absurdities for those who do not see the fun of two men eating crumpets one against the other, or of a whole company provided with copies of the Army List, everyone searching for the name of the father of the foundling who is the chief character in the piece; or of the production of the old black bag, in which the baby, who has grown up to be the chief character of the piece, was left by a careless domestic by mistake for the manuscript of a novel. Some people still like this sort of thing, and some people don't. It must be acknowledged that the house roared over the debauchery in muffins, though I should not like to say whether it was by accident or design that Mr. Allan Aynesworth went on eating the muffins after they had dropped from the dish on to the floor. The meaning – or the absense of meaning – in the dialogue is clearer, for although such remarks as "Divorces are made in heaven," or "People should not wash their clean linen in public," pass with the less intelligent people in the stalls for brilliant epigrams, the trick of the thing is obvious to anybody who will give a moment's thought to it. The secret is simply to turn a popular saying round the other way. For "dirty linen" of the adage substitute "clean," and there you have an epigram in the style of Mr. Wilde, who considers sound, of course, above sense, and relies upon the public not to reflect that clean linen does not usually need washing. Mr. Wilde, to do him justice, is not always so silly as this. In returning to the ways of the old-fashioned farce, he has dished it up with sauce à l'Oscar, and the impudence of the dialogue suggests that he has been trying to write a play in the manner of "Arms and the Man," only he has not the invention nor the sense of character nor the depth of thought of Mr. G. Bernard Shaw. But Mr. Wilde's superficiality is certainly better adapted to the purpose of farce than to any other kind of play, and "The Importance of Being Earnest" is not unamusing, in spite of the fact that all the characters – the hero, the knowing heroine, the ingenuous ward, and even the valet – speak exactly alike.

The two men who have invented each an imaginary person to bear the brunt of his defections from the straight path are the heroes of a hundred farces, though Mr. Wilde, who has, in common with the writers of kitchen literature, a partiality for placing his characters in the "hupper suckles," presents John Worthing and Algernon Moncrieffe in a world of fashion. There is the haughty lady of title, who might have stepped out of one of his earlier masterpieces, whose daughter falls in love with Algernon Moncrieffe because she thinks *his* name is Ernest. Both young ladies frankly acknowledge so much to their lovers in pretty much the same terms, and in scenes that, are pretty well identical. This is a mistake, even if, as I have a sneaking suspicion, Mr. Wilde is only poking fun at the methods of farce by showing us how young ladies supposed to differ in character act in precisely the same manner under given circumstances. Certainly, there is one excellent scene of genuine farce, when Algernon Moncrieffe, pretending to be the imaginary brother Ernest, arrives at Worthing's place, just before Worthing himself returns in deep mourning to announce that his brother Ernest is dead. But Mr. Wilde, who has caught a good idea here, does not seem to be able to hold it tight. It slips away, and just when

you think he has a rich thing in hand he seems bent upon showing that there is nothing in it. This is not deliberate perversity, of course. It is simply miscalculation of effect for the purpose of the stage. After all, action is the cardinal thing in a play, but Mr. Wilde does not seem yet to have realised that. If he had but taken a hint from Algernon Moncrieffe, who is not the man to go on talking when he ought to be getting on with his dinner, "The Importance of Being Earnest" would have fared better still than it did, though the malcontents in the audience were certainly very few, and the calls for "Oscar" – he is Oscar to the pit and gallery – to make a speech at the end of the play almost drowned the counter-cry of "No speech!" If he did not hear it, Oscarissimus acted upon the advice of the minority. For which surprise he is to be commended.

Some doubt appears to exist as to whether "An Ideal Husband" will be played at night at the Haymarket next Tuesday as well as at the five o'clock "morning performance" mentioned by me last week. You may take it from me that it will, for the aforesaid "afternoon" performance will finish at half-past seven, and, after just sixty minutes' interval for refreshment, "An Ideal Husband" will appear again.

OSCAR WILDE AT WORK
"(AS WE MIGHT HAS HE REGARDED)"

"THE IMPORTANCE OF BEING EARNEST"
AT THE ST. JAMES'S THEATRE.

CICELY—"The next day I bought this little ring in your name."

MRS. PRISM—"Poor Ernest! it's a sad blow."

JOHN WORTHING—"I suppose a man may eat his own muffins in his own garden."

GWENDOLEN—"My first impressions of people are never wrong."

Pall Mall Gazette, 15 February 1895

THE THEATRE
"THE IMPORTANCE OF BEING EARNEST," AT THE ST. JAMES'S.

IT is, we were told last night, "much harder to listen to nonsense than to talk it"; but not if it is good nonsense. And very good nonsense, excellent fooling, in this new play of Mr. Oscar Wilde's. It is, indeed, as new a new comedy as we have had this year. Most of the others, after the fashion of Mr. John Worthing, J.P., last night, have been simply the old comedies posing as their own imaginary youngest brothers. More humorous dealing with theatrical conventions it would be difficult to imagine. To the dramatic critic especially, who leads a dismal life, it came with a flavour of rare holiday. As for the serious people who populate this city, and to whom it is addressed, how they will take it is another matter. Last night, at any rate, it was a success, and our familiar first-night audience – whose cough, by-the-bye, is much quieter – received it with delight.

You must understand that this John Worthing, J.P., was found in a bag, a very respectable but by no means imposing two-handled black bag, at Victoria Station. He was a baby at the time. Mr. Cardew took him by mistake, and to save the bother of inquiry adopted him, called him Worthing, after the day's destination, and endowed him with a Manor House. Then, dying without any indecent longevity, he made Cecily Cardew, his grandchild, ward to John Worthing. In the country John Worthing was a quiet man, in London a blade; and to conceal the scandal from his ward and the vicar, he called himself Ernest Worthing in town, and explained in the country that that was his younger brother. And in town he became enamoured of the Hon. Gwendolen Fairfax, who loved him because his name was Ernest, and his ward in the country, who had never seen his brother Ernest, loved that legend for the splendour

of his wickedness. Then Algernon Moncrieffe, cousin to Gwendolen Fairfax, demanding certain explanations from John Worthing (hitherto known to him as Ernest), learns this duplicity – Mr. Alexander should make the confession more pathetic – and learns, too, of the existence of the charming ward. And while Mr. John Worthing, with that virtue of intention that only the first contemplation of matrimony can give, is resolving that his alias, his brother Ernest, must die, Mr. Algernon Moncrieffe is preparing a charming little expedition. He professes to be called away from town by the sickness of a convenient chimera called Bunbury, and rushes down to introduce himself to the charming ward, as the penitent

Messrs. Aynesworth and Alexander

reprobate Ernest. He arrives, meets with the ward and excellent fortune, and disappears into the house with her. She is of altogether Gilbertian artlessness, and explains that she has been relieving the tedium of her existence, under the instruction of Miss Prism, by an imaginary love affair with Ernest, and that they are already engaged. This places things on an easy footing at once. Then – a brilliant situation – arrives John Worthing, dressed like a hearse, to announce to Miss Prism and the Rev. Chasuble, with infinite pathos, that his brother – his long-lost brother – is dead. Miss Prism, hoping against hope, trusts that "he'll profit by it." To whom enter the ward and Algernon Moncrieffe, as the defunct brother.

Then presently arrives Gwendolen Fairfax, in flight from her recalcitrant mother, who objects to a son-in-law with no more family than a handbag; and an amusing but rather too flabby scene follows between Gwendolen and Cecily, the ward. Both imagine they are engaged to the non-existent Ernest. They both attach a magical virtue to the name, and could not possibly love men with any other names. Hence the importance of being Ernest. The scene ends with revelations, four peoples' despair, and the hazardous enterprise of John and Algernon to get christened Ernest forthwith. (Afterwards Lady Bracknell thought this talk of christening "a little premature.")

MISS IRENE VANBRUGH   MISS EVELYN MILLARD

But it all comes right. It was Miss Prism who lost that bag when she was nursemaid to Mrs Moncrieffe. She had written a three-volume novel in her scanty leisure, and, being absent-minded, put that into the perambulator and the baby into a bag, and so it comes out that John Worthing is Ernest after all, Ernest Moncrieffe, Algernon Moncrieffe's brother. "I always said I had a brother," he remarks in the tone of an ill-used man. Gwendolen's mother – who was worse than a Gorgon, because she was "a monster and yet not a myth" – is appeased, and the curtain descends on three happy couples. For Mr. Oscar Wilde, with a commendable regard for dramatic customs, has supplied the Rev. Canon Chasuble, D.D., for the excellent Miss Prism. It is all very funny, and Mr. Oscar Wilde has decorated a humour that is Gilbertian with innumerable spangles of that wit that is all his own. Of the pure and simple truth, for instance, he remarks that "Truth is never pure and rarely simple;" and the reply, "Yes, flowers are as common in the country as people are in London," is particularly pretty from the artless country girl to the town-bred Gwendolen.

Now to act really artistic burlesque is a difficult thing. A more admirable Miss Prism than that of Mrs. George Canninge would scarce be possible; and Miss Leclercq, Miss Vanbrugh, and Miss Evelyn Millard all acted with humour, if with a trifle too much naturalness. But the actors scarcely recognized that it was their business to poke fun at conventional play-acting as the author poked fun at the conventional play-writing. The most successful among them was Mr. Aynesworth as Algernon, but he was funny *in* the part rather than at the expense of the part. Mr. Alexander might with advantage study Mr. Fred Terry's Llewelyn – 'tis a pity his own Guy Domville is inaccessible to him. The part of John Worthing, played with the infinite seriousness of common comedy, with frowns and starts at his guilty secret, brow-clasping remorse, and crescendo emotion, would be irresistible. Mr. Alexander was best in the third act, and his heartrending cry of "Mother!

mother!" – he fancied for a few terrible moments that Miss Prism was his mother – was a moving piece of stage pathos. But he would be better if he mouthed his words more, and stamped a little, and glared. Mr. Vincent, too, as a sympathetic Canon, threw away an excellent chance of dramatic caricature.

How Serious People – the majority of the population, according to Carlyle – how Serious People will take this Trivial Comedy written for their learning remains to be seen. No doubt seriously. One last night thought that the bag incident was a "little far-fetched." Moreover, he could not see how the bag and the baby got to Victoria Station (L.B. and S.C.R. station) while the manuscript and perambulator turned up "at the summit of Primrose Hill." Why the summit? Such difficulties, he said, rob a play of "convincingness." That is one serious person disposed of, at any rate.

On the last production of a play by Mr. Oscar Wilde we said it was fairly bad, and anticipated success. This time we must congratulate him unreservedly on a delightful revival of theatrical satire. *Absit omen.* But we could pray for the play's success, else we fear it may prove the last struggle of its author against the growing seriousness of his dramatic style.

ST. JAMES'S THEATRE

"THE IMPORTANCE OF BEING EARNEST."

The empire of Mr. Gilbert over Topseyturveydom is at last successfully challenged, and Mr. Wilde may now claim to reign

> Beyond dispute
> O'er all the realms of nonsense absolute.

His three-act novelty at the St. James's Theatre, announced as "a trivial comedy for serious people," is a veritable specimen of what, in a more propitious season, might be called midsummer madness. It has not a relish of reason or sparkle of sanity; it is absurd, preposterous, extravagant, idiotic, saucy, brilliantly clever, and unedifyingly diverting. The idea on which Voltaire constructed his "Ingénu," that of an innocent and guileless savage speaking the truth in all presences and under all conditions – a notion subsequently elaborated by Mr. Gilbert in the "Palace of Truth" – is once more employed. This time, however, everybody speaks truth through no magical influence of place, but through a hardened belief that what they think, do, and say is the same as is thought, done, and said by the rest of the world.

John Worthing, Mr. Wilde's hero, has been found in Victoria Station in a leather bag by a rich, elderly, and benevolent gentleman, who on dying has left him a large estate encumbered only with a rich and pretty ward. Living as a bachelor in the country, John Worthing has also chambers in the Albany, which he occupies under the name of Ernest Worthing, a purely imaginary brother, whom he converts into a scapegoat, bearing the blame of all his own iniquities. He has fallen in love with the Hon. Gwendolen Fairfax, to whom, under his town name of Ernest, he proposes marriage. Being accepted by the lady, though refused by Lady Bracknell, her mother, he determines on reformation. When, accordingly, he returns to his country house at Woolton, he goes in deep mourning, and announces solemnly and with tears the death of his brother Ernest. Unluckily for him a pseudo Ernest, whom he cannot possibly repudiate, is already in the house, and has already become affianced to his ward, Cecily Cardew. Cecily had always loved in her heart the disreputable young scamp, concerning whose evil doings she has heard so much, and so soon as his representative turns up, she is prepared to throw herself into his arms. It so chances, however, that what has principally captivated the maidens has been the name of Ernest, which both have assumed, though neither is entitled to it. For a while negotiations are broken off, and an offer on the part of the two suitors to be rechristened does not go far towards settling matters. To tell the means by which the imbroglio is set straight the mystery of John Worthing's birth dispelled, and the way cleared to a brace or, indeed, possibly, to a leash of marriages, would be mere waste of time. The story is as frankly nonsensical as it is diverting.

What really constitutes the attraction is less the scenes of equivoque, though these abound, than the absolutely delicious things which people say to each other. A scene in the second act, in which the two heroines meet for the first time, embrace, and on a sudden thought swear eternal friendship, then, finding that they are both betrothed, as they think, to the same man, the imaginary Ernest, proceed to exercise on each other the coldest civility, or the most cutting irony, is one of the drollest things ever witnessed on the stage. A little too much repetition of motive in the second act is, indeed, all in the way of approximation to dulness with which the play can be charged. Each successive scene elicited roars and shouts of approval, and the audience grew absolutely impatient to hear each succeeding witticism or impertinence the author had in store. Mr. Wilde has the power to make even *fadeurs* diverting. There is not a line without a laugh, and joke, epigram, and parody jostle each other unendingly. Mr. Wilde seems, indeed, to have introduced the piece in part as an Apologia, and makes one of his characters say, when taxed with talking nonsense: "It is much better and rarer to talk nonsense than to listen to it." It is, however, a mistake that everybody, down to the servants, talks in the same vein of *persiflage*. A similar kind of indictment has, however, been brought against Sheridan.

Taking for the first time a farcical character, Mr. Alexander played it with a kind of placid and perverse seriousness that was unlike anything we can recall on the stage. Miss Rose Leclercq played in her best style Lady Bracknell, the one character that had a touch of comedy as distinguished from drollery. Misses Irene Vanbrugh and Evelyn Millard were equally delightful, joyous, and diverting as the two heroines; and Mr. Allan Aynesworth gave an admirable rendering of Algernon Moncrieffe, the second of the two would-be Ernests. Mr. Alexander and Mr. Wilde were enthusiastically summoned, and the whole was a delirious sucess. "In the Season," a sentimental one-act piece, first seen at an afternoon representation at the Strand, served to introduce Miss Elliott Page, an American lady of much beauty and some talent, and to bring before the public Mr. Herbert Waring in a character of which he was the original representative. It was received with great warmth, though it was taken in too slow time, and impressed us less favourably than when first seen.

"THE IMPORTANCE OF BEING EARNEST."

A Trivial Comedy for Serious People
by Oscar Wilde,
Played for the First Time at the
St. James's Theatre,
on Thursday, Feb. 14th, 1895.

John Worthing	Mr GEORGE ALEXANDER
Algernon Moncrieffe	Mr ALLAN AYNESWORTH
Rev. Canon Chasuble	Mr H. H. VINCENT
Merriman	Mr FRANK DYALL
Lane	Mr F. KINSEY PEILE
Lady Bracknell	Miss ROSE LECLERCQ
Hon. Gwendoline Fairfax	Miss IRENE VANBRUGH
Cecily Cardew	Miss EVELYN MILLARD
Miss Prism	Mrs GEORGE CANNINGS

As bright and merry a piece of clever folly as ever was put on our stage was produced at the St. James's Theatre on Thursday, when Mr. Oscar Wilde's "trivial comedy for serious people" was given for the first time with unqualified success. People have found fault with Mr. Wilde for the *naif* pun contained in his title on the name of an imaginary individual in the piece. This is not the spirit in which the task of appreciating a work of this sort should be approached. If Mr. Wilde is pleased by the resemblance in sound between the two words it would be cruel indeed to deny him a harmless gratification which the late H. J. Byron enjoyed so keenly and so often. It is a sad thought, by the way, that of the ephemerality of the vogue of particular kinds of humour. At one time the writer to whom we have just alluded was "the only wear." How we roared at his dialogue! How we admired plays upon words which would now evoke a unanimous groan from the best natured house! Then there was the "cup and saucer" school, when this sort of thing was the rage: – Lord B. – See, we are divided again. BELLA – No (*placing her hand on jug*). The jug unites us. Lord B. – Only for a moment. Roars again. Not long ago what was called "Gilbertian" dialogue was in fashion. No one

needs to be reminded of its merits; but even Mr. Gilbert has realised, with his habitual acuteness, that the old *Pinafore and Patience* methods are out of date, and has given us in *His Excellency* a charming comedy for music. The Wildean style is now in full bloom of fashionableness. We are reminded by some of its samples of Henry Murger's Bohemian journalist, who, wishing to complete a column of paradoxes, wrote "Absolute honesty is only found in the hulks." The fashion of the stage passeth away, and the time will come when *The Importance of Being Earnest* will be as antiquated as *Engaged* is now. Meanwhile, let us enjoy Mr Wilde's work while we can; and certainly those whose lungs were not tickled o' the sere had a merry time of it at the St. James's on Thursday. Mr. Wilde has shown himself fertile in expedient, resourceful in the invention of amusing incident, and unceasingly epigrammatic. Every other line was what actors call a "wheeze," and the audience, so to speak, "waited for" Mr. Wilde every time. After the first act the author was, indeed, in the agreeable position of the brilliant parson who only had to say "Pass the mustard" to set the table in a roar. We are not about to quote any of Mr. Wilde's jests. The point of an epigram lies in the introduction of it, and we have no right to take a good line away from its surroundings, and put it, as it were, under the microscope by itself.

Mr. Wilde's piece was preceded by Mr. Langdon E. Mitchell's one act play entitled

"IN THE SEASON."

Sir Harry Collingwood	Mr HERBERT WARING
Edward Fairburne	Mr ARTHUR ROYSTON
Sybil March	Miss ELLIOTT PAGE

It is interesting to note how certain effects are produced on the stage. On the first night of *The Importance of Being Earnest* at the St. James's many were struck with the realistic watering-pot carried by Miss Evelyn Millard in the second act. From the rose of this what looked like real water was distributed over the mimic garden. The water was merely silver-sand. On Saturday champagne was freely used at the Opera Comique in the first act of *An M.P.'s Wife*. The corks were always drawn off, the noise being made by a pop gun. These are hints for managers on tour.

Here are a few of the inverted axioms and witty lines drafted by Mr. Oscar Wilde into his new piece at the St. James's:—

If our lower orders don't set us a good example, what on earth is the use of them?

You do not propose to set up the asses against the classes.

Divorces are made in heaven.

The truth is rarely pure and never simple.

In married life three is company and two is none.

What with the duties expected during one's lifetime and the duties exacted after one's death, a landowner has a position without the means of keeping it up.

Women only call each other sister when they have called each other lots of other things first.

I am always bored in the country; yes, they call it agricultural depression.

It is a much cleverer thing to talk nonsense than to listen to it.

Cleverness becomes a public nuisance.

To be advanced in years is no guarantee of respectability.

Born in the purple of commerce, or raised from the ranks of the aristocracy.

To wish to be buried in Paris hardly points to a serious state of mind at the last.

To have lost one parent is a misfortune, to have lost both looks like carelessness.

Only such people as stockbrokers talk "business," and then only at dinner.

I hate people who are not serious about meals.

Ignorance is like a delicate exotic fruit. Touch it, and the bloom is gone.

The old-fashioned respect for the young is rapidly dying out.

Nobody ever does talk anything but nonsense.

It is always painful to part from people one has only known a brief time.

I did not know you had flowers in the country. Yes,

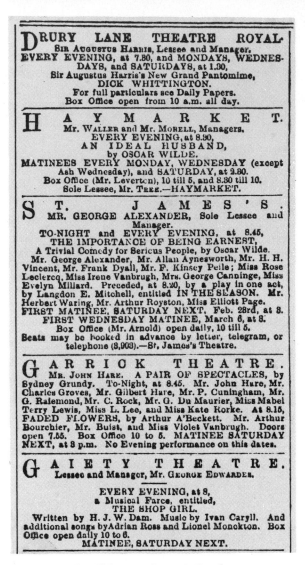

they are as plentiful as people are in London.

If it were my business, I should not talk about it.

I am only serious about my amusements.

No married man is ever attractive to his wife.

The amount of women who flirt with their husbands in London is simply scandalous. It is washing one's clean linen in public.

When I saw Mr. Fred Latham carefully following *The Importance of being Earnest* on its first night at the St. James's, I guessed there was something in the wind. It appears that he has secured the provincial rights of the piece, which he will send on tour later on. He also has bought the rights for the provinces of the new piece by Pinero, which is shortly due at the Garrick.

"THE IMPORTANCE OF BEING EARNEST."

We shall perhaps understand Mr. Oscar Wilde some day, and know whether he wishes to be regarded as a real playwright or merely as a superior kind of practical joker. It appears to me that none of his pieces so far have settled this point, and that, among the rest, *The Importance of Being Earnest* might be very easily mistaken for the impertinence of not being so. There is no doubt, however, that Mr. Wilde has a public – a public of the stalls and boxes – who think him good fun, and do not ask too particularly for good drama. The better seats were filled on the night when we went to the St. James's Theatre, though pit and gallery were the reverse of crowded. The masses want more for their money than the classes do, and with Mr. Gilbert – and Moore and Burgess – they get the same sort of thing, better or worse, with added dance and music. It is impossible not to think of Mr. Gilbert when one follows this production of Mr. Oscar Wilde – as one thinks of Madame de Genlis sometimes when one recalls the origin of the Gilbertian method. But between Mr. Gilbert's

THE MUFFIN DUET.

Mr W. ALLAN AYNESWORTH   Mr GEORGE ALEXANDER

THE BARD OF St. JAMES'S

style and Mr. Wilde's there is the difference between bigness and smallness. The former topsy-turvies set sentences. In *The Importance of Being Earnest*, there are the usual – perhaps more than the usual – number of smart verbal acrobatics – truisms turning somersault, proverbial philosophy high-kicking, platitude vaulting in spangles – and in a literary sense this must content us. Every personage firing off cynical crackers and affecting the same Palace of Truth like frankness of motive, there is very little individuality of character. The three women – the careful mother, the country-bred girl, the fashionable young lady of the period – lose all their initial distinctness of contrast long before the play draws to a close. It is much the same with the two young men who have so many of the same sort of things to say, apart from the similarity of what they have to do. At first, it is true, one of them has such special colour as an insatiable appetite for cucumber sandwiches may give him, but he is not long allowed to retain the monopoly of greediness, for the other gentleman runs him close over a dish of buttered muffins later.

Reynolds's Newspaper, 3 March 1895

LORD QUEENSBERRY ARRESTED.

CHARGED WITH LIBELLING
OSCAR WILDE.

WORDS UNFIT FOR PUBLICATION.

STATEMENT TO THE POLICE.

The Marquis of Queensberry, 50, described as having no occupation, and as residing in Carter's Hotel, Dover-street, W., was charged, at Marlborough-street Police Court, yesterday, on a warrant, "for that he did unlawfully and maliciously publish a certain defamatory libel of and concerning one Oscar Wilde, at Albemarle-street, on February 18, 1895, at the parish of St. George's." Mr. C. O. Humphreys, solicitor, prosecuted and Sir George Lewis, solicitor, appeared for the defence.

OPENING OF THE CASE.

Mr. Humphreys, in opening the case, said that Mr. Oscar Wilde was a married man living on most affectionate terms with his wife and family of two sons. He had been the object of a most cruel

The Marquis of Queensberry, an impression by Phil May in 1889

34

persecution at the hands of Lord Queensberry. In consequence of family affairs, Mr. Oscar Wilde was very unwilling to take any steps of a criminal nature against Lord Queensberry, but he had been so fearfully persecuted by that gentleman, said Mr. Humphreys, that he was compelled to take the step he had now taken for protection and peace of mind.

A MELANCHOLY DRAMA.

The last act in this most melancholy drama was performed on the 18th of last month, but it only came to the notice of Mr. Oscar Wilde the night before last. Mr. Wilde was a member of the Albemarle Club, where both ladies and gentlemen are admitted. Mrs. Wilde was also a member of the club. On the night before last Mr. Oscar Wilde went to this club, and the hall porter presented him with a card, and addressed to "Oscar Wilde, Esq.," explaining that a gentleman had called and requested that the card should be handed over to Mr. Oscar Wilde. The porter was astonished at what was written upon the card, and considered it of sufficient importance to add the date and hour when the card was left. He wrote: "4.30, February 18, 1895." The words written upon the card were of such a character as to be unfit for publication.

The first word written upon the card was of the most objectionable nature. Then there was a word he could not decipher, and then followed, but imperfectly spelt, another objectionable phrase.

The Marquis of Queensberry said the other word is "posing."

Mr. Humphreys (continuing) said that a more frightful, serious, or abominable libel for one man to publish about another he could not conceive. He now proposed to call as witnesses only the hall porter of the club and the officer, Detective-inspector Greet, who executed the warrant. After the evidence he would ask for an adjournment, that the whole matter might be gone into on a future occasion, because he did not propose to rest his case simply upon the question of this libel. He proposed to go into other cases which had occurred before February 18, and after they had

THE HALL PORTER.

been investigated would ask the Magistrate to commit the defendant to take his trial.

Mr. George Lewis asked that before any evidence was taken the case should be adjourned, so that he might consult with his client and have more time to consider the matter.

Mr. Humphreys said that he only proposed now calling two witnesses, whose evidence would be very short, and the whole matter could be gone into next week.

THE HALL PORTER'S EVIDENCE.

Sidney Wright, hall porter of the Albemarle Club, Piccadilly, said that the defendant presented himself at the club on February 18, and handed to him the card produced. He wrote the words on the card in his (witness's) presence, excepting the letter "A." He said, "Give that to Oscar Wilde." He (witness) wrote on the back of the card the date and hour when it was given him. He put the card into an envelope, so that it should not be lost. On February 28 Mr. Oscar Wilde called at the club.

In reply to the Magistrate, Witness stated that he did not seal the envelope down.

35

The Albermarle Club, 37 Dover Street

Continuing, Witness said he knew that Mrs. Wilde was a member of the club. When Mr. Wilde called he handed him the envelope containing the card, and said that Lord Queensberry had left the card for him.

Cross-examined: He made it quite evident that the card was to be delivered to Mr. Wilde. He knew nothing of the circumstances preceding the delivery of the card.

THE ARREST OF LORD QUEENSBERRY.

Inspector Greet, C Division, deposed that he arrested the prisoner at Carter's Hotel that morning at nine o'clock. He told him that he held a warrant for his arrest. He then read the warrant to him. He (the Marquis) said, "In these cases I thought proceedings were usually taken by summons, but I suppose it is all right. What is the date?" He (Greet) told him February 18. He (the Marquis) then said, "I have been wanting to find Mr. Oscar Wilde for nine or ten days. This thing has been going on for about two years." He made no reply when charged at Vine-street Police Station.

Sir George Lewis: Let me say one word, sir. I venture to say that when the circumstances of this case are more fully known that Lord Queensberry acted as he did under feelings of great indignation, and—

Mr. Newton (interrupting): I cannot go into that now.

Sir George Lewis: I don't wish this case to be adjourned without its being known that there is nothing against the honour of Lord Queensberry.

Mr Newton: You mean to say that you have a perfect answer to the charge.

Sir George Lewis: I ask you, sir, to allow his lordship to be at large on his entering into his own recognizances in £1,000.

Mr. Humphreys: I should like to have a surety.

The Magistrate: The case will be adjourned for a week, and the defendant will have to find one surety in the sum of £500, and enter into his own recognizances in the sum of £1,000.

Mr. William Tyser, a merchant, of Gloucester-square, then went into the witness-box, and tendered the necessary bail, and the Marquis of Queensberry left the court with his friends.

All of the newspapers are, and will be, decently reticent about the message.

Far less literarily adept than Wilde, the Marquis, meaning to write, 'Posing as a sodomite,' has written: 'Posing as Somdomite'.

According to a rumour presently scuttling about the Inns of Court, Charles Russell, the solicitor retained by the Marquis, was advised by his father, the lately-appointed Lord Chief Justice of England, to offer the defence brief to the Dublin-born barrister, Edward 'Ned' Carson. Certainly, after some humming and hawing, Carson has accepted the brief. His hesitancy may have been due to the fact that he and Wilde were classmates at Trinity

College, Dublin. (Wilde's response to the news that he is to be cross-examined by Carson: 'No doubt he will perform his task with all the added bitterness of an old friend.')

A more probable reason for Carson's hesitancy is that he felt that the brief, as first presented to him, left the Marquis without a leg to stand on. Charles Russell is making every effort, with no expense spared, to garner evidence in support of the Marquis's allegation: the West End seems suddenly crowded with quizzical private investigators, each prepared to offer surreptitious fees for confidences from acquaintances of, or gossip from menials in hotels frequented by, Wilde. Strange to relate, the most industrious – and yet unrecompensed – ally of the Marquis is Charles Brookfield. Having initially retailed to Russell a fund of ugly anecdotes apropos of the man whom he has 'travestied' – and in whose play, *An Ideal Husband*, he is appearing – Brookfield is scavenging high and especially low for titbits of information that may further the Marquis's cause. It is said that he is revengeful against Wilde on account of a snub. One wonders, however, whether he harbours some other motive for malice of so extreme a kind.

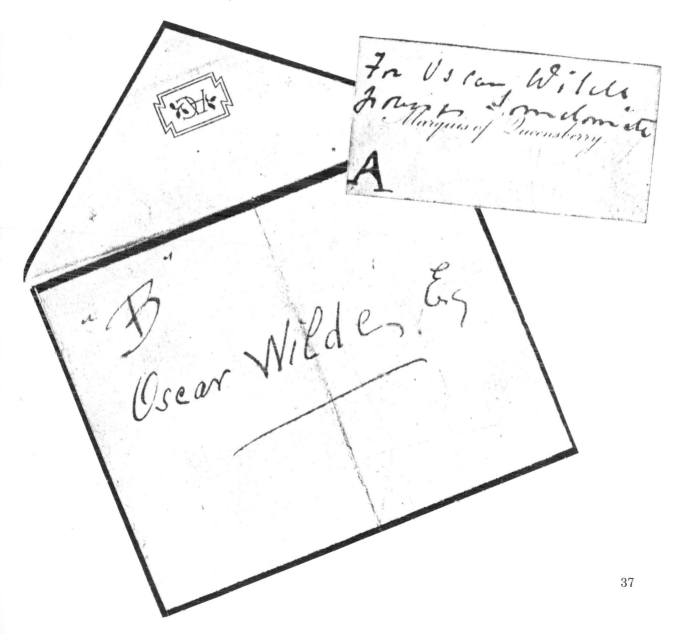

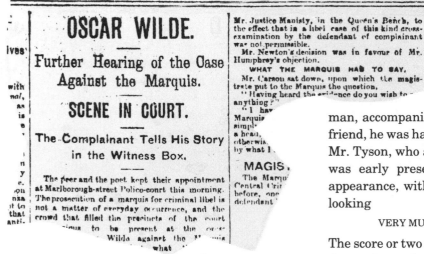

OSCAR WILDE.

Further Hearing of the Case Against the Marquis.

SCENE IN COURT.

The Complainant Tells His Story in the Witness Box.

The peer and the poet kept their appointment at Marlborough-street Police-court this morning. The prosecution of a marquis for criminal libel is not a matter of everyday occurrence, and the crowd that filled the precincts of the court anxious to be present at the ca... Wilde against the M... what

Mr. Justice Manisty, in the Queen's Bench, to the effect that in a libel case of this kind cross-examination by the defendant of complainant was not permissible.

Mr. Newton's decision was in favour of Mr. Humphrey's objection.

WHAT THE MARQUIS HAD TO SAY.

Mr. Carson sat down, upon which the magistrate put to the Marquis the question,

"Having heard the evidence do you wish to ... anything?"

"I hav... Marquis simpl... a head, otherwis... by what I...

MAGIS...

The Marqu... Central Crit... before, one... defendant...

The Evening News, 9 March 1895

OSCAR WILDE.

Further Hearing of the Case
Against the Marquis.

SCENE IN COURT.

The Complainant Tells His Story in
the Witness Box.

The peer and the poet kept their appointment at Marlborough-street Police-court this morning. The prosecution of a marquis for criminal libel is not a matter of everyday occurrence, and the crowd that filled the precincts of the court all anxious to be present at the *cause célèbre* of Oscar Wilde against the Marquis of Queensberry was just what the court authorities might have expected and prepared for. Whether the police expected them or not, it is certain they made no preparations, and the whole of the Press were kept waiting in the evil-smelling waiting-room until half-past 11, the time for which the case had been fixed. There were very few present who could be identified as friends of either side, and when Oscar Wilde drove up in a carriage and pair, a magnificent turn-out with coachman and cockaded foot-

man, accompanied by Lord Alfred Douglas and a friend, he was hardly recognised outside the court. Mr. Tyson, who acted as Lord Queensberry's bail, was early present, an elderly man of French appearance, with white moustache and imperial, looking

VERY MUCH LIKE HENRI ROCHEFORT.

The score or two of the general public who filled up the nooks and crannies left unoccupied by the Press, were packed worse than sardines in a tin.

Mr. E. H. Carson, M.P., who possesses the distinction of being a Q.C. both at the English and the Irish Bar, was present as leader of the defence, his junior, Mr. Gill, not putting in an appearance, but the prosecution was still in the hands of Mr. C. O. Humphrey, the solicitor who conducted the case last week.

"OSCAR."

Looking round the Court during the few moments that elapsed between the filling and the case being called on, the noticeable feature was the utter absence of the fashionable West-end element which might have been expected *en evidence* when such a *cause célèbre* is to be tried.

It seemed as if an unanimous decision had been arrived at to stop away, and let the parties fight it out alone. It was 11.40 when Mr. Newton took his seat, and the Marquis in a long brown Melton coat, trimmed with fur, came in from the opposite side to that from which advanced Oscar, smiling and debonnaire, accompanied by Lord Alfred Douglas.

WILDE IN THE BOX.

Immediately Oscar was called into the witness-box, and took the oath with an aesthetic grace. Most straightforwardly and without any striving after epigrammatic effect, but with a conscious pose, he said he was a dramatist and author and lived in Tite-street. He knew the Marquis of Queensberry and many members of his family. He believed he first became acquainted with Lord Queensberry in 1892, and he remembered on one occasion in October, 1892, when he was lunching with Lord Alfred Douglas at the Café Royal, the Marquis of Queensberry came into the room where they were lunching, and by his son's invitation came to their table.

This cleared the preliminary ground, and matters took a more serious turn. In March 1894, again Mr. Wilde was lunching with Lord Alfred at the Café Royal, and again Lord Queensberry came in and joined them. This incident was just after Lord Alfred's return from Egypt, and the conversation ran somewhat in the direction of the Pyramids. Shortly after that Lord Alfred Douglas showed him a letter.

Mr. Newton stopped the examination. In what direction, he asked, did this tend?

Mr. Humphrey proposed to put in other libels in addition to the card.

Mr. Carson: I hope the letter will be put in. I am anxious to show that Lord Queensberry was acting in the interest of his son.

"You cannot go into that here," replied Mr. Newton.

The argument was continued for some minutes but in spite of the wish of both sides Mr. Newton wished the letter not to be dealt with.

The learned magistrate was obviously unwilling that

ANYTHING SENSATIONAL SHOULD COME OUT

in his court, and perhaps neither side was particularly desirous of hearing the letters read in Court, though each side professed the utmost anxiety to have them put in.

References were made to the name of "exalted personages" that were mentioned in the letters, and Mr. Humphrey suggested that it was most desirable that these should not be mentioned.

While the legal luminaries were wrangling, Oscar ran his fingers through his hair and gazed curiously round, being recalled to the matter in hand by Mr. Humphrey resuming his examination.

The letters being dropped, the matter of the present libel was at once gone into. On Thursday, February 28, Mr. Wilde drove up, he said, to the Albemarle Club. It was his first visit to the club after his return from Algiers. As he passed in, the hall porter handed to him an envelope, and Oscar identified the envelope, square and black-edged. At the same time the porter said, "Lord Queensberry desired me, sir, to hand this to you when you came to the club." Oscar straightway opened the envelope and took from it a card.

Lord Queensberry, who had left the dock and was sitting behind his counsel,

FOLLOWED EVERY WORD OF EVIDENCE

with head bent forward as Oscar went on to say that on the back of the card were the figures "4.30, 18/2/95," and on the front were certain words, which he read. He at once communicated with his solicitor, and on the following day a warrant was applied for for Lord Queensberry's apprehension.

"That is all I ask," said Mr. Humphrey, and sat down.

At once rather an unexpected course was taken by the Bench. "Mr. Humphrey," said Mr. Newton, "will you and Mr. Carson come into my room?"

The three left the Court, Oscar passed a note down to the solicitors' table, and a buzz of conversation filled the court. What was the reason for the retirement, was the case to be nipped in the bud in the interest of "exalted personages" once or twice so distantly referred to, or was the conference but the prelude to a committal? Every one had to wait and see.

In about 10 minutes the parties returned.

"That is all I propose to ask Mr. Wilde," repeated Mr. Humphrey, Mr. Wilde's counsel, on retaking his seat in court.

Mr. Carson rose and commenced to cross-examine Mr. Wilde with the question, "How long have you known Lord Alfred Douglas?"

An objection was raised to the cross-examination by Mr. Humphrey.

Mr. Carson explained that all he desired to do was to prove that the Marquis was justified in the action he took, and that he was entitled, if he thought it necessary, in the interests of the

MORALITY OF HIS OWN SON

to do everything in his power to put a stop to the acquaintanceship between him and Mr. Wilde.

Mr. Carson went on to say that as to the matter of justification, that was a plea the full responsibility of the effect of which Lord Queensberry was prepared to accept if sent for trial.

Mr. Humphrey cited a ruling of the late Lord Chief Justice Cockburn, Mr. Justice Lush, and Mr. Justice Manisty, in the Queen's Bench, to the effect that in a libel case of this kind cross-examination by the defendant of complainant was not permissible.

Mr. Newton's decision was in favour of Mr. Humphrey's objection.

WHAT THE MARQUIS HAS TO SAY.

Mr. Carson sat down, upon which the magistrate put to the Marquis the question,

Edward Carson

"Having heard the evidence do you wish to say anything?"

"I have simply, your worship," replied the Marquis, "to say this, that I wrote the card simply with the intention of bringing matters to a head, I having been unable to meet Mr. Wilde otherwise, and to save my son, and I abide by what I said, what I wrote."

MAGISTRATE'S DECISION.

The Marquis was committed for trial at the Central Criminal Court, bail being accepted as before, one surety (Mr. Tyson) in £500 and the defendant himself in £1,000.

Really, our London stage promises to be more poly-glot than ever this year. Not only have we the Parisians upon us next week – with a programme from which all French work is carefully excluded in favour of the Norwegian and the Belgian drama – but Sir Augustus promises to show us, in the doings of the Saxe-Coburg theatre, how far the German "provinces" are ahead of our own; and there have been rumours – in which it is not too easy to believe – of a company of Chinese actors, who will prove how flowery the Flowery Land can be by their performance of *The Green Dragon*, partly in Chinese and partly, strange to say, in French!

Mr. E. H. Vanderfelt, the representative of the opium-eating poet in *John-a-Dreams* at the Theatre Royal, Norwich, this week, had a serious accident whilst taking a drive round Norwich last Tuesday. He was accompanied by his brother, Mr. Sydney G. Vanderfelt, and Mrs. Tremayne. Whilst turning a corner at Mulbarton, a dog ran out barking, frightening the horses. The driver did his best to steady the team, but they ran up a steep bank, completely overturning the waggonette. Several of the inhabitants were quickly on the spot, and extricated the unfortunate travellers. Mr. Vanderfelt was much bruised and shaken, sustaining severe contusions about the face. Mrs. Tremayne's wrist was sprained, and she was much upset. The Rev. J. J. Cumming, who was passing at the time, conveyed Mr. Vanderfelt and party to the rectory, where they were medically attended, returning to Norwich by train. The vehicle was smashed to pieces, but the horses

were uninjured. Mr. Vanderfelt, although visibly suffering, went through his performance manfully the same night.

In consequence of Miss Fanny Brough leaving the Haymarket company to appear at Terry's Theatre, the part of Lady Marbury, on Monday and during the remainder of the run of *An Ideal Husband*, will be sustained by Miss Vane Featherstone, and that of Lady Basildon by Miss Enid Spencer-Brunton.

At the Columbus, New York, last week, during the performance of the play called *On the Mississippi*, a performer called Henry Arnold was marching as a Zulu Chief, carrying a torch, at the head of a procession, when somebody stumbled against him, and in a moment his dress was in a blaze. A woman screamed; the cry of "Fire!" was raised, and a panic and crush seemed inevitable, while poor Arnold danced and writhed in pain. A policeman's presence of mind saved the audience. Rushing down the centre aisle, he shouted, "Keep your seats! Don't be alarmed! It's all in the play!" The audience looked at each other, laughed a little, sat down, and began to applaud the realism. The play proceeded, the people enjoyed the songs and dances, and none of them knew that they had seen a man severely burnt.

The proceedings at the annual general meeting of the members of the Actors' Association, to be held at the Lyceum Theatre on Friday next, with Mr. Henry Irving in the chair, are likely to be interesting. A large number of prominent actors and actresses will be present, and some "burning questions" will be discussed.

Sir Augustus Harris has engaged Miss Sophie Larkin and Miss M. A. Victor to represent the ugly sisters in *Cinderella* at Drury-lane next Christmas; so that, somewhat unusually, those diverting personages will be played not by men, but by women. This, of course, will do away with any possible objections on the part of over-particular people; though it must be owned that, as a rule, our female impersonators are as free from offence as they are ingenious.

There is no quite obvious conection between sanitation and Mr. Oscar Wilde; but the Medical Officer of Health for the Borough of Cambridge has discovered sufficient to induce him to preface his "Report on the Sanitary Condition of the Borough of Cambridge" by a twenty-line quotation from *A Woman of No Importance*. It is true this excerpt is followed by half-a-dozen lines from a famous French novelist; but the association in the officer's mind of Zola with drains is easily understood.

We regret to hear that Mr. Charles Wyndham last Tuesday, in the second act of *Rebellious Susan*, directly after, as Sir Richard Kato, he had dismissed Pybus and Elaine with a sentence of judicious advice, was attacked by a sudden vertigo, and fell down in a fainting fit. He was unable to resume his part, and was taken home, Dr. Ransford and a trained nurse being immediately sent for. On Wednesday Mr. Wyndham was much better; and it is hoped that, with complete rest, he will soon be restored to health. Meanwhile, his part is being played very effectively by Mr. Frank Atherley.

for admission, and the junior Bar passed in on its wig and choked all the passage ways. The indictment charges John Sholto Douglas, Marquis of Queensberry, with writing and publishing a false and defamatory libel of and concernig Oscar Fingall O'Flaherty Wilde. This, however, will become the smallest part of the case. The defendant has undertaken to justify the libel, and if rumour is to be trusted in the smallest degree the plea of justification, which was delivered on Saturday, involves charges of the most serious kind against Mr. Wilde. Counsel for the plaintiff

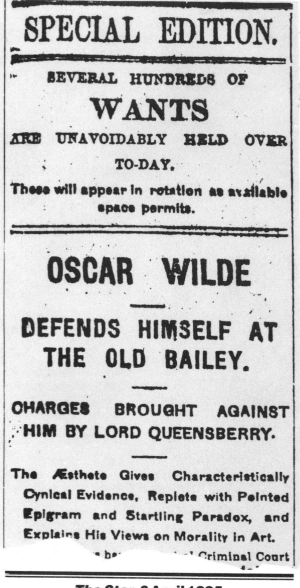

SPECIAL EDITION.

SEVERAL HUNDREDS OF
WANTS
ARE UNAVOIDABLY HELD OVER
TO-DAY.

These will appear in rotation as available space permits.

OSCAR WILDE

DEFENDS HIMSELF AT THE OLD BAILEY.

CHARGES BROUGHT AGAINST HIM BY LORD QUEENSBERRY.

The Æsthete Gives Characteristically Cynical Evidence, Replete with Pointed Epigram and Startling Paradox, and Explains His Views on Morality in Art.

· b· ·' Criminal Court

The Star, 3 April 1895

The Aesthete Gives Characteristically Cynical Evi-The Aesthete Gives Characteristically Cynical Evidence, Replete with Pointed Epigrams and Startling Paradox, and Explains His Views on Morality in Art.

Not for years has the Central Criminal Court at the Old Bailey been so densely crowded as it was this morning. People begged, bullied, and bribed

Sir Edward Clarke

the defendant was called upon to surrender, and entered the dock by the steps at the left-hand side of the dock. Standing there in a dark-blue overcoat, short and dark, and mutton chop whiskered, with his arms on the ledge at the front of the dock, while the clerk read to him the indictment. He pleaded not guilty to the charge of libelling the plaintiff, and that the publication of the words complained of was for the public benefit.

Sir Edward Clarke plunged at once in medias res. He first read to the jury the card which Lord Queensberry left open with the porter of the Albemarle Club for the plaintiff – containing a very grave and serious allegation against Mr. Wilde's character – and pointed out that it seemed to stop short of actually charging the plaintiff with the commission of one of the most serious of offences. By the pleas which the defendant had put before the court

A MUCH GRAVER ISSUE

was raised. He said the statement was true, and that it was for the public benefit it was made, and he gave particulars. There was no allegation that

are Sir Edward Clarke, Q.C., Mr. Charles Mathews and Mr. Travers Humphreys. Lord Queensbury is represented by Mr. Carson, Q.C., Mr. C. F. Gill, and Mr. A. Gill. Mr. Besley, Q.C., with whom is Mr. Monckton, holds a watching brief for Lord Douglas of Hawick, elder son of the Marquess. The judge, Mr Justice Collins, arrived at half-past ten. Mr. C. F. Gill was the first of the counsel to arrive.

MR. OSCAR WILDE ENTERED

the court, accompanied by Mr. C. O. Humphreys, his solicitor, about a quarter past ten. He wore a dark Chesterfield coat, and silk hat, and a dark tie. He did not on this occasion sport the white flower which was conspicuous in his lapel at the police-court. So crowded was the court that some difficulty was experienced in finding a place for a mere principal. A commonplace-looking jury was sworn in. As soon as the judge had taken his seat,

MARQUIS OF QUEENSBERRY.

LORD DOUGLAS.

But defendant's plea raised a much graver issue, for in that plea it was alleged that the complainant had solicited various persons to commit an offence. It was for those who

Mr. Wilde had been guilty of the offence mentioned, but there was a series of accusations, mentioning the names of a number of persons and alleging that Mr. Wilde had solicited them to the commission of the offence and had been guilty of indecent practices with them. The statement, Sir Edward added, was put in this form in order that the persons named, whilst they would assist much in cross-examination, might not have to admit that they had been guilty of the gravest of possible offences. It was for those who had taken the grave responsibility of putting in such a plea to justify it. Mr. Oscar Wilde was a gentleman 38 years of age, the son of Sir William Wilde, a very distinguished Irish surgeon and oculist, who died some years ago. The plaintiff's mother, Lady Wilde, is still living. The plaintiff went first to Trinity College, Dublin, where he

GREATLY DISTINGUISHED HIMSELF

for classical knowledge. He passed to Magdalen College, Oxford, and again greatly distinguished himself, taking the Newdigate Prize among other honours. Leaving the university, he devoted himself to literature in its artistic side, and many years ago became a very public person indeed, laughed at by some, appreciated by many, as representing a particular aspect of culture – the aesthetic cult. In 1884 he married the daughter of the late Mr. Horace Lloyd, Q.C., and has lived with her and their two children at Tite-st., Chelsea. Both are members of the Albemarle Club, to the porter of which this offensive card was delivered. Here he made the acquaintance of Lord Alfred Douglas, and from 1891 had been the friend of that young gentleman as well as of his mother, the Lady Queensberry who was the wife of the defendant till she obtained release on the ground of the defendant's misconduct. Mr. Wilde had repeatedly been her guest at Wokingham, and at Salisbury, and Lord Alfred Douglas has been the accepted friend in Mr. Wilde's own house in Chelsea, and at Cromer and Worthing and elsewhere. Until the early part of 1893 Mr. Wilde did not know the defendant except that they met once, about 1880 or 1881, an incident of which Lord Queensberry

Left: Lord Alfred Douglas
Below: Oscar Wilde
Facing page: Café Royal

44

reminded Mr. Wilde when they met at luncheon. In November, 1892, Mr. Wilde and Lord Alfred Douglas were

LUNCHING TOGETHER

at the Café Royal when Lord Queensberry came into the room. Mr. Wilde was aware there had been strained relations between Lord Alfred and his father, and he suggested that this was a good opportunity for making it up. Lord Alfred acted on the suggestion, brought Lord Queensberry to the table and introduced him to Mr. Wilde, and the three lunched together. Lord Queensberry remained chatting with Mr. Wilde after his son left, and invited the prosecutor to visit him at Torquay. After that they saw nothing of each other till the early part of 1894, when Mr. Wilde became aware that certain statements were being made –

not by Lord Queensberry – affecting his character. A man named Wood had been given some clothes by Lord Alfred Douglas, and he alleged that he found in the pocket of a coat four letters from Mr. Wilde to Lord Alfred Douglas. Whether he did find them there or whether he stole them is matter for speculation, but the letters were handed about, and Wood asked Mr. Wilde to buy them back. He represented himself as being in need and wanting to go to America. Mr. Wilde handed him £15 or £20, and received from him three of somewhat ordinary importance. It afterwards appeared that only the letters of no importance had been given up (Sir Edward Clarke made the remark quite innocently), and the letter of some importance had been retained. At that time "A Woman of No Importance" was in rehearsal at the Haymarket Theatre,

Mr. C.W. Matthews

and there came to Mr. Wilde through Mr. Beerbohm Tree a document which purported to be a copy of the retained letter. It had two headings – one Babbicombe Cliff, Torquay, and the other 16 Tite-st. Shortly afterwards a man named Allen called on Mr. Wilde, and demanded ransom for the original of the letter. Mr. Wilde

PEREMPTORILY REFUSED.

He said, "I look upon the letter as a work of art. Now I have got a copy I do not desire the original. Go." Almost immediately afterwards a man named Claburn brought the original and surrendered it, saying it was sent by Mr. Wood. Mr. Wilde gave him a sovereign for his trouble. It was supposed to be a letter of an incriminating character, and someone had taken the trouble to copy it, with mistakes, and put it about. Mr. Wilde still says that he looks upon this letter as being a kind of prose sonnet, and on 4 May, 1893, it was published in sonnet form in the *Spirit Lamp*, an aesthetical and satirical magazine, edited by Lord Alfred Douglas. Here is the letter:-

"My Own Boy, – Your sonnet is quite lovely, and it is a marvel that those red-roseleaf lips of yours should be made no less for the madness of music and song than for the madness of kissing. Your slim-built soul walks between passion and poetry. No Hyacinthus followed Love so madly as you in Greek days. Why are you alone in London, and when do you go to Salisbury? Do go there and cool your hands in the grey twilight of Gothic things. Come here whenever you like. It is a lovely place and only lacks you. But go to Salisbury first. Always with undying love, – Yours, OSCAR."

When Sir Edward Clarke read this letter there was a momentary and involuntary outburst of merriment. Sir Edward said it might provoke mirth in those used only to the terms of commercial correspondence, but Mr. Wilde denied that it was open to any unclean interpretation, or was more than the letter of

ONE POET TO ANOTHER.

On 14 Feb. another play of Mr. Wilde's, "The Importance of Being Earnest," was about to be produced at the St. James's Theatre. In the course of the day certain information was given to the management of certain intentions of Lord Queensberry. It is a matter of history, said Sir Edward, that when the late Laureatic play, "The Promise of May," was produced, Lord Queensberry got up in the theatre, and in his character as an agnostic took objection to the exposition which had been made of agnostic principles in that play in the character played by Mr. Hermann Vezin. It would have been still more serious to have had a scene, and charges affecting Mr. Wilde's character made in the theatre. Lord Queensberry had booked a seat, but his money was returned and police were retained at the theatre in the evening. Lord Queensberry attended, with a large bouquet made of vegetables. His intention can only be conjectured, but when he was refused admission to the theatre he left the bouquet at the box-office "for

Mr. Justice Collins

bring into prominence the relations between Lord Queensberry and his family, and would not now do so more than was actually necessary.

The next day Lord Queensberry was arrested. The police-court proceedings are already public property.

Sir Edward said he would not refer in detail to the accusations made against Mr. Wilde, and mention the names which he believed must have been hastily included. He would do

NOTHING TO EXTEND THE RANGE

of the case beyond the radius which was inevitable. But two of the allegations were so strange that he was bound to notice them. The first that in July 1890, Mr. Wilde published "a certain immoral and obscene work entitled 'The Picture of Dorian Grey,'" designed and intended to describe the relations, intimacies, and passions of certain persons of unnatural habits, tastes, and practices. The second was that in December, 1894, he published a certain other immoral and obscene work in the form of a magazine entitled "The Chameleon," containing similar references and "certain immoral maxims entitled 'Phrases and Philosophies for the Use of the Young.'" With regard to the magazine, Mr. Wilde was only a contributor, and in no way responsible for any part of it except the "Phrases," which were only such epigrammatic sentences as lent brilliancy to his plays. But on seeing the magazine he found that it contained a story, "The Priest and the Acolyte," which was a disgrace to literature, an amazing thing to be written by anyone, or published by any decent publisher, and he at once saw the editor and insisted on its withdrawal. As to "Dorian Grey," it has been for five years on bookstalls and in libraries, and all Sir Edward need say of it was that it was the

STORY OF A YOUNG MAN

of good birth, with great wealth and much personal beauty, whose friend, a distinguished painter, paints a portrait of him. He expresses the strange wish that as life goes on he might be allowed to

Mr. Wilde." Sir Edward could not understand how his lordship could condescend to such a pantomimic expedient, even if he had cause for attacking the character of Mr. Wilde, and whether Lord Queensberry was always and

ALTOGETHER RESPONSIBLE FOR HIS ACTIONS

would be open to doubt. No notice was taken of this intended insult. He tried to get into the gallery, but the police had their instructions, and he was not able to get into any part of the theatre. On 28 Feb. Mr. Wilde went to the Albemarle Club, where the porter, a very sensible man, handed him an envelope containing the card he had received from Lord Queensberry as long before as the 18th. This was the first publication by Lord Queensberry of the accusation he was making against Mr. Wilde, and it was now incumbent on Mr. Wilde to take action in the matter. Short of actual publication Mr. Wilde would not have done anything to

possess the undiminished beauty of his youth, while the picture should age and fade. The strange wish is granted; his conduct in life leaves its record on the picture, not on himself. He plunges into dissipation and crime, and the portrait, which is locked up from every eye but his own, grows more hideous till he can stand it no longer, but takes a knife and strikes at the picture. He instantly falls dead himself, and those who come into the room find the picture again amazingly beautiful, and on the floor a hideous and unrecognisable body of an old man. "I have read the book – for the purposes of this case," said Sir Edward, "and I shall be surprised if my learned friend can point to any passage other than such as the novelist must write to describe life and produce a work of art."

This was all Sir Edward had to say.

Sidney Wright, porter, of the Albemarle Club, was the first witness. He deposed that on 18 Feb. the defendant handed to him a card on which were written the words complained of, saying, "Give that to Oscar Wilde." Witness made a note of the day and hour at the back of the card, and placed it in an envelope, which he handed to Mr. Wilde on 28 Feb., which was the first occasion on which he saw the prosecutor.

Mr. Oscar Wilde was himself the next witness. Ponderous and fleshy, his face a dusky red, and his hair brushed away from a middle parting in smooth waves, he folded his hands on the front of the witness-box, and replied in carefully modulated monosyllables, accentuated by nods of the head, to Sir Edward Clarke's leading questions about his early life, already described. In 1882, he added, he published a first volume of poems, and he had since lectured both in America and England. During the last few years he had devoted himself to such dramatic literature as "Lady Windermere's Fan," "A Woman of No Importance," "The Importance of Being Earnest," and "The Ideal Husband," all of which were written between February, 1892, and February, 1895,

AND HAD ALL BEEN SUCCESSFUL.

He had also written a French play, "Salomé,"

which is at the present time in preparation in Paris, and had also written essays and occasional articles. He made the acquaintance of Lord Alfred Douglas in 1891, when he was brought to Tite-st., by a friend of Lady Queensberry, whose acquaintance he made later. He also came to know Lord Douglas of Hawick, and the late Lord Drumlanrig, who was the eldest son. Mr. Wilde went on to describe the Café Royal luncheon party in November, 1892, and repeated that it was at his suggestion Lord Alfred made friendly overtures to his father, from whom he had been estranged. After that he did not see Lord Queensberry till March, 1894. In the meantime the episode of the four letters had begun. The man Wood said he had found them in a suit of clothes which Lord Alfred Douglas had given to him. "I read the letters," said Mr. Wilde, "and I said, 'I do not consider these letters of any importance.'" Wood said, "They were stolen from me by a man named Allen, and I have been employed to get them back, as they wished to extort money from you." Witness repeated that they were of no use, and Wood proceeded, "I am very much afraid, as they are threatening me. I want to get away to America." "He made a very strong appeal to me to enable him to go to New York, as he could find nothing to do in London. I gave him £15." Long afterwards, on 23 April, 1893,

MR. BEERBOHM TREE

handed him the copy of the other letter which had been read, and a man named Allen afterwards called and witness said, "I suppose you have come about my beautiful letter to Lord Alfred Douglas. If you had not been so foolish as to send a copy of it to Mr. Beerbohm Tree I would gladly have paid a very large sum of money for the letter, as I consider it to be a work of art." He replied, "A very curious construction has been put on that letter." Witness replied, "Ah, art is rarely intelligible to the criminal classes." Allen said he had been offered £60 for it. Witness said, "Take my advice. Go to that man and sell my letter to him for £60. I myself have never received so large a sum for any prose

Savoy Hotel

work, and that very small work, but I am glad to find there is anyone in England who considers that a letter of mine is worth £60." "He was somewhat taken aback," added Oscar. "I said, 'I can only assure you on my word of honour that I will not pay one penny for that letter, so if you dislike this man very much you should sell my letter to him for £60.' He then, changing his manner, said he hadn't a single penny, was very poor, and had been many times to try and find me. I said I would gladly give him half a sovereign. He took it and went away. I also told him, 'This letter, which is a prose poem, will shortly be published in sonnet form in a delightful magazine, and I will send you a copy,' In fact the letter was made

THE BASIS OF A SONNET

in French, which was published in the *Chameleon*. Allen had no sooner gone than the man Cliburn came with the letter. He said, 'Allen said you were kind to him, and there is no good trying to "rent" you, as you only laugh at us.' The letter was very much soiled and I said, 'I think it quite unpardonable that better care was not taken of a manuscript of mine.' He said he was very sorry, but it had been in so many hands. I said to him, 'I am afraid you are leading a wonderfully wicked life.' He said, 'There is good and bad in every one of us.' I told him that was more than possible."

All this Oscar told with the blandest air of sangfroid, caressing his tan gloves between his hands. Sir Edward passed on to the incidents of 1894. At the end of June there was an interview at 16, Tite-st., with Lord Queensberry and another gentleman – "whose name is of no importance." Lord Queensberry said, "Sit down!" Oscar replied, "I don't allow you to talk to me like that. I suppose you have come to apologise for the statements you have made about my wife and me in relation to your son. I could have you up any day I choose for criminal libel for writing such letters. How dare you say such things about your son and me!" Lord Queensberry replied, "You were both kicked out of the Savoy Hotel at a moment's notice for your scandalous conduct." Oscar said, "That is a lie!"

Lord Queensberry continued, "You have taken and furnished rooms for him in Piccadilly." Oscar replied, "Someone has been telling you a series of lies." Lord Queensberry said, "I hear you were thoroughly well blackmailed last year for a disgusting letter that you wrote to my son." Oscar replied, "The letter was

A BEAUTIFUL LETTER

and I never write except for publication." Oscar said, "You accuse me of leading your son into vice." Lord Queensberry replied, "I don't say you are it, but you look it and you pose as it."

An applausive tapping in the gallery followed this statement. "If I hear the slightest repetition of that noise I will have the court cleared," said the judge.

Mr. Wilde continued, "Lord Queensberry said, 'If I catch you and my son together again I will thrash you." I said, 'I do not know what the Queensberry rules are, but the Oscar Wilde rule is to shoot at sight.' I then told him to leave my house. He said that he would not do so. I told him I would have him put out by the police." The scene ended with recriminations of a similar kind. Mr. Wilde went into the hall and said to his servant, "This is the Marquess of Queensberry, the most infamous brute in London. Never allow him to enter my house again. Should he attempt to come in, you may send for the police."

Was it a fact that you had taken rooms in Piccadilly for his son? – No.

Was there any foundation for the statement that you and any of his sons were expelled from the Savoy Hotel? – It is perfectly untrue.

Mr. Wilde. briefly denied responsibility for the character of the *Chameleon*, and said he knew nothing about the story of "The Priest and the Acolyte" till he saw the magazine, and expressed his disapproval of it to the editor. As to "Dorian Grey," the moral of that was that the man who tried to destroy his conscience destroyed himself. There was no truth whatsoever in any one of the accusations of misconduct made in the plea of justification.

The Daily Telegraph, 4 April 1895

CROSS-EXAMINATION OF THE PROSECUTOR

Cross-examined by Mr. Carson: You stated your age as thirty-nine. I think you are over forty?

The Witness: I am thirty-nine or forty. You have my certificate, and that settles the matter.

You were born in 1854 — that makes you somewhat over forty? — Very well.

Do you happen to know what age Lord Alfred Douglas is? — Lord Alfred Douglas is about twenty-four, and was between twenty and twenty-one years of age when I first knew him. Down to the interview in Tite-street Lord Queensberry had been friendly. I am quite sure I did not receive a letter in which Lord Queensberry desired that my acquaintance with his son should cease. After the interview I had no doubt that such was Lord Queensberry's desire. Notwithstanding Lord Queensberry's protest my intimacy with Lord A. Douglas continues to the present moment.

You have stayed with him at many places? — Yes.

Edward Carson

At Oxford, Brighton — on several occasions — Worthing? — Yes.

You never took rooms for him? — Never.

Were you at other places with him? — Well, at Cromer and Torquay.

And in various hotels in London? — Yes. One in Albemarle-street and one in Dover-street, and at the Savoy.

Did you ever take rooms yourself in addition to having your house in Tite-street? — Yes, at 10 and 11, St. James's-place. I kept the rooms from the month of October, 1893, to the end of March, 1894. Lord Douglas has stopped in those chambers, which were not far from Piccadilly. I have been abroad with him several times, and even lately to

51

Monte Carlo. With reference to these books, it was not at Brighton in the King's-road that I wrote my contribution in the "Chameleon." I observed that there were also contributions from Lord Alfred Douglas, but these were not written in Brighton. They were written whilst he was an undergraduate at Oxford.

He had shown them to you before he sent them to the "Chameleon"? — No (doubtfully). I had seen them. I thought them exceedingly beautiful poems, one was in "Praise of Shame" the other "Two Loves."

The Two Loves are two boys? — Yes.

One calls his love true love and the other boy's love as Shame? — Yes. Are you quoting from the poem?

Mr. Carson quoted a few lines ending with the words "I am the love that dare not speak its name." (To witness:) Did you see in that any improper suggestion? — No; none whatever.

You read "The Priest and the Acolyte"? — Yes.

You have no doubt whatever that was an improper story? — From the literary point of view it was highly improper. It is impossible for a man of letters to judge it otherwise, by literature meaning treatment, selection of subject, and the like. I thought the treatment wrong and the subject wrong.

You are of opinion there is no such thing as an immoral book? — Yes.

May I take it that you think "The Priest and the Acolyte" was not immoral? — It is worse, it is badly written. (Laughter).

Mr. Carson was proceeding to examine as to the nature of the story, when Sir Edward Clarke objected, but his lordship held that Mr. Carson had a perfect right to examine as to the reasons for the witness's disapproval of the book.

Sir E. Clarke: We are not dealing here with matters of literary criticism.

Mr. Carson: That is the very point. We are not. Is not that the story of a priest who fell in love with a boy who attended him at the altar, and a scandal arose?

The Witness: I have only read it once. You cannot cross-examine me as to the details of the story. I don't care for it; it does not interest me.

Do you think the story blasphemous? — I think the end — the death — violated every artistic canon of beauty.

That is not an answer. — It is the only one I can give.

I want to see the position you pose as. — I do not think you should use that.

I have said nothing out of the way. I wish to know whether you thought the story blasphemous? — The story filled me with disgust.

Answer the question, sir. Did you or did you not consider the story blasphemous? — I did not consider the story a blasphemous production. I thought it was disgusting.

I am satisfied with that. You know that when the priest in the story administers poison to the boy that he uses the words of the Sacrament of the Church of England? — That I entirely forgot.

Do you consider that blasphemous? — I think it is horrible; the word "blasphemous" is not a word of mine.

In further cross-examination upon passages which Mr. Carson read, the witness said he did not think that they were intended as blasphemous by the writer. Mr. Wilde added: I disapprove of the tone, the treatment, and the subject from beginning to end.

Sir Edward Clarke objected to the reading of these extracts, the witness having declared the story to be horrible, and there could be no possible object except for the sake in some way of identifying Mr. Wilde with the passages and so affecting the case.

The judge held that Mr. Carson was in order in testing the witness's view of the production. It was germane to the inquiry.

Sir Edward Clarke: His view has been expressed.

Mr. Carson (to witness): Was it only from the literary point of view that you disapproved of the death scene?

Witness: I think it is disgusting twaddle.

I think that you will admit that anyone who was connected, or would allow himself to approve, of that article would be posing as a felon? — No, certainly not. It was written by another person in the magazine.

I am asking you, supposing the person had been connected with the production of it, or had approved it in public, would he be posing as a felon? — I should say he would be displaying a very bad literary taste. I don't know why I should be cross-examined on a thing that I object to.

You disapprove of this story from a literary point of view. Did you ever do any public act to inform the public that you disapproved of the "Chameleon?" — No, I never did.

And notwithstanding the article — a portion of which has been read — being in the paper to which you yourself had contributed, you did not think it in the least necessary to disassociate yourself from it? — You mean by a public letter. I thought it would be beneath my dignity as a man of letters to disassociate myself from the work of an Oxford undergraduate. I have no doubt it was circulated among the undergraduates of Oxford.

Do you think that these phrases and philosophies of yours — your contribution – were axioms likely to tend to morality among young men? — My work never aims to produce anything less than literature.

May I take it that you are not concerned whether it has a moral or immoral effect? — I do not believe that any book or work of art ever produced any effect upon conduct at all.

You do not consider the effect in creating morality or immorality? — Certainly not.

So far as your work is concerned you pose as not being concerned about morality or immorality? — I won't use the word "pose."

Pose is a favourite word of your own? — Is it? I have no pose in the matter. My own work in writing a play or a book is concerned entirely with literature — that is, with art. The aim is not to do good or evil, but trying to make a thing that will have some quality or form of beauty, wit, emotion, and so on.

Listen, sir. Here is one of the "Phrases and Philosophies for the Use of the Young": "Wickedness is a myth invented by good people to account for the curious attractiveness of others." You think that true? — I rarely think that anything I write is true.

Did you say rarely? — I said rarely. I might have said never; not true in the sense of correspondence with the actual facts.

"Religions die when they are proved to be true." Is that true? — Yes, I hold that. It is a suggestion towards a philosophy of the absorption of religions by science, but it is too big a question to go into now.

Do you think that was a safe axiom to put forward for the use of the young? — It was a most stimulating thought. (Laughter.)

"If one tells the truth one is sure, sooner or later, to be found out." — That is a pleasing paradox, but I do not set very high store on it as an axiom.

Is it good for the young? — Anything is good that stimulates thought in whatever age.

Whether moral or immoral? — There is no such thing as morality or immorality in thought. There is immoral emotion.

"Pleasure is the only thing one should live for: nothing ages like happiness," — I think that the realisation of oneself is the prime aim of life, and to realise oneself through pleasure is finer than to do so through pain. I am on that point entirely on the side of the ancients.

"A truth ceases to be true when more than one person believes it"? — Perfectly. That would be my metaphysical definition of truth; something so personal that the same truth could never be appreciated by two minds.

"The condition of perfection is idleness"? — Oh, yes, I think so. Half of it is true. The life of contemplation is the highest life, and so recognised by the philosopher.

"There is something tragic about the enormous number of young men in England who at the present moment are starting life with perfect profiles, and end by adopting some useful profession?" Is that phrase philosophy for the young? — I should think that the young would have enough sense of humour.

You think that is amusing? — It is an amusing paradox — an amusing play of words.

What would anybody say would be the effect of "Phrases and Philosophies" taken in connection with such an article as "The Priest and the Acolyte"? — Undoubtedly it was the idea that might be formed that made me object so strongly to the story. I saw at once that maxims that were mere nonsense, paradoxical, or anything you like — several of them have appeared in my plays — might be read in conjunction with it.

After the criticisms that were passed on "Dorian Grey," was it modified a good deal? No. Additions were made. In one case it was pointed out to me — not in a newspaper or anything of that sort, but by the only critic of the century whose opinion I set high, Mr. Walter Pater — that certain passages were liable to misconstruction in respect to the nature of Dorian Grey's sin, and I made one addition.

This is your introduction to "Dorian Grey": "There is no such thing as a moral or immoral book; books are well written or badly written." That expresses your view? — My view on art, yes.

May I take it that no matter how immoral the book was, if it was well written it would be a good book? — If it were well written it would produce a sense of duty, which is the highest feeling man is capable of. If it was badly written it would produce a sense of disgust.

Then a well written book, putting forth certain views, might be a good book? — No work of art ever puts forward views of any kind. Views belong to people who are not artists.

Is "Dorian Grey" open to a certain interpretation? — Only to brutes and the illiterate. The views of the Philistine on art are incalculably stupid.

The majority of people would come within your definition of Philistines and illiterates? — I have found wonderful exceptions.

Do you think the majority of people live up to the pose you are giving us? — I am afraid they are not cultivated enough.

Not cultivated enough to draw the distinction you have done between a good book and a bad book? — Certainly not. It has nothing to do with art at all.

You don't prevent the ordinary individual from buying your books? — I have never discouraged it. (Laughter.)

Mr. Carson said he proposed to ask questions of the witness with reference to further passages in "Dorian Grey."

Sir E. Clarke raised a question as to the edition of the work which was being quoted; but after a conversation with Mr. Oscar Wilde, who left the box for that purpose, intimated that his client was indifferent as to which edition was challenged.

Mr. Carson then read a passage describing the introduction of the artist to Dorian Grey, and asked: Do you consider the feeling there described as a proper or an improper feeling?

Witness: I think it is the most perfect description possible of what an artist would feel on meeting a beautiful personality that he felt in some way or other was necessary to his art and his life.

You think that this is a moral kind of feeling for one man to have towards another? — I say it is the feeling of an artist towards a beautiful personality.

You have never known the feelings you describe there? — No. I have never allowed any personality to dominate my art.

The passage I am quoting says: "I quite admit that I adore you madly." Have you had that feeling? — I have never given admiration to any person except myself. (Laughter.) The expression was, I regret to say, borrowed from Shakespeare. (Laughter.)

Then we read, "I want to have you all to myself." — I should consider that an intense bore. (Laughter.)

People who have not the views you have might form another opinion of these passages? —

Undoubtedly; but don't cross-examine me about the ignorance of other people. (Laughter.) I have a great passion to civilise the community.

You describe the gift of a novel, which affected for evil the mind of Dorian Grey. You had a book in your mind? — Yes, "A Rebours." I consider it badly written, but it gave me an idea.

Was "A Rebours" a moral book? — It was not well written. I would not call it moral.

Mr. Carson put to the witness a marked passage in the book in question.

Witness: I don't think you have a right to cross-examine me on the works of another artist.

Mr. Carson pressed the point, and Sir E. Clarke objected.

Mr. Justice Collins: I don't think it is admissible. Mr. Wilde has repudiated "A Rebours," and has said that all the book did was to suggest a plot to him.

Mr. Carson (to witness): You don't think that one person can exercise influence on another? — I don't think, except in fiction, there is any influence, good or bad, of one person over another. It is a mere philosophic point.

I want to ask you a few questions about your letter to Lord Alfred Douglas. Where was he staying then? — At the Savoy Hotel, and I was staying at the Babbicombe, Torquay. It was in answer to a poem which he had sent me.

Was it an ordinary letter? — Certainly not. I should think not. (Laughter.) It was a beautiful letter.

Apart from art? — I cannot answer any question apart from art. A man who is not an artist could never have written that letter.

Was it an exceptional letter? — Unique, I should think.

Was it the ordinary way in which you carried on correspondence with Lord Alfred Douglas? — No, it would be impossible. One could not. It was like writing a poem.

Have you written others of this class of letter? — There is no class in that letter.

Have you written others like this? — I don't repeat myself in style. (Laughter.)

Here is another letter which I believe you also wrote to Lord Alfred Douglas: "Savoy Hotel. — Dearest of all Boys — Your letter was delightful red and yellow wine to me, but I am sad and out of sorts. You must not make scenes with me; they kill me. They wreck the loveliness of life. I cannot see you, so Greek and gracious, distorted by passion. I cannot listen to your carved lips saying hideous things to me. Don't do it; you break my heart. I had sooner — (here Mr. Carson said he could not decipher the letter) — than have you bitter, unjust, horrid. I must see you soon. You are the divine thing I want; the thing of grace and genius; but I don't know how to do it. Shall I come to Salisbury? There are many difficulties. My bill here is £49 for a week. I have also got a new sitting-room over the Thames; but you — why are you not here, my dear, my wonderful boy? I fear I must leave; no money, no credit, and a heart of lead. — Ever your own, OSCAR."

Is that an extraordinary letter? — I think everything I write is extraordinary. I don't pose as being ordinary, great heavens! Ask me any question you like about it.

Is it the kind of letter a man writes to another man? — It is the kind of letter I wrote to Lord Alfred Douglas. What other men write to other men I know nothing about, nor do I care. It is not like the other — a prose poem.

Were you living at the Savoy then? — Yes, I think I was there about a month.

Had you a house in Tito street at the same time? — Yes.

Had Lord Alfred Douglas been staying with you at the Savoy immediately before that? — Yes.

You said a man named Wood came to see you about certain letters found in Lord Alfred Douglas's coat. Who made the appointment? — It was made through Mr. Alfred Taylor.

He is an intimate friend of yours? — A friend — not an intimate friend.

When did you last see Taylor? — Yesterday.

Before you brought about the appointment with

Wood had you gone to Sir George Lewis, and got him to write a letter to Wood? — Yes.

And Wood had refused to go to Sir George Lewis? — That I don't know. He did not go.

Were you anxious about these letters? — About my private correspondence! Yes, I should think so. What gentleman isn't?

How long had you known Wood? — I think I met him at the end of January, 1893. It was at the Café Royal. Lord Alfred Douglas had telegraphed me from Salisbury, asking me to help Wood.

Was Wood living with Taylor? — I don't know.

You used subsequently to go to 13, Little College-street, where Taylor lived? — Yes, on many occasions.

Was Wood there at any time you were there? — No.

There were tea parties? — Yes.

They were all men at the tea parties? — Yes.

Did you dine at the Florence Restaurant in Rupert-street with Wood? — No. The first time we met, it was about nine o'clock. I asked him if he had dined, and we went round to the Florence and I ordered some supper for him.

What was Wood's occupation? — As far as I know, he had none. He was looking for some. He told me he had had a clerkship.

I suggest it was Taylor who introduced Wood to you? — No; he was introduced to me through this telegram from Lord Alfred Douglas.

Did you become intimate with Wood? — No; I met him three or four times.

Was he ever at Tite-street? — Never.

Had you ever a servant called Ginger? — Never.

Why did you go round from the Café Royal to the Florence? — Because I had been in the habit of supping there. I considered it a pleasant place and I could get cheques cashed there. I got a cheque cashed that evening.

Did you give any money to Wood? — I gave him £2 because Lord Alfred Douglas had asked me to be kind to him. I gave the money to him at the Café Royal. I got a cheque cashed at the Florence for my own convenience, the next day being Sunday.

Was Wood an artist or literary man? — No.

Did you ever go to see Wood? — Never in my life.

When he came to you about these letters, did you consider he intended to levy blackmail on you? — Yes; and I was determined to face him.

And the way you faced it was giving him the £16 to go to America? — I thought he was going to produce letters of mine and Lord Alfred Douglas to extort money. I said the letters were of no interest. Then he told me a long story, and then, very foolishly, perhaps, but out of pure kindness, I gave him the money.

I suggest that you gave him £30? — No; he told me that his passage cost more than he expected, and I gave him £5 in addition. I did it out of kindness.

You suggest that you gave this £21 out of charity? — I say I undoubtedly felt his having possession of these letters, and, after the story he told me, I candidly confessed he behaved rather well.

Did you have a champagne lunch with him before he went off? — No champagne. I never drink in the middle of the day. We lunched at the Florence.

A farewell lunch to the man you thought had attempted to blackmail you? — Yes; he had convinced me that it was not so.

Was it then and there that you gave him the £5? — Yes: because he said the £15 I had given him would land him almost penniless in New York.

When Wood was in America did he write to you for money? — No.

Did Taylor tell you Wood had written to him to ask for money? — No.

Did you know Taylor was in communication with him in America? — No.

Is this Wood's handwriting? (letter produced) — I should think so.

Did Wood call Taylor Alfred? — Yes; they were great friends.

Did Wood call you Oscar? — Yes.

And you called him Alf.? — No; I never use abbreviations. I called him Alfred. I also called

Taylor by his Christian name, Alfred.

You, Wood, and Taylor all called each other by your Christian names? — Yes. I am afraid everybody, with few exceptions, calls me by my Christian name, and I like calling people by their Christian names.

Wasn't it a curious thing that a man with whom you were on such intimate terms should come and blackmail you? — I thought it was monstrous. In fact, I did not believe it.

Did Allen come and see you afterwards? — Six or seven weeks after.

He came bringing one of the letters? — Yes.

You knew he had stolen it from Wood? — Wood assured me that the letters had been stolen from him and that he had recovered them all.

What position in life was Allen? — A blackmailer.

You complained of the loss of your beautiful work of art? — No; I said that it wasn't a loss any longer, as he had sent a copy to Mr. Beerbohm Tree.

Did you give this man, whom you knew as a blackmailer, 10s? — Yes.

What had he given you? — Nothing; he sent the letter round.

Why did you give it to him? — I gave it him to show my contempt. (Laughter.)

The way you show your contempt is by giving 10s? — Very often. (Laughter.) I did it really to show I didn't care twopence for him, (Laughter.)

When he had gone, Clyburn came to the door? — Yes.

Did you think he was a blackmailer? — I thought he was connected with it.

You immediately were kind to him? — Yes; he brought back the letter, and I gave him half-a-sovereign.

You complained to him about this beautiful manuscript? — I was annoyed at the soiled way in which it was returned.

Did you tell this blackmailer that this beautiful letter was about to be published as a sonnet? — No; I told that to Allen.

And did you tell him that when it was published you would send him a copy? — Yes, to show him how little I cared whether I had the letter or not.

You told Clyburn about the wicked life he was leading? — I am afraid I did make an observation. I thought he was mixed up in this attempt to blackmail me.

You told me you have written a good many beautiful letters. Do you happen to have any one of them except the one which was found out, and which was turned into a sonnet? — I should require to read the whole of modern poetry to answer that. (Laughter.) At the moment I cannot recollect any.

In February, 1892, when you were staying at the Albemarle Hotel, did you become acquainted with a young man named Edward Shelley? — Yes, he was employed by the firm who were then my publishers. He often dined with me.

Was that an intellectual treat? — Yes, for him. (Laughter.)

Did you ever give him any money? — Yes, on two or three occasions. The first time it was £4. The second time it was £3, which I sent for his railway fare to Cromer, where my wife and I had asked him to stay with us. He did not come. The third time I gave him £5.

He kept the £3? — There were continual references to his struggling to support his mother, or something of that kind; and I wrote and told him not to trouble to send it back. I gave him copies of my works.

Why were you on such intimate terms with this young Shelley? — Because he had high literary ambitions, and also because he admired my works.

You became intimate with a young lad named Alphonso Conway at Worthing? — Yes.

He sold newspapers at Worthing Pier? — Never.

What was he? — Enjoying himself by being idle.

He was a loafer, wasn't he? — I call him happy. You may call him what you like.

He had no occupation? — His mother had a house there.

Was he a literary character or an artist? — No.

How did you come to know him? — When I was

at Worthing Lord Alfred Douglas and I were in the habit of going out in a sailing-boat, and one afternoon, while the boat was being dragged down the beach, Conway and a younger boy in flannels helped. I suggested to Lord Alfred Douglas that we should take them out for a sail.

Was Conway's conversation literary? — On the contrary, it was quite simple and easy to be understood. He was a pleasant, nice creature.

What did you know of him? — He said that hiis father had been an electrical engineer, and had died young; that his mother kept a lodging-house, or, at least, she had one lodger; that he himself had been sent to school, where, naturally, he did not learn much, and that his desire was to go to sea as an apprentice in a merchant ship.

Did you give him anything? — Oh, yes. (Laughter.) I do not think I ever gave him any money.

Did you not give him sums amounting to £15? — Good heavens, no! I have given him a cigarette-case, my photograph, a book, "The Wreck of the Grosvenor," and a walking-stick.

It is a handsome stick for a boy of that class? — I do not think it is a beautiful stick myself. (Laughter.)

You dressed him up in a blue serge suit and a straw hat, in order that he might look more like your equal? — Oh, no; he never looked that. (Laughter.)

You took him to Brighton? — Yes. I had promised him an excursion.

The cross-examination of the witness had not been concluded when the Court rose. Lord Queensberry was liberated on his own recognisance of £500.

ALLEGED LIBEL ON MR. OSCAR WILDE.

CROSS-EXAMINATION OF THE PROSECUTOR.

SPEECH FOR THE DEFENCE.

The Marquis of Queensberry yesterday morning again surrendered at the Central Criminal Court, before Mr. Justice Henn Collins, to take his trial upon the charge of having unlawfully and maliciously written and published a defamatory libel on Mr. Oscar Wilde in the form of a card directed to him, and left at the Albemarle Club.

Sir Edward Clarke, Q.C., M.P., Mr. Charles Mathews, and Mr. Travers Humphreys, instructed by Messrs. C. O. Humphreys, Son, and Kershaw, appeared for Mr. Wilde; Mr. Carson, Q.C., M.P., Mr. C. F. Gill, and Mr. A. Gill, instructed by Mr. Charles Russell, defended the Marquis of Queensberry; and Mr. Besley, Q.C., and Mr. Monckton were present to watch the case at the instance of Lord Douglas of Hawick.

Mr. Oscar Wilde was recalled for cross-examination by Mr. Carson, and in reply to questions said he had continued to be intimate with Taylor, who ar-

The Daily Telegraph, 5 April 1895

The Marquis of Queensberry yesterday morning again surrendered at the Central Criminal Court, before Mr. Justice Henn Collins, to take his trial upon the charge of having unlawfully and maliciously written and published a defamatory libel on Mr. Oscar Wilde in the form of a card directed to him, and left at the Albemarle Club.

Sir Edward Clarke, Q.C., M.P., Mr. Charles Mathews, and Mr. Travers Humphreys, instructed by Messrs. C.O. Humphreys, Son, and Kershaw, appeared for Mr. Wilde; Mr. Carson, Q.C., M.P., Mr. C.F. Gill, and Mr. A. Gill, instructed by Mr. Charles Russell, defended the Marquis of Queensberry; and Mr. Besley, Q.C., and Mr. Monckton were present to watch the case at the instance of Lord Douglas of Harwick.

Mr. Oscar Wilde was recalled for cross-examination by Mr. Carson, and in reply to questions said he had continued to be intimate with Taylor, who arranged the meeting between him and Wood with reference to the letters, at his house, 13, Little College-street, which he gave up in 1893. Taylor occupied the upper part of the house. Witness had gone there to tea parties in the afternoon.

Do you know what rent he paid? — I had not the slightest idea; not very high, I should think. He had no servant; he used to open the door himself.

Did he use to do his own cooking? — That I don't know. I have never dined there. I don't know there was anything wrong in it.

Have I suggested that there was anything wrong? — No, cooking is an art.

Another art? — Yes.

Did his rooms strike you as being peculiar at all? — No, except that they displayed more taste than usual.

It was rather elaborate furniture for that class of house? — I did not say it was elaborate. I said it was in good taste.

It did not occur to you that the rooms were luxurious? — I thought them most pretty.

He never admitted any daylight into them? — I really don't know what you mean.

Was there always either candles or gas light there? — No.

Did you ever see them lighted other than by gas or candle, whether day or night? — (After a pause) Yes, certainly.

Did you ever see the curtains drawn back in the sitting-room? — When I went to see Mr. Taylor it was in winter, usually at five o'clock, when, naturally, it was dark, but I am under the impression of having seen him earlier in the day, when it was daylight.

It would not be true, then, to say that he had always got a double set of curtains drawn across the window, and day and night always kept the room lighted by candles or gas? — It would be certainly untrue.

Can you recall any time specifically when you saw daylight in the room? — Yes. Mr. Taylor was there. It was in the month of March, at noon.

Were the rooms strongly perfumed? — I don't know what you mean. He used to burn perfumes, just as I do in my rooms.

Just as you do. Did you ever see Wood there? — No, never, except on the one occasion when I met him there.

Did you ever see Sidney Mavor there? — Yes.

How old was he? About twenty-five or twenty-six.

Is he still your friend? — I have not seen him for a year now. He dined with me a year ago. I have not the remotest idea where he is now.

Did you have any communication with him since, either directly or indirectly? — To him, yes. I asked Mr. Taylor to go down there on last Sunday to the house of Mr. Mavor's mother, as I wished to see him. He was not there, but it was said he would

The Marquis of Queensberry

be back on Monday. I asked Taylor to write to him.

Well, have you found him since? — What do you mean by "finding him"? I object to the phrase. I have not seen him since.

Did you know whether Mr. Taylor had a lady's costume there? — No, he has never told me so, and I have never heard of it, or seen him in fancy dress.

You frequently communicated with him by telegraph. Had you any business with him? — No, none at all. He was a friend of mine.

Was he a literary man? — He was a young man of great taste and intelligence, and had been brought up at a very good English public school. I have never seen any created work of his.

Was he a literary man? — What do you mean by a literary man?

Did you discuss literature with him? — He used to listen on the subject.

I suppose that he used to get an intellectual treat also? — Certainly.

Was he an artist? — Not in the sense of creating anything. He was very artistic, intellectual, clever, and pleasant, and I liked him very much.

Used you to get him from time to time to arrange dinners for you to meet young men? — No. I have dined with him and young men perhaps ten or twelve times at Solferino's, the Florence, and Kettner's. We usually had a private room, as I prefer dining in private rooms.

Did you send Taylor this telegram on March 7, 1893: "Could you call at six o'clock? — OSCAR, Savoy"? — Yes. I had received an anonymous letter saying that Alfred Wood was going to blackmail me for certain letters that he had stolen from Lord Alfred Douglas. The matter of my meeting Wood was discussed then.

When you were at Goring you also telegraphed to him, on Aug. 21, 1893, "Cannot manage the dinner to-morrow; am sorry, – OSCAR"? — Yes.

Who was Fred? — Fred? He was a young man to whom I was introduced by the gentleman whose name you handed me yesterday. His other name was Atkins.

You were very familiar with him? — What do you mean by being familiar? I liked him.

You told me yesterday that you called persons by their Christian names? — Always when I like them. If I dislike people I call them something else.

Had you any trouble about Fred? — Never in my life.

Did you on March 10, 1893, telegraph to Taylor, "Obliged to see Tree at five o'clock, so do not come to Savoy. Let me know at once about Fred. — OSCAR"? I do not remember what I wanted to know about Fred.

Did you know that Taylor was being watched by the police? — No, I never heard that.

At his rooms there? — Never.

Do you know that Taylor and Parker were arrested together in a raid made on a house in Fitzroy-square? — Last year, yes.

Did you know Parker? — Yes. I do not think that I have seen him at Taylor's rooms, but when Taylor moved to Chapel-street I have seen him there.

How many young men has he introduced to you? — You can hardly ask me to remember. Do you mean people mentioned in the indictment?

No. Young men with whom you afterwards became intimate? — I should think six, seven, or eight. I became friendly with about five.

Such men as you would call by their Christian names? — Yes.

Were they all about twenty years of age? — Twenty or twenty-two. I like the society of young men.

Had they any occupation? — That I really do not know.

To how many of them did you give money? — I should think to all five I gave money or presents.

Did they give you anything? — Me! No.

Did Taylor introduce you to Charles Parker? — Yes; he was one of those I became friendly with.

Was he a gentleman's servant out of employment? — I have no knowledge of that at all. I never heard it; nor should I have minded. I should become friendly with any human being that I liked.

How old was he? — Really, I do not keep a

census. He may be sixteen or forty-five. Don't ask me. What is the good of cross-examining me on what I don't know? He may be about twenty. He was young, and that was one of his attractions. I have never asked him his age. I think it vulgar to ask people their age.

Was he a literary character? — Oh, no!

Was he an artist? — No.

Was he an educated man? — Culture was not his strong point. (Laughter.)

Did you ever ask this man with whom you were so friendly what his previous occupation was? — I never inquire into people's pasts.

Nor their future? — Ah, that is problematical.

Sir E. Clarke: There is no use in inquiring about that.

Mr. Carson: Where is Parker now? — I have not the remotest idea. I have lost sight of him.

How much money did you give Parker? — I should think altogether £4 or £5.

For what? — Because he was poor. He had no money, and I liked him. What better reason could I have?

Where did you first meet him? — At Kettner's, with Alfred Taylor. His brother was also there.

Did you become friendly with his brother? — They were guests at my table.

On the first occasion you saw them? — Yes. It was Taylor's birthday, and I asked him to dinner and told him to bring any of his friends.

Did you know that one was a gentleman's valet and the other a gentleman's groom? — I did not know it, and if I had I should not have cared. I do not care twopence about social position.

What enjoyment was it to you to be entertaining grooms and coachmen? — The pleasure of being with those who are young, bright, happy, careless, and original. I don't like the old.

Taylor accepted your invitation by bringing a valet and a groom? — That is your account of them, not mine.

Were they persons of that class? — I am surprised at your description, as they seemed not to have the manners of that class. They seemed to be very pleasant and nice. They spoke of a father at Datchet who was a person of wealth, or not exactly of wealth, but of some fortune, and Charley Parker said that he was anxious to go upon the stage.

Did you call him Charley on the first evening? — Certainly.

Had you a good dinner? — I forget the menu, but it was Kettner at his best. (Laughter.)

And the best of Kettner's wine? — Yes.

All for the groom and valet? — No, for Mr. Alfred Taylor.

You did the honours to the groom and the valet in a private room? — I entertained Mr. Taylor and his friends in a private room.

Did you give them also an intellectual treat? — They seemed deeply impressed. (Laughter.)

During the dinner you became more familiar with Charley than the other one? — Yes. I liked him better.

Did Charles Parker call you Oscar? — Yes. I like to be called either Oscar or Mr. Wilde.

You put him at his ease at once? — At once.

Did you give them plenty of champagne? — They had as much as they wanted.

As much as they could drink? — If you imply by that that I forced wine upon them, I did not.

You did not stint them? — What gentleman would stint his guests?

Mr. Carson: What gentleman would stint the valet and the groom?

Witness and his counsel objected to this comment.

In reply to further questions the witness denied that Parker went back with him to the Savoy Hotel, and had whiskies and sodas, or two small bottles of iced champagne.

Is that a favourite drink of yours? — Yes; strongly against the doctor's orders.

Never mind the doctor's orders. — No, I don't. (Laughter.)

Witness denied that he had given Parker £2 after the dinner at Kettner's, but did so in December, 1893. He did not ask Taylor what those young men were; it was sufficient for him that they were friends of his. Taylor did not say that he had met them in the St. James's Restaurant. In October, 1893, to April, 1894, he had rooms in St. James's-place, which he described.

Did Parker come there to tea? — Yes, five or six times.

What was he doing there? — Nothing.

What was he doing? — Visiting me.

Visiting you. Was he alone? — Sometimes he came with Taylor, and sometimes alone. I like his society.

Did you give him presents? — I gave him a Christmas present.

Did you give him a chain gold ring? — No; but I gave him a silver cigarette case, and also £3 or £4, as he was hard up.

Did you give it to him all at once? — Yes, all at once.

What did he do when he came to tea? — You asked me what a young man would do in that time. Why, have his tea, smoke a cigarette, and enjoy himself.

What was there in common between this young man and you? — I like to be in the society of people much younger than myself, and who may be called idle and careless. I recognise no social distinctions of any kind, and to me youth, the mere fact of youth, is so wonderful that I would sooner talk to a young man for half an hour than even be cross-examined in court. (Laughter.)

Yes! Do I understand that even a young boy you would pick up in the street would be a pleasing companion? — I would talk to street arabs with pleasure.

And take them to your private room? — Yes, if they interested me. Charles Parker had no employment during the time I knew him. He had an allowance from his father, of the smallness of which he complained. I knew he lived at 7, Camera-square. I don't know if that is near Tite-street. I never got clothes for him.

Did you take him to lunch at various places? – Oh, yes; he lunched with me at the Café Royal and at St. James's-place, and dined with me at Kettner's. We did not have a private room. I am quite sure of that for particular reasons. We went then to the Pavilion, but we did not go back to St.James's-place. I have never been to see him at Camera-square.

Why? — Well, it really would not have interested me to go to see him; while it would interest him to see me. (Laughter.) Going to see him is a very different thing to his coming to tea with me.

You remember Parker leaving Camera-square to go to 50, Park-walk? – No; I don't know where Park-walk is.

Did you write to him any beautiful letters? — I don't think I have ever written to Charles Parker a beautiful letter.

Have you any of his letters to you? — There is only one.

The letter (produced) was dated from "7, Camera-square, Thursday," and ran: "Dear Oscar — May I have the pleasure of dining with you this evening? If so, kindly send a message or wire whether we cannot spend the evening together. — With very kind regards and apologies, CHARLES PARKER."

Sir E. Clarke: I should like to see the hand-writing.

Mr. Carson: We will see all about that. Parker himself will be here, which is better.

Sir. E. Clarke: I should like his lordship to see the handwriting.

Mr. Carson: It depends who wrote it. (To witness:). Did you go in March or April last year, one night at 12.30, to visit Parker at 50, Park-walk? — No.

Do you know where Park-walk is? — In Chelsea.

Five or ten minutes' walk from Tite-street? — Oh, I never walk.

In paying your visits to your friends you would keep your cab outside? — Oh, yes, certainly — if it was a good cab.

When did you last see Parker? — Not since February last.

February, 1894? Are you quite sure of that? — That is my recollection. I took him to the Crystal

Palace at Christmas, 1893. I have heard that he has enlisted in the Army as a private.

You told me that you heard that he and Taylor were arrested together? — I read that in the newspapers in August, 1894.

Did you read that when they were arrested they were in the company of several men in women's clothes? — My recollection is that two men in women's clothes — music-hall singers — drove up to the house and were arrested outside. I asked Taylor about it, as I was very much distressed; but the magistrate seemed to have a different view, and dismissed the case.

But some were fined? — I don't know.

Witness was asked whether he had ever heard of Preston, whose name was in the list of the persons arrested, and he replied in the negative.

When you saw that Taylor was arrested in the company of these people, did it make any difference in your feelings towards him? — When I read it I was greatly distressed, and I wrote and told him so. I did not see him again till this year; but it has made no difference in my feelings, and he came to my house last Tuesday.

When did you first know Fred Atkins? — In October, 1892. He told me that he was connected with a firm of bookmakers. I did not come into contact with him through making bets. He was then nineteen or twenty. I cannot be cross-examined about that. I met him at a dinner given by the gentleman whose name you wrote down. I think Taylor was there. We called each other by our Christian names at that dinner.

You said he was in the employ of a bookmaker? — But he apologised, and said he neglected his business.

Did he seem to be an idle kind of fellow? — Oh, yes; a charming kind of fellow. He had an ambition to go on the music-hall stage. I thought him very pleasant.

Did he discuss literature with you? — No, I did not allow him.

That was not his line? — The art of the music-hall was as far as he got. On a subsequent Sunday I saw him and the gentleman mentioned – who was then about twenty-three or twenty-four years of age – lunching at the Café Royal, and they came and had their coffee and cigarettes at my table. I intended to go to Paris the next day to arrange for the publication of a book, and the gentleman, who was also going with Atkins, suggested that we should go together. It was arranged that we should go on the Monday; but on that Sunday the gentleman told me that he could not go until Tuesday or Wednesday, and asked me, as Atkins seemed very disappointed at his stay in Paris being shortened, if I would take him over. I said, "With the greatest pleasure."

How long had you known him? — About a fortnight.

You went to Paris on Nov. 20 by the Club train? — Yes. I paid for his ticket, but was afterwards repaid by the gentleman. Atkins did not go in the capacity of my secretary. I was going over to see a French publisher. It is childish to ask me such a question. I took him to the rooms where I was staying, at 29, Boulevard des Capucines — an hotel. I did not, after our arrival, ask Atkins to copy out a page of MS. I took Atkins to lunch at the Café Julien. He was my guest then, and certainly I paid for his lunch.

He had not the means to pay himself? — Certainly not — not the sort of lunch I like.

After lunch did you suggest that he should have his hair curled? — No; he suggested it, and I said I thought it would be very unbecoming, (Laughter.) I still think I was right in that opinion.

Did he get his hair curled? — I should have been very angry if he had. (Laughter.) It would have been a silly thing to do.

Did he get his hair curled at Pascal's, under the Grand Hotel? — I have no recollection.

You gave him an excellent dinner in the evening? — I never had anything else.

And plenty of wine? — If you ask me whether I plied him with wine I say it is perfectly monstrous, and I won't have it. (Laughter.)

I have never suggested it. — But you have

suggested it before.

After dinner did you give Atkins a sovereign to go to the Moulin Rouge? — Yes.

Did the other gentleman whose name has not been disclosed come to Paris two days afterwards? — He came on the Wednesday, and we all three returned together on the Saturday.

Did you the next day but one after your arrival give Atkins a cigarette-case? — I gave him one in Paris.

Shortly after arriving in London did you ask Atkins to call at your house in Tite-street? — I think I wrote to the other gentleman asking him to bring Fred Atkins. I was ill in bed, and they called, I think, together. I thought it was very kind of Atkins to come. It is not everybody in the world who is grateful.

Did you ask Atkins to give you back the letter you had written to him? — No; I have no recollection of any letter.

Did you ask him to say nothing about the visit to Paris? — Certainly not. I thought it the great event of his life, and it was.

You have been in correspondence with Atkins up to the present year? — I have written to him on several occasions, and have sent him tickets for my theatre on two occasions.

What is his present address? — It is 25, Osnaburgh-street.

You have been to tea there? — Yes.

Was there any one else there at the time? — Yes. An actor about twenty years of age.

Did you give Atkins any money? — I gave him £3. 15s to buy his first song for the music-hall stage. He told me that poets who wrote for the music-hall stage never take less. (Laughter.) I had the pleasure of meeting one of the poets.

Was he alone? — When Atkins came to St. James's-place I think he was accompanied by a young actor. I thought him a very pleasant, good-natured fellow, and as he was going on the music-hall stage I bought him a song and encouraged him. I heard him sing at a dinner at a restaurant. All that interested me.

Did you know Ernest Scarfe? — I met him in 1893. Mr. Taylor introduced him. He was a young man about twenty, and had no occupation; but had been in Australia. I did not know he had been a valet, nor do I know he is employed as that now in a situation.

Did he appear to be an educated young man? — He appeared a very pleasant spoken young man. Education depends upon what one's standard is.

Did you ever meet him in society? — I have never met him in society, certainly not; but he has been in my society, which is more important. (Laughter.) I have seen him with Taylor. Taylor introduced him to me at St. James's-place.

How did he come to bring that young man there? — Shall I tell you? He told me he knew a young man who had met on board ship going out to Australia Lord Douglas of Harwick. They had met at a skating-rink, and Taylor brought him to see me.

The honour was quite unexpected? — It was no shock, but I did not expect him. It was in the early afternoon. I made an appointment for them to dine with me on another day. We dined at Kettner's. I forget whether it was in a public or private room.

Why did you ask him to dinner? — Because I am very good natured, and because it is one of the best ways of pleasing anyone not of your social position. (Laughter.)

Did you give him any money? — No. I gave him a cigarette-case; it was my custom. (Laughter.) I gave it him as a Christmas present. I last saw Scarfe in February, when he dined with me at the Avondale Hotel. He was then employed as a clerk at a place in St. Paul's-churchyard.

When did you first know Sidney Mavor? — In September, 1892. I do not know where he is now. I never gave him any money nor a cigarette-case.

You deal at a shop in Bond-street, Thornhill's? — Yes.

Did you not tell them to send a cigarette-case, value £4 11s 6d, to S. A. Mavor? — Well, if it is there, perhaps I did so. I give people presents because I like them.

But you only knew Mavor a month? — Quite long enough to get to feel an interest in him.

Did you ask him to dine with you at the Albemarle Hotel? — Yes. He stayed the night there.

When was that? — In October, after I had given him the cigarette-case. I was on my way from Scotland, and I stayed one night there, and he met me at the station when I arrived, and I asked him to stay at the same place. Mavor was living at Notting-hill or West Kensington.

What should he stay at the hotel the night for? — Because I had asked him to stay for companionship. It was an amusement and a pleasure to him to stay the night at an hotel. The evening was passed with me, and in the morning we met at breakfast. I liked to have people staying with me.

Did you pay for the rooms? — Oh, yes, certainly; I had asked him.

He could have got home to Notting-hill in half an hour? — Yes, but he amused me and pleased me because he was a very nice, charming fellow. He brought luggage with him because I had invited him to stay the night.

Do you know Walter Granger? — Yes, he was a servant at a certain house in High-street, Oxford, and was about sixteen. They were the rooms of Lord Alfred Douglas, and I have stayed there several times.

Were you on familiar terms with Granger? Did you have him to dine with you? — No, he waited at table.

Did you ever kiss him? — He was a peculiarly plain boy. He was, unfortunately, very ugly. I pitied him for it.

Do you say that in support of your statement that you never kissed him? — No; it is such a childish question to ask me.

Do you suggest that he was too ugly? — (Warmly): I did not say that.

Why did you mention his ugliness? — The question seemed to me merely an intentional insult on your part, such as I have been going through the whole of this morning.

Why did you mention his ugliness? I am obliged to ask you these questions. — It is ridiculous to imagine that any such thing could have possibly occurred under any circumstances.

Then why did you mention his ugliness? — For that reason. If I was asked why I did not kiss a doorpost, I should say, "Because I do not like to kiss doorposts," and then am I to be cross-examined because I do not like it?

Why did you mention his ugliness? — (Excitedly): You stung me by an insulting question.

Was that a reason that you should say that the boy was ugly? — Pardon me, I say that you sting me and insult me, and try to unnerve me in every way, and at times one says things flippantly when one should speak more seriously. I admit it.

Then you mentioned his ugliness flippantly? That is what you wish to convey now? — Oh, do not say that I want to convey anything. I have given you my answer.

But is that it? It was a flippant answer? — Yes, certainly, it was a flippant answer.

In June, 1893, did you go to Goring? — Yes, I took The Cottage there. I engaged Granger as under-butler, and he occupied a little room next to mine, because we were crowded.

After other questions the cross-examination ended.

Sir Edward Clarke in re-examination: You were asked whether Lord Queensberry had objected to your acquaintance with his son being continued. Will you take these letters and tell me, first, whether they are written by Lord Queensberry? — Yes.

Secondly, whether these letters were communicated to you by the persons who received them? — Yes; but with one exception. It was brought to me, but not by the person to whom it is addressed.

Was it from these letters that you gathered the statement which you made to my learned friend that Lord Queensberry objected to your continued association with his son? — Yes.

Several letters written by Lord Queensberry

were read. The first, dated "Carter's Hotel, Albemarle-street, Wm, Sunday, April 1," was addressed to his son Alfred, and complained in very strong terms that the young man was doing nothing to qualify himself for any position in life. Disapproval was expressed of Lord Alfred's association with Mr. Oscar Wilde. The next letter was also dated from Carter's Hotel, and addressed by the Marquis to his son Alfred, and in it complaint was made of the impertinence of the young man to his father, threatening to stop his allowance. The third letter read was dated from "Skindle's, Maidenhead Bridge, Berks," on July 6. It was addressed to Mr. Alfred Montgomery, father of Lady Queensberry. In it the Marquis further protested against his son's acquaintance with Mr. Oscar Wilde, and urgently requested Lady Queensberry not to encourage the young man in disregarding the wishes of his father. There were two other letters, dated in the month of August, 1894, and containing expressions of regret that his son, Lord Alfred Douglas, should still be defying his father, in spite of the latter's requests to give up the acquaintanceship with the prosecutor.

Sir E. Clarke to witness: Having regard to the contents and the nature of these letters, you thought it right to take no notice of Lord Queensberry's wish that your acquaintance with his son should cease? I thought it entirely right to disregard it.

Sir Edward Clarke then put several questions as to the reviews of "Dorian Grey" and correspondence resulting therefrom. In further re-examination the witness said that Taylor was introduced to him in October, 1892, by the gentleman whose name had been written down. That gentleman was a person in high position, of good birth and good repute. It was now two years since he had been in England or since witness had seen him. He knew that Taylor had lost a great deal of money that he had inherited, but had still a share in a very important business. He was educated at Marlborough.

Have you ever had reason to think that Taylor was a disreputable person? — None whatever.

What was the explanation Taylor gave you about his arrest? — He told me that it was a benefit concert, for which he had been given a ticket. When he arrived at the house there was dancing going on, and he had been asked to play the piano. Two music-hall singers were expected to come in costume. They were not in the house at the time, but suddenly the police entered and arrested everybody.

And knowing that the charge had been dismissed, and having heard Mr. Taylor's account of what had happened, was there the slightest imputation resting on your mind as regards Taylor? — No; I thought his arrest was monstrous. I was extremely sorry for him.

Who introduced you to Shelley? — Mr. John Lane, the publisher of my books.

He expressed great admiration of your works? — Yes; he was very well acquainted with them and very appreciative.

And you gratified that appreciation by presenting him with a copy of your books? — Yes.

It seems that the books you have given him have the fly-leaves torn out. Did you ever write an inscription upon any book given by you to Mr. Shelley that you would have any objection to the whole world reading and knowing? — Never in my life.

Mr. Shelley dined with you at Tite-street with Mrs. Wilde? — Yes.

Was he in every way a gentleman that you were content to introduce to your wife at your own table? — In every way.

Sir E. Clarke read several letters from Edward Shelley to Mr. Wilde asking for money on account of ill-health and the inadequate payment he was receiving at a commercial house in the City. (To witness): Were there ever any relations between you and Shelley other than the relations between a man of letters and one who admired his works and had been brought into connection with him on business matters? — Never.

With regard to Alfonso Conway, did you ever hear that he had been employed as a newspaper boy? — No, I never heard that he was connected with literature in any form. (Laughter.)

Did Mrs. Wilde see Conway at Worthing? — Oh, yes, constantly. She knew him quite well. I have not seen him since I was at Worthing, but I wrote him a letter in November with reference to his entering the merchant service.

When was it you first met Wood? — At the end of January, 1893.

You have seen him at Taylor's rooms? — Yes, but only on the occasion of the letters.

Had you any idea of what the occupation had been of the Parkers? — They told me they were looking for employment. Charles Parker was anxious to go on the stage. It was represented to me that their father was a man of means, who made them allowances.

Atkins was introduced to you by a gentleman whose name has not been mentioned, but was passed to you on paper? — Yes; that was the first time I knew Atkins at all.

When these persons were introduced to you, had you any reason for suspecting them of being disreputable persons? — None whatever. Nothing has ever come to my knowledge that led me to think so.

You heard of the arrest of Charles Parker? — I read the case, which was dismissed, and I did not think there was anything against him. I have not seen him since.

Have you ever seen Charles Parker at the Savoy? — Never in my life.

Have you ever been to 17, Camera-square? — Never.

Or to 50, Park-walk? — Never.

With regard to Granger, how long was he in your service at Goring? — Two or three months. He was in ill-health during a part of that time.

How was it that after your interview with Lord Queensberry, and those further letters coming to your knowledge, you did not take steps earlier? — On account of the very strong pressure put upon me by the Queensberry family, which I did not feel myself able to resist.

Did you early in July have an interview with a member of Parliament who represented the Queensberry family? — Yes; on the Wednesday following the visit of Lord Queensberry to my house.

Mr. Carson remarked that there was one letter read by his learned friend which referred to a postcard from Lord Alfred Douglas. He desired to have the postcard put in.

Sir E. Clarke objected, but Mr. Justice Collins overruled the objection, on the ground that there was evidence that the postcard was brought to the notice of Lord Queensberry.

Mr. Carson then read the postcard, which was in the following terms,

"As you return my letters unopened, I am obliged to write on a postcard. I write to inform you that I treat your absurd threats with absolute indifference. Ever since your exhibitions at O. W's house I have made a point of appearing with him at many public restaurants, such as Berkley's, Willis's Rooms, the Café Royal, &c., and I shall continue to go to any of these places, and with whom I choose. I am of age, and my own master. You have disowned me at least a dozen times, and have very meanly deprived me of money. You have, therefore, no rights over me, either legal or moral. If O.W. were to prosecute you for libel in the criminal courts you would get seven years' penal servitude for your outrageous libels. Much as I detest you, I am anxious to avoid this for the sake of the family, but if you try to assault me I shall defend myself with a loaded revolver, which I always carry, and if I shoot you, or if he shoots you, we should be completely justified, as we should be acting in self defence against a violent and dangerous rough, and I think if you were dead not many people would miss you. — A.D."

Sir E. Clarke remarked that if he had known that the postcard was legible he should not have objected.

The following correspondence between Mr. Oscar Wilde's solicitors and Lord Queensberry was then read:

"Giltspur-chambers, Holborn Viaduct, E.C.,
July 11, 1894.

"My Lord Marquis — We have been consulted by Mr. Oscar Wilde with reference to certain letters written by your lordship, in which letters you have most foully and infamously libelled him, and also your son, Lord Alfred Douglas. In these letters your lordship has mentioned exalted personages, and Mr. Oscar Wilde, not being desirous to wound their feelings by a publication of your letters, has instructed us to give you the opportunity of retracting your assertions and insinuations in writing, with an apology for having made them. If this be done at once it may prevent litigation, but unless done forthwith no other course will be left open to us but to advise our client the proper course to adopt to vindicate his character. — Awaiting your reply by return of post, we have the honour to be, &c.,

"C. O. HUMPHREYS, SON, and KERSHAW."

"Skindle's, Maidenhead Bridge, July 13.

"Sir — I have received your letter here with considerable astonishment. I certainly shall not tender to Mr. Oscar Wilde any apology for letters I have written to my son. (The writer proceeded to say that he made no direct accusations against Mr. Oscar Wilde, but desired to stop the association so far as Lord Alfred Douglas was concerned). — Yours faithfully,

"QUEENSBERRY."

"Skindle's, Maidenhead Bridge, July 18.

"Sir — Since meeting you this morning I have heard that the revolver has been given up. I shall therefore not insist on taking the step I threatened to do to-morrow morning of giving information to the police authorities. However, if this is to go on, and I am to be openly defied by Mr. Wilde and my son by further scandals in public places. I shall have no other resort but to do as I have threatened, and give information at Scotland-yard as to what has happened. — Yours faithfully,

"QUEENSBERRY."

A Juryman (to Mr. Oscar Wilde): Was the editor of the "Chameleon" a friend of yours? — I had never seen him at the time he wrote to me from Oxford to ask me to contribute. I subsequently saw him, I think in the month of November, in the rooms of a friend in the Albany. I wrote to him that I could give him some aphorisms out of my play — some that were unpublished. Some of those quoted yesterday are out of the play at present being performed at the Haymarket Theatre, and there have been no complaints at the box-office of any moral deprecia-tion of the audience. (Laughter.)

Was the "Chameleon" for private circulation? — Oh, no.

Sir E. Clarke: We will hand in a copy. Only 100 copies were to be printed. They were for the public.

Another juryman (to witness): Had you seen this article "The Priest and the Acolyte" before its publication? — No; it came upon me as a terrible shock.

Sir E. Clarke intimated that this concluded the evidence for the prosecution, subject, of course, to evidence by way of rebuttal.

Mr. Carson, in opening the case for the defence, said that so far as Lord Queensberry was concerned, whether as regarded any act he had done, any letter he had written, or the card which had put him in the present position, he withdrew nothing. Lord Queensberry did what he did premeditatedly, for he was determined at all risks and at all hazards to try and save his son. Whether he was right or wrong the jury probably now had to some extent information on which to found a judgement, and he (Mr. Carson) must claim for Lord Queensberry that, notwith-standing any elements of prejudice which Sir Edward Clarke had thought it right to introduce into the case, his conduct had been absolutely consistent all through, and not only was he justified in putting a stop to what must, or probably might, prove a disastrous acquaintance, but he was bound to take every step which could suggest itself to bring about such an inquiry as would lead, at all events, to the acts of Mr. Wilde being made public. It was said that the names of eminent persons were introduced into Lord Queensberry's letters. For his (Mr. Carson's) own part, he was glad that those letters had been read, and he thought Sir Edward Clarke took a proper course in having them read, because the suggestion apparently had been that at some time the names of these distinguished persons were in some way or other in Lord Queensberry's letters mixed up with his charge against Mr. Oscar Wilde. It was clear, now that the letters were before the Court and jury, that if there ever was any impression of that kind, the letters connected with these distinguished individuals were quite distinct from the allegations as regarded Mr. Wilde; that they were related to purely political matters, arising out of the fact that one of Lord Queensberry's sons, Lord Drumlanrig, had been made a member of the House of Lords, of which Lord Queensberry was not a member, and felt aggrieved that such an honour should be conferred upon his son while not given to him; and that was why these names of eminent politicians were introduced. From beginning to end Lord Queensberry had been influenced as regarded Mr. Wilde by one hope, and one hope alone, that he might save his son.

What had been proved with regard to Mr. Oscar Wilde's life? It had been shown that he had been going about with young men who were not his co-equals in age or station; that he had been associating with whom it might be proved, before the case was over, were well known as some of the most disreputable characters in London. They knew that on Tuesday last, Taylor was in company with Mr. Wilde at his house; yet Sir Edward Clarke had not put him into the box, to enable them to learn what course of life he led. Taylor was found afterwards at Fitzroy-square in company with Parker, and was arrested with a number of notorious characters by the police. As the evidence showed that Taylor was practically the right-hand man of Wilde in all his orgies, he (Mr. Carson) thought they would have had an opportunity of cross-examining him as to what was going on at Fitzroy-square. Taylor was really the pivot of the case; for the jury would feel that surely the man who introduced these men to Mr. Wilde was, above all others, the man who could have thrown some light upon their antecedants. Mr. Wilde undertook to prove sufficient to send the Marquis of Queensberry to gaol and to brand him as a criminal. Therefore it was, above all things, necessary, when they had so much proved by his own admissions, that Mr. Wilde should bring any witness he could to bear out his explanations. They had heard a great deal of a gentleman whose name was written down. On each occasion when it was convenient to introduce somebody, this was the name which Mr. Wilde gave, because he was out of the country. But Taylor was in the country, and he was still the friend of Wilde. Where was Taylor? The jury would hear more about him and the kind of life he led as the case proceeded, and the extraordinary den that he kept in Little College-street.

In relation to his books Mr. Wilde took up the position of an artist; that he wrote only in the language of an artist for artists. Contrast that with the position which he took up as regarded his acquaintances. They included Parker, a gentleman's servant; Conway, a boy who sold papers on the pier at Worthing; and Scarge, who was also a gentleman's servant. Then Mr. Wilde's case was no longer that he was dwelling in the regions of art, but that he was such a noble, such a democratic soul — (laughter) — that he drew no social distinction, and that it gave him exactly the same pleasure to have a sweeping boy from the street to lunch or drive with him as to sit down with the best educated artist or the greatest littérateur in the whole kingdom. His position in these respects was absolutely irreconcilable. He (Mr. Carson) thought that if they rested this case on Mr. Wilde's literature alone they would have been amply justified in the course they had taken. Take the "Chameleon". He was not going to say that Mr. Wilde was responsible for everything that appeared in it, but, at all events, he contributed to the publication. Mr. Wilde made no complaint of "The Priest and the Acolyte." As he had said, he drew no distinction between a moral and an immoral book. Nor did he care whether the article was in its very terms blasphemous. All that Mr. Wilde said was that he did not approve of the story from a literary point of view. The same idea that ran through that story ran through those two letters which Mr. Wilde called beautiful, but which he (Mr. Carson) called disgusting. Moreover, there was in this same "Chameleon" a poem which showed some justification for the apprehensions Lord Queensberry entertained for his son. The poem was written by Lord Alfred Douglas, and was seen by Mr. Wilde before its publication. Was it not a terrible thing that a young man on the threshold of life, who had been for several years dominated by Oscar Wilde, should thus show the tendency of his mind. With regard to "Dorian Grey," from which the learned counsel proceeded to read extracts, Mr. Wilde admitted that there were passages which might be misunderstood by people who did not appreciate the artistic bearing of the language; but he should have accepted that better as a defence if Mr. Wilde had ensured that his book fell into the hands of those only who would put an artistic meaning upon it.

As to the letter to Lord Alfred Douglas, which had been called a sonnet, a more thinly disguised attempt to cover its real nature had never been attempted in a court of justice. He had some difficulty in understanding why his learned friend had referred to it at all. Perhaps he thought the defence had the letter, and that it was better to give an explanation of it; but if that was so it was futile, because for the letter which the defence did possess his learned friend had no explanation. Sir Edward Clarke had referred to "a man of the name of Wood" as being supposed to have taken out of a pocket of Lord Alfred Douglas correspondence which had passed between him and Wilde. Why, Wood was "Fred," one of Wilde's bosom companions; one of the Little College-street lot. When he (Mr. Carson) told the jury of the previous relations of the parties before Wood got possession of the letters, they would get the key of the situation. Wood was not the innocent friend, assisted by Wilde out of the largeness of that great heart which he had told them he had. (Laughter.) He was one of the men introduced by Taylor, and when Wilde heard that Wood had got possession of the letters, he probably felt that if Wood turned against him the letters would be strange corroboration. What other reason could be suggested for giving him £16 to go to America with? He was shipped off, and Wilde thought he would never be heard of again; but Wood was there, and would be examined before the jury. With regard to what Mr. Wilde called this beautiful letter, he (Mr. Carson) thought that Mr. Beerbohm Tree acted rightly in every way when he received a copy of it.

Sir E. Clarke: I quite agree.

Mr. Carson took leave to make that statement, because he had received a cable from Mr. Tree, who was in America, and had already seen his name mentioned in connection with the reports of the case. It would be unnecessary for him to read the cable.

Mr. Justice Collins: There is not the slightest ground for making any suggestion whatever adverse to Mr. Tree.

Mr. Carson: Thank you, my Lord. My view is that his action was exactly what it ought to have been.

Mr. Justice Collins: Mr. Tree acted with the most perfect propriety.

Mr. Carson, continuing, observed that Mr. Tree sent for Mr. Wilde, and gave him the copy of the letter; and Wilde then began to think, when the letter was discovered, how he should get out of it. A short time afterwards Allen, the blackmailer, called, and had a most extraordinary conversation with Wilde, who then said he had made up his mind to publish the letter as a sonnet. When did he make up his mind? Not when he sent it to Lord Alfred Douglas, for he did not ask him to preserve it. He envied the credulity of the jury if they believed this abominable composition was written as a sonnet.

THE CASE ENDS

With a Verdict Against Oscar.

SIR EDWARD CLARKE

Asks to Withdraw From the Prosecution.

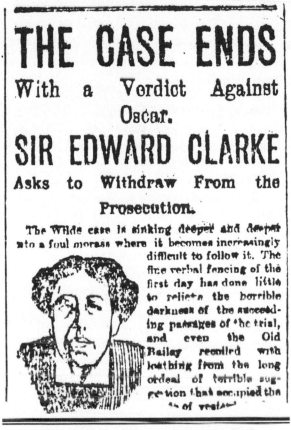

The Wilde case is sinking deeper and deeper into a foul morass where it becomes increasingly difficult to follow it. The fine verbal fencing of the first day has done little to relieve the horrible darkness of the succeeding passages of the trial, and even the Old Bailey recoiled with loathing from the long ordeal of terrible suggestion that occupied the

The Evening News, 5 April 1895

The Wilde case is sinking deeper and deeper into a foul morass where it becomes increasingly difficult to follow it. The fine verbal fencing of the first day has done little to relieve the horrible darkness of the succeeding passages of the trial, and even the Old Bailey recoiled with loathing from the long ordeal of terrible suggestion that occupied the whole of yesterday when the cross-examination left the artistic literary plane and entered the dim-lit, perfumed rooms where the poet of the beautiful joined with valets and grooms in the bond of the silver cigarette case. And when Oscar Wilde left the box the little light that had relieved the awful sombreness of the picture died out, as Mr. Carson went on to paint a horrid nocturne of terrible suggestions, a thing of blackness, only half defined, but wholly horrible.

Curiosity, however, was as strong to-day as ever, and brought together if possible a larger crowd than that which on the two preceding days had filled the court. It was known that the defence had a large number of witnesses, though how many were to be called of the 15 persons as to whom Mr Wilde was examined was unknown.

THE ABSENT OSCAR.

Day by day, in the miserable hour of waiting that precedes the sitting of court, the scene is curiously the same. Everyone is in the same seat, wedged in the same angle, or standing in the same corner; looking around, not a face seems missing that was present on the morning the trial begun. As the time wears on, Lord Queensberry enters and leans nonchalantly against the dock, and after looking about him a moment climbs inside and sits down to read a paper. Everyone is looking for the prosecutor, who does not put in an appearance in court, though several letters addressed to "Oscar Wilde, Old Bailey, London," are awaiting him.

When the Judge takes his seat he is handed a cablegram from America, which he reads slowly.

FOR THE DEFENCE.

Mr. Carson at once went on with his speech. He had dealt fully, he said, with the literature in the case, and almost hoped that, so far as Lord Queensberry was concerned, he was absolutely on that ground alone in bringing to a climax the connection between Mr. Wilde and his son. The rest of his duty was more painful, to comment on the remaining portion of the case. He had to bring before them the young men, one after the other, to tell their tales, for an advocate a most distasteful task. One word he would say — let those who would blame these young men remember they were more sinned against than sinning. Mr. Carson then dealt with Mr. Wilde's admissions in cross-examination.

The learned judge sat with his face hidden in his hands, never raising it till Mr. Carson relieved the awful character of his speech by a protest against the flippancy of Mr. Wilde's answers in the box.

71

"No doubt he thought he was making smart repartees, scoring off counsel, that is as it may be." Then to the terrible stories again.

In the middle of Mr. Carson's speech, Sir Edward Clarke rose and interposed. At once there was an electric shock, and everyone knew something had happened.

Sir Edward, looking pale, said: "Mr Lord, I interpose with a sense of great responsibility to make a statement as to what my friend said yesterday in addressing the jury on the question of the literature involved in this case and upon inferences he had drawn from the admissions with regard to the letters by Mr. Oscar Wilde yesterday. My friend began his address this morning by saying he hoped yesterday that he had said enough, dealing with these topics, to induce the jury to relieve him from this necessity of dealing in detail with the other issues. Those who represent Mr. Oscar Wilde in this case have before them a very terrible anxiety. They could not conceal from themselves that a judgment might be formed that the literature and the conduct which has been admitted would not improbably induce the jury to say that Lord Queensberry in using the word "posing" was using words which there was sufficient justification to entitle him to use, and that he should be relieved from any criminal charge in respect of them. As in our clear view that would be bound to be the result, I and my friends have to look forward to this, that the verdict which might be given for the defendant on that part of the case might be interpreted outside as a conclusive finding with regard to all the issues in the case; and the position in which we stood was this, that without expecting to obtain a verdict in this case we should be going through day after day, it might be, matters of the most appalling character. Under these circumstances I hope your lordship will think I am taking a right course, which I take after communicating with Mr. Oscar Wilde, and that is to say that, having regard to what has already been referred to by my learned friend in respect of matter connected with the literature and the letters, I feel we could not resist a verdict of Not guilty, the Not guilty having references to the words "posing as."

Under these circumstances I hope your lordship will think I am not going beyond the bounds of duty, and am doing something to save, and prevent what may be a most terrible task, when I ask, on behalf of Mr. Oscar Wilde, to be allowed to withdraw from the prosecution, or if not allowed to, to submit to a verdict of Not guilty, having reference to that part of the particulars in connection with the literature of the case.

Mr. Carson, in a few words, raised no objection, but insisted on the point that Lord Queensberry had justified the libel, had said it was for the public benefit it should be published, and the verdict must be taken on those issues.

The learned Judge then said that if both parties acquiesced it was not within his province or that of the jury to stand in the way of taking a course which would avoid going into prurient details. But there could be no limitation of the verdict. The libel is either justified or not: there can be no limitation to the terms of the verdict and I shall direct the jury to return a verdict that the libel was true in substance and in fact, and that it was for the public benefit that it was published.

After a few moments' consultation together on the part of the jury, the foreman intimated that they had arrived at their verdict that the libel was true.

The Clerk of Arraigns: Do you find the plea of justification proved? — Yes.

Mr. Carson: Lord Queensberry may be discharged?

Mr. Justice Collins: Oh, certainly.

Lord Queensberry at once stepped out of the dock and joined his solicitor in the well of the court.

MR. OSCAR WILDE

MR. CARSON, Q.C. CROSS-EXAMINES WILDE

SIR EDWD. CLARKE WITHDRAWS FROM THE CASE.

LORD A. DOUGLAS.

AT THE OLD BAILEY

LORD QUEENSBERRY HEARS THE VERDICT.

There was applause in court, which, in contradiction to usual custom, was not immediately suppressed. There was little excitement outside the Court, very few people being present.

WHERE OSCAR WAS.

Oscar Wilde went to the Old Bailey, but did not enter the court. He had a consultation with Sir Edward Clarke in a room off the court, and while the learned gentleman was making his statement to the judge Wilde hurriedly left the building. The Exchange Telegraph Company has authority for stating that no warrant has been applied for, but on leaving the Court Mr. Charles Russell, Lord Queensberry's solicitor, addressed the following letter to the Public Prosecutor:

"37, Norfolk-street, Strand.

"The Hon. Hamilton Cuffe, Esq.,

"Director of Prosecutions.

"Dear Sir — in order that there may be no miscarriage of justice I think it my duty at once to send you a copy of all our witnesses statements, together with a copy of the shorthand notes of the trial.   "Yours faithfully,

"CHARLES RUSSELL,   "The Treasury, Whitehall."

AT THE HOLBORN VIADUCT.

When Oscar left the Old Bailey he drove, in company with a companion, in his carriage which was waiting, to the Holborn Viaduct Hotel. Shortly afterwards he was joined by Lord Alfred Douglas and another person and the four remained closeted in a private room. At one o'clock the four ordered luncheon to be served in another private room. Wilde's carriage remains outside the hotel.

LETTER FROM WILDE.

He Gives His Reasons For Closing the Case.

The Evening News has received the following letter from Oscar Wilde, written on the notepaper of the Holborn Viaduct Hotel.

TO THE EDITOR:

It would have been impossible for me to have proved my case without putting Lord Alfred Douglas in the witness-box against his father.

Lord Alfred Douglas was extremely anxious to go into the box, but I would not let him do so.

Rather than put him in so painful a position I determined to retire from the case, and to bear on my own shoulders whatever ignominy and shame might result from my prosecuting Lord Queensberry.

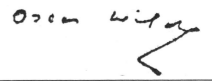

Instead of celebrating with a dinner-party, the Marquis of Queensberry arranged an after-theatre supper — the reason being that his guests of honour, Charles Brookfield and Charles Hawtrey, were required to be at the Theatre Royal, Haymarket, for the evening performance of *An Ideal Husband*.

THE DAILY TELEGRAPH.

LARGEST CIRCULATION IN THE WORLD.

The Daily Telegraph, 6 April 1895

Hardly had the Queensberry libel trial recommenced yesterday, at the Old Bailey, when SIR EDWARD CLARKE withdrew from the hopeless task of maintaining his unworthy client's case, and the miserable impudence of the prosecutor's charge collapsed. The jury, directed by the Court, wanted not so much as one minute's consideration to find that the statement made by the Marquis of Queensberry was true in fact, and that its publication, in the form of the alleged libel, was for the public benefit, with the consequent verdict of "Not guilty." The Judge did not attempt to silence or reprove the irrepressible cheering in the court which greeted the acquittal of this sorely-provoked and cruelly-injured father. As for the prosecutor, whose notoriety has now become infamy, he made no appearance yesterday upon the scene, and he has since been arrested at the instance of the Treasury on a charge of a very grave character. This being so, as regards any further influence which he can exercise upon social, literary, or artistic matters, and the contempt and disgust felt for such a character being fully met by the hideous downfall of the man and of his theories, we may dismiss the prisoner without further remark. We have had enough, and more than enough, of Mr. OSCAR WILDE, who has been the means of inflicting upon public patience during the recent episode as much moral damage of the most offensive and repulsive kind as any single individual could well cause. If the general concern were only with the man himself — his spurious brilliancy, inflated egotism, diseased vanity, cultivated affectation, and shameless disavowal of all morality — the best thing would be to dismiss him and his deeds without another word to the penalty of universal condemnation. But there is more than the individual himself to be considered in the matter. The just verdict of yesterday must be held to include with him the tendency of his peculiar career, the meaning and influence of his teaching, and all those shallow and specious arts by which he and his like have attempted to establish a cult in our midst, and even to set up new schools in literature, the drama, and social thought.

In these aspects the public will have patience, and we must endeavour to find courage, to contemplate a little longer the evil figure which disappears from London society. It will not be considered an exaggeration to state that OSCAR WILDE and those who imitated him have attempted to found, and have partly succeeded in founding, a new school or style of ethical and literary principle. To the fantastic beginnings of this no particular objections could be urged. If there were people who could not admire the beauty of our floral world without going into pretended raptures over a sunflower or a lily, or finding the crown of creation in a green picotee, that could be very well dealt with by satire and laughter. The pranks of POSTLETHWAITE and his congeners were innocent so long as they were merely aesthetic. But, in spasmodic search for ancient graces and what was falsely thought the classic vein, the worst and boldest of these innovators set themselves to import into healthy and honest English art and life the pagan side of bygone times, with all its cynicism, scepticism, and animalism. Every scholar is aware how false it is to pretend that art and literature move in the true classical path when they are tainted by vice and by disbelief in law and morality. If Rome had nameless sins and shameful pleasures, she also had a JUVENAL to scourge and stigmatise their votaries. And, if it were not so, to go back publicly and of purpose to the times and tenets of early civilisations would be to throw away deliberately half the blessings and the teachings of Christianity, and to hold the monstrous doctrine that the race must advance by moral retrogression. Nevertheless, these men, linking a certain real sense of beauty with profligate tastes and profane mockery, have undoubtedly exercised a visible influence upon the generation cursed by their presence. You may trace them to-day — we are ashamed to declare — in the outlying regions of the Press, where a certain class of publication strives to exist which has for its inspiration a salacious impulse to go perpetually as close as it can to the limits of public decorum, and to show its smartness by irreverence, veiled indelicacy, and, as far as it dares, by the violation of the sacredness of private life. The trail of this fetid fashion has penetrated to our theatres, where it is too much the mode to borrow from the French stage the motives and combinations which season the drama to the jaded appetites of Parisians. The shame and disgrace of it have invaded art, and we are asked to admire nowadays specimens from the impressionist and fleshly galleries which are of true and serious art merely the burlesque and the mockery. It has passed, with heavy damage to good taste and rightful amusement, into the domain of fiction, so that we see novel after novel aspire to a moment's popularity mainly on the grounds of prurient sexuality or of ignorant disbelief. We abstain, and intend to abstain, from naming examples in all these branches of the mischief, deadly and subtle, wrought upon the present generation by the showy paradoxes and false glitter of this school of "poseurs." Everybody can see and read for himself, and every honest and wholesome-minded Englishman must grieve to notice how largely this French and Pagan plague has filtered into the healthy fields of British life. If we would observe its ultimate results, have we to look further than to the declining population of France; the decay there of religion, reverence, obedience, and legality; the restless changes of her systems; nay, even the aspect of her picture-shops and advertisements? There also, as here, the vast body of social and civil life is no doubt sound and sober; but he who loves France most and wishes best to her must deplore the extent to which cynicism, scepticism, irreverence, and lubricity have misled the noble gifts of much in French genius and French invention.

It will be a public benefit, compensating for a great deal that has been painful in the reports of this trial, if the exposure of a chief representative of the immoral school leads to a clearer perception of its tendency and a heartier contempt for its methods. There is nothing difficult to understand in the principles of such people or in the results to which these lead. The aestheticism that worships a green carnation or a perfume has lost so much the sense of what is precious in parental and filial relations that we saw in this case a son addressing his father in terms which in ancient days would have involved his death. The superfine "Art" which admits no moral duty and laughs at the established phrases of right and wrong is the visible enemy of those ties and bonds of society — the natural affections, the domestic joys, the sanctity and sweetness of the home. We may judge this curse of an outrageous cult best when we find it the sworn and desperate opposite of that sacred verse which runs, "Whatsoever things are true, whatsoever things are honest, whatsoever things are just, whatsoever things are pure, whatsoever things are lovely, whatsoever things are of good report, if there be any virtue, and if there be any praise, think on these things." A nation prospers and profits by precisely those national qualities which these innovators deride and abjure. It goes

SIR E. CLARKE — OSCAR WILDE. A CONSULTATION ABOUT THE DEFENCE.

swiftly to wreck and decay by precisely that brilliant corruption of which we have just had the exposure and the demonstration. All the good literature and the noble art in our own and other countries has been sane, moral, and serious in its object; nor can life be wholesomely lived under guidance of brilliant paradoxes and corrosive epigrams. To those who know how to observe, this man WILDE in the act of his defence condemned himself and his system by his vanity, egotism, artificiality, and distorted perceptions, before the Judge and jury had pronounced upon him the indirect sentence which eliminates him from the society he has disgraced. We shall have purchased the pain and shame of such an exhibition at a price, perhaps, not too high if it lead the youth of our generation, on the one hand, to graver thoughts of duty and propriety, and the public, on the other, to a sterner impatience with those who, under the name of Art, or some other pretence, insidiously poison our stage, our literature, our drama, and the outskirts of our press.

The Star, 6 April 1895

WHAT WE THINK.

A CHECK TO CANT.

Nothing is easier or more common than to exaggerate the importance, in the general scheme of things, of the incident of the hour, the startling episode of yesterday or the day before yesterday. THUCYDIDES himself, though he believed strongly in the doctrine of "the greatest war for the greatest historian," perceived that people were apt to regard the war in which they were at the moment involved as more important than any that had preceded it. The error is doubtless entertaining to those serene judges who see life steadily and see it whole. On the other hand, it is only a cheap cynicism which would uniformly regard the present as a matter of no importance, and refuse to draw any general inference from the events of the moment. We shall, at any rate, be greatly surprised if the criminal case which has attracted public attention during the past few days is void of effect, not indeed upon the trend of English literature — even to mention the two things in the same breath seems grotesque and outrageous — but upon the precious "movement" which imagines, in its haste, that it is a part of literature and, in its vanity, an important part. It would be absurd to suggest that the general course of what is called in the slang of the day the "literature of the decadence" or "fin de siècle-ism" will or can be arrested upon the warrant of a stipendiary magistrate. The "literature of the decadence" contains much that is admirable and something that will live. To that extent, and only to that extent, it is literature. But nobody will deny that there has existed a parasite, an excrescence, an aberration which diligent advertisement had made more or less familiar to the public against its will. More than that, we have of late been deluged with cant about "Art for Art's sake" — an unexceptional canon within its proper limits but,

when it is reduced to cant, capable of any ludicrous exaggeration. This is the tendency which will, we hope and believe, receive a check. We may expect to be driven back upon what is more wholesome because licence has come to produce a sense of nausea. It is easy for the artist to say that art and morals are widely different. In the sense that art is not primarily didactic the proposition is so true as to be the baldest commonplace. The point is that the artist, especially if he be a poet, a playwright, or a novelist, has to do with conduct and, whether he will or no, his work implies, where it does not express, a standard of conduct. The fact has been brought home a little vividly, and the cheap paradoxes, the inverted commonplaces, the complete and calculated cynicism of a small section of parasitic writers and their clique have come by their own. When LEWIS CARROLL, through the mouth of the grandfather, was instructing the juvenile poet in his art, he reminded him that abstract substantives begin with capitals always:

> The True, The Good, The Beautiful,
> Those are the things that pay.

Unwholesomeness masquerading in the garb of the capital letter will hardly pay so well, for a time at least. That mysterious person, the philistine, will doubtless enjoy a momentary triumph. But the ultimate effect of recent disclosures should be to strengthen health and right reason — that kind of art which PLATO had in his mind when he spoke the winds that blow from healthy regions.

The Illustrated Police News, 6 April 1895

The principal actors in this most gruesome tragedy of the nineteenth century, which has excited the curiosity of tens of thousands of English men and women, are the Marquis of Queensberry, a man of considerable notoriety by reason of his boldly-avowed views on religious matters — views which, without doubt, have kept him out of his seat in the House of Lords, where he was an elected representative peer for Scotland. He is also notorious for his patronage of the prize ring, but he is a man, despite his peculiarities, to be admired for the fact that he has had in his public life the courage of his convictions, and thus stands head and shoulders above the majority of hereditary personages of his own rank. And of his accuser, Mr. Oscar Wilde, what can be said? He is a man who started life with a distinguished and brilliant college career, and has since been distinguished as a poet, a writer, and a dramatist of undoubted ability and cleverness, a man whom a month ago thousands would have been glad to have known, a man who was fawned and cringed to and lionised by many, and to-day stands without a friend in the world.

The Pall Mall Gazette, 6 April 1895

We begin to breathe a purer air. The sensational close of the noisome Wilde-Queensberry case has relieved those responsible for the conduct of daily papers of a very oppressive and painful burden. It is a very difficult question to decide whether in such cases absolute reticence or modified publicity is the better in the interests of public morality. On the one hand we are spared the appalling details which even the most careful revision can only half conceal; on the other we lose the preventive effect which publicity has upon the infamous gang with which London and other great cities are infested. We do not yet include Wilde amongst them, for he has to stand his trial. But we cannot overlook the fact that the jury yesterday found a verdict of guilty against him on his own admissions, and before any witnesses were called. For the nominal positions yesterday were the reverse of the real positions. Lord Queensberry was really the prosecutor and Wilde the defendant, and Lord Queensberry's plea of justification was virtually the indictment of Wilde. And the jury found that the charges in that indictment were true, and were made for the public benefit. More than that, mercifully, we need not at present say.

The Echo, 6 April 1895

LORD QUEENSBERRY

And so a most intolerable case is ended. Lord Queensberry is triumphant, and Mr. Oscar Wilde is "damned and done for." He may now change places with Lord Queensberry, and go into the dock himself, and have Lord Queensberry's evidence against him. He appears to have illustrated in his life the beauty and truthfulness of his teachings. He said, in cross-examination, that he considered there was no such thing as morality, and he seems to have harmonised his practice with his theory. The counsel for the prosecution, the judge, and jury are entitled to public thanks for abruptly terminating the trial, and so preventing the publication of probably revolting revelations. The best thing for everybody now is to forget all about Oscar Wilde, his perpetual posings, his aesthetical teachings, and his theatrical productions. If not tried himself, let him go into silence, and be heard of no more.

SATURDAY, APRIL 13, 1895.

OSCAR WILDE'S ARREST.

FULL DETAILS OF HIS CAPTURE.

events casting their shadows before them. Mr. Wilde did not enter the court in which the trial was taking place. He was, however, about to do so when he was met by his solicitor who conducted him to a private room in the building. A conference was held in that room—a conference that will become almost an historical one—between Sir Edward Clarke, Q.C., M⸺ ⸺⸺⸺ ⸺⸺⸺, Mr. Humphrie⸺ (the legal

nine copies of evening papers, which had evidently been hastily scanned and then thrown aside. Inspector Richards said, "We are police officers, and hold a warrant for your arrest." Ob, really." Inspector Rich⸺ to accompan⸺ shall ."

cultivated affectation, a shameless disavowal of all morality, and the Great M⸺ ⸺⸺ ⸺sthetic passed his first⸺ cell.

The Illustrated Police Budget, 13 April 1895

OSCAR WILDE'S ARREST.

FULL DETAILS OF HIS CAPTURE.

[BY OUR SPECIAL REPORTER.]

POLICE COURT PROCEEDINGS.

"Pick Oscar Wilde up to-morrow morning and never leave him until he either goes abroad or is arrested." These few words comprised the brief instructions given me late on Thursday night by the far-seeing Editor of the *Police Budget*.

Now it was extremely difficult to find out where Oscar was living during the time his charge of slander against Lord Queensberry was being heard at the Old Bailey. The police themselves were unaware of his then whereabouts. I chanced, however, to alight on a private detective of my acquaintance. Luckily he had to keep watch on Oscar, and in confidence confided to me the fact that he (Mr. Wilde) was sleeping at his own house in Tite Street, Queen's Road, Chelsea.

Punctually at seven o'clock on Friday morning I was in Tite Street. The houses are all of the Queen

Elizabeth style of architecture, and No. 16 – Mr. Wilde's house – is painted, so far as wood work goes, from top to bottom with cream coloured paint. Tite Street runs from the Queen's Road to the Embankment. At the corner is a cab rank, and I had little difficulty by keeping on the blind side of the cabs in watching Mr. Wilde's house. There were, however, two other watchers — the private detectives employed by Lord Queensberry. Shortly before nine o'clock a smart brougham, drawn by a pair of brown cobs, pulled up outside Mr. Wilde's house. At five minutes past the hour the great Oscar himself emerged from his house and entered the carriage. He was dressed in the long cloth overcoat so familiar to the *habitués* of the Old Bailey, a very highly-glazed top hat, wore suede gloves, and carried in his hand a small walking-stick. Between his lips was the ever favourite cigarette. The brougham no sooner started on its journey than two cabs were employed to follow it. One cab contained the private detectives, the other the *Budget* reporter.

SIR JOHN BRIDGE

Mr. Wilde drove by way of Sloane Square to the Cadogan Hotel, a place of the highest respectability in Sloane Street. At the door of the hotel he was met by Lord Alfred Douglas, who had rooms in the building. Mr. Wilde entered the Hotel, and proceeded upstairs. He opened and read some letters which had arrived for him. He stayed in the place about twenty minutes, and then re-entered his carriage and drove direct to the Old Bailey. The brougham pulled up opposite to the private entrance to the criminal court, a gateway leading to Old Newgate Prison Yard, and an entrance through which the prisoners are taken. Mr. Wilde at that time could not have realised the adage that his last entrance to the Old Bailey as a free man, considering the doorway by which he went in — of coming events casting their shadows before them. Mr. Wilde did not enter the court in which the trial was taking place. He was, however, about to do so when he was met by his solicitor who conducted him to a private room in the building. A conference

16 Tite Street, Chelsea

was held in that room — a conference that will become almost an historical one — between Sir Edward Clarke, Q.C., Mr. Charles Matthews, Mr. Humphries (the legal advisers of Oscar), and Mr. Wilde. The result of the discussion was seen some twenty minutes later by Sir Edward Clarke publicly withdrawing from the case. Mr. Wilde, immediately the conference was ended, left the precincts of the Old Bailey and drove in his carriage to the Holborn Viaduct Hotel, where Lord Alfred Douglas had reserved a special room for him, and who was in waiting to receive his friend. Mr. Wilde on entering the hotel proceeded directly to his room, and soon after his arrival (about half past eleven) was joined by Lord Douglas of Hawick. At half-past twelve the party had lunch served, and at half-past one o'clock paid the bill and made arrangements for departure. On emerging from the hotel Mr. Wilde re-entered his carriage, and was followed by the two Douglas's. The party drove

BITER BIT

THE ARREST OF OSCAR WILDE.

PET OF LONDON SOCIETY, ONE OF OUR MOST SUCCESSFUL PLAYWRITERS AND POETS, ARRESTED ON A HORRIBLE CHARGE.

The Cadogan Hotel

to Ely Place, and Mr. Wilde personally delivered a letter at the offices of Sir George Lewis. Outside Ely Place, Lord Alfred and Lord Douglas of Hawick left the brougham and entered a cab. Mr. Wilde, however, drove on in his carriage and the cab followed close behind. The procession at this time was an interesting one. Mr. Wilde leading in his brougham, then the Lords Douglas in a cab, next two private detectives in another cab, then the *Budget* man in another cab, and then about four other cabs containing more newspaper men. In this order the procession proceeded to Ludgate Circus, up Fleet Street and the Strand to St. James's Square. The cab containing the Lords Douglas stopped at a bank and they entered and cashed a large cheque. Mr. Wilde, however, drove on, and eventually alighted at the Cadogan Hotel. Soon after, he was joined by Lord Alfred Douglas. The time was now shortly after three o'clock, and as I ascertained from the porter of the hotel that Mr. Wilde had dismissed his carriage and had expressed a desire to stay at the hotel until the evening, I determined to drive back to the City and find out how matters were proceeding there.

The first news I obtained was to the effect that immediately on the termination of the trial at the Old Bailey, Mr. Charles Russell (Lord Queensberry's solicitor) had sent the following letter to the public prosecutor; — "In order that there may be no miscarriage of justice, I think it my duty at once to send you a copy of all our witnesses' statements, together with a copy of the shorthand notes of the trial."

The Hon. Hamilton Cuffe, the present Director of Public Prosecutions, is a very different man to his predecessor. He does not take a month to decide any question of grave importance. Immediately he saw the purport of the documents Mr. Russell had forwarded to him, he sent for that gentleman and requested him to attend at the Treasury immediately. Mr. Russell did so, and the result of the interview was shown in the fact that he left the Treasury with Mr. Angus Lewis, one of the solicitors to the Public Prosecutor, and a Detective Inspector Brockwell. The party proceeded to Bow Street Police Court, and asked for a private interview with Sir John Bridge. This was granted, and Sir John returned with the party to Whitehall.

Sir John Bridge

The magistrate then read the documents supplied by Mr. Russell, and returned to Bow Street. At five minutes to five o'clock he signed a warrant for the arrest of Mr. Oscar Wilde, and handed it to Detective Inspector Brockwell for immediate execution. The inspector proceeded by cab to Scotland Yard and instructed Detective Inspector Richards and Detective Sergeant Allen to go at once to the Cadogan Hotel and effect the arrest. The two officers took a cab, and I followed them. Arrived at the hotel, they had a moment's conversation with one of the private detectives, and then entered the hotel. What took place inside is best described in the words of an eye-witness, who was present from the time the police officers entered the hotel until Wilde came out in their custody. My informant said, "The detectives entered here (the Cadogan Hotel) about 6.20 p.m. Addressing the hall porter, one of them asked, 'Is Oscar Wilde staying here?' They were answered in the affirmative. 'Will you show us to his room?' they asked, notifying that they were police officers. The porter, somewhat flurried, summoned the waiter, who conducted the two detectives to Wilde's sitting-room, No. 53, where they found their man. In the room were two young men. Wilde was seated by the fireplace in a saddle bag chair, calmly smoking a cigarette and drinking a brandy and soda. He raised his inquiring eyes to the intruders. Inspector Richards said, 'Mr. Wilde, I believe?' Wilde languidly responded. 'Yes, yes.' The floor of the room was strewn with some eight or nine copies of evening papers, which had evidently been hastily scanned and then thrown aside. Inspector Richards said, 'We are police officers, and hold a warrant for your arrest.' Wilde replied, 'Oh, really.' Inspector Richards added, 'I must ask you to accompany me to the police station.' 'Whither shall I be taken?' inquired Wilde. 'To Scotland Yard,' replied the inspector, 'and thence to Bow Street.' 'Shall I be able to obtain bail?' plaintively said Wilde. The officer sternly replied, 'That is a matter for the magistrate.' With a deep sigh, he dropped an evening-paper, and

raising himself by the aid of the arms of the chair into standing position, he remarked with characteristic nonchalance to the officers, 'Well, if I must go I will give you the least possible trouble.' Wilde then passed over to a couch, picked up his overcoat, and was assisted in putting it on by one of the young men present. Carefully he lifted and adjusted his hat. He grasped his suede gloves in one hand and seized his stick with the other. Then he picked up from the table a copy of 'The Yellow Book,' which he placed in security under his left arm. He then threw away the end of a cigarette, and taking a fresh one from his silver case, lit it by a match given him by one of his young friends. Before departing with the police officers, he asked one of the young men present to go to his house and obtain some clean linen and forward it to the police station whither he was to be conveyed. Then he said to the detectives, 'I am now, gentlemen, ready to accompany you.'

"Detective Allen, acting upon this condescension, ran down the stairs and hailed a four-wheel cab (No. 15,034) from the rank in Cadogan Square. When the party came down to the hall the porter, by force of habit, politely opened the door, while the waiter as politely showed them into the cab."

When Mr. Wilde emerged from the hotel he looked considerably flushed, but he did not appear in any way to have lost his self-possession, and he never for one moment relaxed his grasp of the "Yellow Book." One of the young men referred to as having been in the room of the hotel — a sallow complexioned young fellow, wearing a fur lined coat and a silk hat — exhibited the intention of entering the cab, but, on a strong hint from one of the detectives, he desisted. The detectives and Wilde were now fairly seated in the growler. Detective Allen directed the cabman to drive by the shortest route to Scotland Yard. The driver accordingly proceeded by way of Cadogan Square, and as he passed the cab rank he cried out to some of his brethren, "I've got him inside." The man was evidently animated by the full glory that he had captured a distinguished fare. The four wheeler then proceeded by way of Hobart Place, Buckingham Palace Road, and St. James' Park to Scotland Yard.

Detective Allen alighted first, and Wilde came next. In alighting he missed the carriage step and nearly fell to the stone pavement. Quickly recovering his position and still retaining between his teeth the cigarette which he was smoking, he dived his hand into his pocket and pulled out some money for the purpose of paying the cabman. Detective Allen interposed, "I'll pay." "No! No!" said Wilde. "Allow me if you please," but on being informed that it was a way they had at Scotland Yard of paying for the conveyance of prisoners, Wilde returned the coins to his pocket. Wilde was then hurried by the two detectives into "the Yard," where he was detained for some time, and subsequently removed to Bow Street, arriving shortly after eight o'clock. Up to this time Wilde had not been charged, and consequently as he drove along in the cab, accompanied by Detective Inspectors Brockwell and Richards, he was allowed to smoke. Arrived at the chief police station in London, Wilde was taken into the charge room and placed in the dock. Inspector Brockwell read the warrant to him and Mr. Digby took the charge. Whilst all this formality took place, Wilde leant over the side of the dock, smiled occasionally, looked extremely bored, and said nothing except asking for the dates mentioned in the warrant to be repeated. He was then searched, and twenty £5 notes found in his pocket-book, his cigarette case and matches taken from him. Lord Alfred Douglas offered bail for Mr. Wilde, but it was refused. He was then conveyed to one of the police cells, and a constable told off to watch him. He was provided with rugs on which to make his bed — a kindness not extended to all prisoners. Wilde, however, slept little, and for more than half the night he paraded his cell. About six o'clock he called the constable on duty and asked if he could smoke. When told it was against the rules, he seemed much surprised. Wilde next gave orders for some breakfast to be sent for from the Tavistock Hotel in Covent Garden. A waiter brought it across on a tray, but Wilde ate hardly any of the toast and eggs, but he drank all the tea, and, in fact, when a second breakfast ordered by mistake arrived, he partook of some more tea, but not one atom of food did he allow to pass his lips. Thus did the man who has cultivated affectation, a shameless disavowal of all morality, and the Great Mogul of the aesthetic craze, passed his first night and early morning in a prison cell.

After the police constable, who had been in attendance on Oscar during the night, had removed his breakfast things he asked the author of "all that's beautiful" if he would like to wash himself. Mr. Wilde replied in the affirmative, and taking off his top coat and placing it on his bed he followed the police officer from the cell, along a passage, and across the yard at the back of Bow Street Police Station, where a lavatory is fitted up. Here Mr. Wilde doffed his silk-lined frock coat, turned up the cuffs of his shirt, took off his collar and tie and had a good sluice in the basin of water the constable prepared for him. Having washed and dried himself, he brushed his massive head of hair with a nearly worn-out brush. He next replaced his collar, and then arranged his tie, carefully putting his gold pin in the cravat. His toilet finished, he retraced his steps back to the police cell, arriving shortly before nine o'clock. He was then locked in and left to his own meditations. At half-past ten o'clock, Gaoler Bush came hurriedly to Mr. Wilde's cell door, unlocked it, and asked the prisoner to follow him. Accompanied by Bush and three constables, Oscar was conducted across the police station yard to the prisoners' entrance to the Police Court. The party ascended by a private staircase to the cells behind the Extradition Court. About twenty minutes to eleven o'clock the door by which prisoners enter the Court was opened, and Oscar, hat in hand, and his suede gloves between his fingers, entered the Court. He was conducted by Mr. Bush to the iron dock, at each end of which stood a policeman. Immediately he was in the dock Mr. Wilde placed

ARREST OF WILDE AT THE CADOGAN HOTEL

his silk hat on the seat provided for the convenience of prisoners and his gloves inside it. He then leant over the front of the dock, and with clasped hands had a short but animated conversation with his solicitor, Mr. Travers Humphreys. The Court, small and oppressive, presented at this moment a scene that will one day become historic.

The Echo, 6 April 1895

OSCAR WILDE.

ARRESTED AT CHELSEA.

How completely have the tables been turned in the Queensberry case! The man who for two days parried the verbal attacks of counsel, who lolled indolently and smilingly in the witness-box at the Old Bailey, who gave vent to his polished paradoxes with careless nonchalance, and who condescendingly expressed his utter contempt for all things mundane, is now in the hands of the police, charged with one of the most heinous crimes that can be alleged against a man — a crime too revolting to be spoken of even by men.

The
A Weekly News.

ARREST OF OSCAR WILDE.

PROCEEDINGS AT BOW-STREET.

The arrest of Oscar Wilde on Friday evening, briefly referred to elsewhere, was made by Insp. Richards at the Cadogan Hotel,

WILDE IN THE DOCK.

On Saturday morning Wilde was brought before Sir J. Bridge, charged with various acts of indecency. A small crowd, chiefly composed of representatives of the press, assembled round the doors of the court some time before the opening. It was supposed that the case would be heard in the large court, but after waiting for nearly half an hour it was rumoured that the remand would be taken in the small room upstairs. This sudden change of venue resulted in a stampede of pressmen and public. The magistrate took his seat at 11 o'clock, and immediately afterwards prisoner was brought into the court, which was densely crowded. He was dressed as at the time of his arrest, in a dark suit with dark overcoat and silk hat. Mr. Gill appeared on behalf of the public prosecutor; Mr. Humphreys defended prisoner.—Mr. Gill said that the actual charge on which he would ask the magistrate to commit prisoner for trial would depend upon the disclosures which were made when the case was fully inquired into. The charge he proposed to go into first related to the conduct of prisoner in regard to a young man named Charles Parker.—Charles Parker, a clear-faced youth, stated that he was 19. He related how he met Taylor at St. James's Restaurant, and was there first treated to drink and afterwards introduced to Oscar Wilde.—In reply to Mr. Humphrey, Sir J. Bridge said he proposed to sit as long as the prosecuting solicitor thought reasonable. It was very desirable that the case should be disposed of as speedily as possible.

ANOTHER ARREST.

The man Taylor whose name was mentioned so prominently in the case, was arrested early on Saturday morning and taken to Bow-street.

THE ARREST OF TAYLOR.

The Illustrated Police News, 27 April 1895

THE AUTHOR AND HIS WORK.

Some theatrical managers have removed the name of Oscar Wilde from their programmes, though they continue the performance of his plays. In reference to this compromise with prudery Mr. Sydney Grundy writes: I wonder on what principles of law, or justice, or common sense, or good manners, or Christian charity, an author's name is blotted from his work. If a man is not to be credited with what he has done well, by what right is he punished for what he has done ill?" Mr. Grundy has nailed a characteristic English instance of moral pretence. The omission of the author's name from the playbills is the weakest kind of compromise. It would evince moral courage to keep the play running as the work of a man whose name at the present moment is unsavoury in the mouth of society, and it will be an act of high principle to withdraw the piece. But to retain the benefit of the dramatist's work and to suppress his name is mere moral humbug.

The Daily Telegraph, 8 April 1895

Reuter's New York correspondent telegraphs that at the Lyceum Theatre, where Oscar Wilde's play "An Ideal Husband" is now running, it has been decided to remove the author's name from the bills and programmes. Miss Rose Coghlan, who has been playing "A Woman of No Importance" in the Western States, has resolved to omit the play from her répertoire. A later despatch states that the directors of the Lyceum Theatre have decided to discontinue the performance of Oscar Wilde's play, "An Ideal Husband," after this week.

Translation of an item on the front page of *Le Figaro* (Paris), 11 April 1895.

ENGLISH PRUDISHNESS

DIRECTOR OF AN ENGLISH THEATRE, *to his secretary* — My dear fellow, you can say what you like. I may be tired of this affair as an impresario, but as an Englishman I am proud of it.

SECRETARY — In that capacity, I too am proud of it.

DIRECTOR — If I had gone on presenting Oscar Wilde's play, there would not have been a single spectator in my theatre — and all the theatres are in the same situation. That's what I find so wonderful about this country of ours.

SECRETARY — It is the only country in which even scandals serve to highlight public morality. Oscar Wilde is not only finished as a gentleman but also as a playwright.

DIRECTOR — In France, if such a thing had happened to a dramatist, it would have given his play enormous publicity. Box-office receipts would have shot up over-night.

SECRETARY — Yes?

DIRECTOR — I wouldn't want money acquired like that. . . . By the way, what are we going to put on now? How would you feel about a play by D'Ennery?*

SECRETARY — It would seem pretty pallid.

*Adolphe Philippe D'Ennery, prolific French melodramatist.

The New York Times, 8 April 1895

Aside from the depravity that it has been necessary to make public in the downfall of Oscar Wilde, people who met him here, and accepted his letters of introduction as an accredited English gentleman, are curious to know something of his family, his mother, his wife, his children, and almost everybody else upon whom he has brought absolute ruin.

Every Irishman is interested in Oscar Wilde because he is a born Irishman. His mother, who is now a tottering old lady in her seventies, was one of the earliest advocates of the home-rule cause. So long as she was able to write she wielded a trenchant pen. In this way she managed to earn enough money to educate her two sons, who were the idols of her heart. Oscar was the elder.

No woman in London society for the last decade has commanded more respect than Lady Wilde. The best people in the most exclusive social set used to go to see her despite the almost intolerable mannerisms of the sons to whom she was a most devoted mother.

Oscar Wilde was born in Dublin about forty years ago. His father was a skilled surgeon-dentist, frequently called upon by the Queen for professional services. But somehow or other he never seemed to accumulate any money. He was a man of letters, a skilled statistician, and a man whose experiments in dentistry are still an authority in his profession; but he seemed to lack thrift. Oscar Wilde was the first one in the family to develop it, and the success he has achieved as a playwright and man of letters is mainly due to the devotion of his mother. She deprived herself of necessities in order that he might be liberally educated.

In a primitive school at Enniskillen, Ireland, Oscar Wilde was sent to get the rudiments of an education. He soon outgrew the school, and was sent to Trinity College, Dublin. Here, again, he distinguished himself with such marked success that he was sent to Oxford. He won prize after prize. This was ten years before he came to America as the apostle of a new "cult," and attained the celebrity that brought in the almighty dollar. Whatever personal humiliation the caricature in "Patience" involved, it put money in Oscar Wilde's pocket, and placed the entire family in a position of personal independence that it had never known before.

Almost every man and woman who has figured in London society for the last thirty years knew and respected Lady Wilde. Prominent people were only too glad to attend her receptions in the home that, by courtesy, was called Cadogan House. It is located in the most fashionable part of London, and despite pecuniary reverses Lady Wilde has always managed to retain possession of it.

At one time the family was so poor that the blinds were kept closed in broad daylight in order to conceal the shabbiness of the furniture. By a skillful arrangement of draperies Lady Wilde always managed to make a creditable appearance by candlelight. In those days Oscar used to appear before his mother's guests arrayed in a curious garment of white cloth calculated to display his fine figure to its best advantage. He had only begun to evolve the singular ideas that soon made him world-famous as an apostle of the "lily" culture. His mother and all her friends encouraged it, but assuredly without any dream that it would lead to the disgrace that has been the talk of London and almost every other part of the civilised world within the last few days.

Oscar Wilde never hesitated to say that it was his American "experience" and the plump bank account that he was able to take home after delivering more than 200 lectures here that taught him that is "paid" to be a crank with a "fad" that people were interested in. he said that once t a public dinner. With all his peculiarities, he was a shrewd business man, with a sharp eye to pecuniary results. He made money much faster than he expected, and it is only just to say that he was quite unselfish in sharing his prosperity with

other members of his family who had not been so fortunate.

A wife and two children must also share the shame brought upon Oscar Wilde by the exposures of the last few days. About eleven years ago he married the daughter of Horace Lloyd, a conspicuous member of the English bar, who had been honored with the title of Queen's Counsel. Since her marriage Mrs. Oscar Wilde has been a notable member of London society, an enthusiastic "first nighter" at the theatres, with a belief in her husband's ability as a novelist and playwright that amounted almost to idolatry. She has two children.

Americans who have had occasion to visit London know Oscar Wilde's mother, his wife, and children very well. It is the effect that his disgrace will have upon them that excites sympathy here just now.

Oscar Wilde at Bow Street

ARRIVAL OF WILDE (B24) AT BOW STREET
HE IS HOOTED BY THE MOB —

WILDE AND TAYLOR IN THE DOCK

WILDE IS ILL IN PRISON

THE LIBERATOR CASE
JABEZ AT LAST SAILS FOR ENGLAND

JABEZ SPENCER BALFOUR

— SAFE ON BOARD THE TARTAR PRINCE

OSCAR WILDE PROSECUTION.

COMMITTAL.

The magisterial examination of Oscar Wilde and Alfred Taylor, on the serious charges brought against them by the Public Prosecutor, was resumed and concluded at Bow Street on Friday, and the accused now stand committed for trial at the Old Bailey. The indictment in the case of Wilde charges him only with misdemeanour, for which the maximum penalty is two years' hard labour, but against Taylor a more serious indictment has been entered. A much larger crowd than on the previous hearings assembled in Bow Street on Friday morning to witness the arrival of the prisoners, through which those whose duties took them to the court had literally to fight their way. The fortnight's confinement in Holloway Gaol has told severely on Wilde. He has lost a great deal of flesh. His face looked almost bloodless, and his eyes

Travers Humphreys.

heavy and weary. He entered the dock with faltering steps, and, having obtained Sir John Bridge's permission to be seated, sank with a sigh of relief upon the narrow oak plank which does duty for a seat in the dock. Taylor, on the other hand, was looking as fresh and happy as ever.

Mr. C. F. Gill again appeared for the prosecution, and Mr. Travers Humphreys, in the absence of Sir Edward Clarke, defended Wilde, while Mr. Arthur Newton appeared on behalf of Taylor; and Mr. J. P. Grain held a watching brief on behalf of the witness, Sidney Mavor.

Charles Parker was recalled and examined by Mr. Gill as to his relations with Taylor. It was with great reluctance that the witness could be got to state what the nature of those relations were. He pleaded first that it was a long time ago, and his

TAYLOR
CHARLES PARKER
OSCAR WILDE
SHELLEY
ATKINS

Mr. Gill then called two clerks from the London and Westminster Bank, who produced certified copies of the prisoners' banking accounts.

After some formal evidence as to Wilde's stay at the Savoy Hotel, Frederick Curley, a superannuated detective-inspector, produced a batch of papers found at Taylor's lodgings in Chapel Street. Among the papers were two cheques made payable to Sidney Mavor, and several telegrams from Wilde to Taylor. In one of these, dated August 9, 1893, Wilde said, "Cannot manage dinner to-morrow. So sorry. — OSCAR"; and in another, "Obliged to see Tree at five o'clock, so do not come to Savoy. Let me know about Friday." The packet also contained a Christmas card from Mavor to Taylor.

This being the whole of the evidence for the prosecution, Mr. Gill asked for the committal of the prisoners upon a series of about a dozen charges, which were carefully perused by Sir John Bridge, and then read by the clerk to the prisoners, after which the usual caution was administered, and they were asked by the magistrate whether they

Above: Arthur Newton.
Right: Charles Gill.

memory was not very vivid as to what happened. "You have already made a statement to the solicitors which I have here in writing," said Mr. Gill, and added, "you must say what occurred, you know." Still the witness was silent, and it was not until Sir John Bridge interposed with a demand that he should speak up and relate what occurred that the witness could be induced to repeat the statement he had previously made.

William Parker, brother of the last witness, was recalled, and gave evidence to the effect that his relations with Taylor were of the same nature as his brother's. It was upon these two statements that Mr. Gill obtained the committal of Taylor upon the more serious charge.

OSCAR WILDE COMMITTED.

OSCAR TAKING HIS CONSTITUTIONAL

SIR JOHN BRIDGE: "HAVE YOU ANYTHING TO SAY, WILDE?"
OSCAR: "NOTHING AT PRESENT, YOUR WORSHIP."

wished to say anything in answer to the charges.

Wilde merely replied: "Not at present, your worship," and Taylor stated through Mr. Newton that he also reserved his defence.

Mr. Newton had previously submitted that as the only evidence against Taylor on the more serious charge — he said nothing about the misdemeanour — had been given by discredited witnesses, no case to justify a committal for the abominable offence had been established, but Sir John Bridge had decided that "it is certainly enough to convict on."

Mr. Humphreys then renewed his application for bail on behalf of Wilde. He said that substantial bail would be forthcoming, and as it was a case which required that the prisoner should see the witnesses he wished to call, he ought to be allowed out on bail. It was necessary that he should see persons who would probably make statements to him that they would not to anyone else. He pointed out that no charge of felony had been made, and said there was not the slightest reason to believe that the prisoner would attempt to escape.

Mr. Newton also asked that Taylor might be admitted to bail.

Sir John Bridge said the question of bail was a matter in his discretion. The two things to be considered were the gravity of the offence and the nature of the evidence. With reference to the first point, there was to his mind no graver offence than that with which the prisoners were charged, and as to the evidence he would not say more than that he did not think it was slight, and he should refuse bail.

The prisoners were then removed in custody.

93

OSCAR

IN PRISON.

CAN YOU IMAGINE WHAT THE MENTAL AND PHYSICAL SUFFERINGS OF A MAN OF THE OSCAR WILDE TEMPERAMENT MUST BE?

3 Temple Gardens,Temple,19 April 1895

My dear Cuffe,

I have considered the question as to whether a prosecution ought to be instituted against Lord Alfred Douglas . . . and have come to the conclusion that no proceedings should be taken upon the evidence we have in the statements of the different witnesses.

Having regard to the fact that Douglas was an Undergraduate at Oxford when Wilde made his acquaintance — the difference in their ages — and the strong influence that Wilde has obviously exercised over Douglas since that time, I think that Douglas, if guilty, may fairly be regarded as one of Wilde's victims.

. . . I am afraid there is little room for doubt that immoral relations existed between them, yet if an attempt were made to prove anything definite, it would be found, I think, that the evidence available only disclosed a case of grave suspicion. . . .

Comments will no doubt be made as to Douglas not being prosecuted, but these comments are made by people who do not understand or appreciate the difficulties of proving such a case. . . .

Part of a letter to the editor of the The Star from Lord Alfred Douglas, 19 April:

SIR, — When the great British public has made up its great British mind to crush any particular unfortunate whom it holds in its power, it generally succeeds in gaining its object, and it is not fond of those who dare to question its power, or its right to do as it wishes. I feel, therefore, that I am taking my life in my hands in daring to raise my voice against the chorus of the pack of those who are now hounding Mr. Oscar Wilde to his ruin; the more so as I feel assured that the public has made up its mind to accept me, as it has accepted everybody and everything connected with this case, at Mr. Carson's valuation. I, of course, am the undutiful son who, in his arrogance and folly, has kicked against his kind and affectionate father, and who has further aggravated his offence by not running away and hiding his face after the discomfiture of his friend. It is

NOT A PLEASANT POSITION

to find oneself in with regard to the public, but the situation is not without an element of grim humour, and it is no part of my intention to try and explain my attitude or defend my position. I am simply the "vox in the solitudine clamantis" raising my feeble protest; not in the expectation of making head against the wave of popular or newspaper clamour, but rather dimly hoping to catch the ear and the sympathy of one or two of those strong and fearless men and women who have before now defied the shrieks of the mob. To such as these I appeal to interfere and to stay the hand of "Judge Lynch." And I submit that Mr. Oscar Wilde has been tried by the newspapers before he has been tried by a jury, that his case has been almost

HOPELESSLY PREJUDICED

in the eyes of the public from whom the jury who must try his case will be drawn, and that he is practically being delivered over bound to the fury of a cowardly and brutal mob. . . .

ALFRED DOUGLAS.
Chalcott House, Long Ditton, 19 April.

Part of a letter to the editor of The Star from Robert Buchanan (poet, playright and novelist), 19 April:

I am sure that Lord Queensberry, who has himself suffered cruelly from the injustice of public opinion, is quite as sorry as I am for his fallen foe, and is quite as anxious as I am that he should be dealt with fairly, justly, and even mercifully. Personally, I would not condemn even a dog on the kind of tainted evidence

ROBERT BUCHANAN

which has been foreshadowed during the recent preliminary inquiry, but the case, as I said, is still only sub judice, and none of us yet know with any certainty whether or not a jury of Englishmen will pronounce Mr. Wilde guilty.

This being the case, I should like to ask on what conceivable plea of justice or expediency an accused person, not yet tried and convicted, is subjected to the indignities and inconveniences of a common prison, and denied, while a prisoner, the ordinary comforts to which he has been accustomed when at large? Why should his diet be regulated unduly? Why should he be denied the sedative of the harmless cigarette, more than ever necessary to a smoker in times of great mental anxiety? Why should not his friends visit him? Why, in short, should he not enjoy, as far as is practicable, all the privileges of an innocent man? Innocent he presumably is until he is tried and found guilty. If it be argued that the case is a serious one, in so far as the magistrate refuses bail and the evidence is considered strong against the prisoner, the reply is that many a case which

looked far blacker has ended in an acquittal; and, at any rate, we have no right whatever to

ASSUME THE GUILT

beforehand. Assume for a moment that the prisoner is acquitted, what amends can be made for treatment which is as unjust as it is abominable? As matters stand, we may shatter a man's health, torture his mind and his body, drive him into madness or imbecility, and then, finally, if it turns out we are mistaken, all we can do is say, "We're very sorry! — we beg your pardon! — you can go!"

I commend this system of things to the attention of the Marquess of Queensberry. It is only possible, I think, in a country where Christianity has got the better of justice and common–sense, and where a man may be lynched by a Christian Press and a Christian public long before he is really put on trial. I have too much sympathy with his lordship's creed to think that the man who holds it would approve of such a system. So far from thinking him "notoriously corrupt," I think him notoriously brave and honest, anxious that all men should have, under Queensberry and all rules, a fair trial and fair play; and I would certainly be the last man in the world to offer him disrespect. — Yours, &c.,

19 April   ROBERT BUCHANAN

The Star, 21 April 1895

SIR, — I chanced to read two letters in your issue of this evening, one from Lord Alfred Douglas and another from Mr. Buchanan, in connection with the proceedings against Wilde in the law courts.

With regard to the sentiments of the first named, it is perhaps not altogether surprising that — because the offence with which Wilde is charged happens to be classified as a misdemeanor — his lordship should characterise it as "comparatively trifling." The statute at least provides for it a term of two years' imprisonment with hard labour, this being the maximum period of hard labour, if I mistake not, that our Legislature allows to be imposed for any offence whatever, it being considered the most that any human being is capable of enduring. I apprehend, however, that the majority of decent English folk will fully endorse Sir John Bridge's sentiments as to the gravity of the offence with which Wilde is charged. Be that, however, as it may, it seems to me that Lord Alfred Douglas is the very last man on the face of creation who is entitled to express an opinion on the case whatever. His allegation of unfairness against Sir John Bridge — one of the kindest-hearted and most just of magistrates that ever sat on the Bench — will be met by your readers with the disdain it merits.

With Mr. Buchanan the matter assumes an entirely different aspect. His position, disinterestedness, and ability entitle his utterances to receive respectful attention at all hands. With any little difference of opinion between him and Lord Queensberry I am not concerned in dealing. If he considers that the régime of our prisons, as regards persons awaiting their trial, is unduly severe, he has every right to say so; and for aught I know there may be much to be advanced both from his and other points of view. As a general question it is one that may very properly be discussed, but why it should in any way be attached to the case of Wilde more than to that of any poor wretch who is awaiting "presentation at court" I altogether fail to see. I am not aware that it has been alleged that Wilde has been subjected to different treatment from that accorded to any other individual in precisely similar circumstances. If there were any such evidence, there might be some grounds for raising the question in connection with this case, but as I believe there is none, I should advocate relegating the discussion of the matter to some more opportune moment. I daresay Wilde misses his cigarettes, but not one whit more than "Bill Sykes" would his "clay." I confess my sympathies would be rather with the latter; but that, again, is neither here nor there. Of one thing, however, I am convinced, and that is — if there is to be a dispassionate consideration of the merits or demerits of the existing régime of prison treatment, the surroundings of Wilde's case are peculiarly unfitted for attaining that end. — Yours, &c.,

London 20 April.   COMMON SENSE.

[We have received a host of other letters bearing on the Wilde case, which, for various reasons, we have decided not to publish. — Ed. *Star*.]

The Star, 22 April 1895

OSCAR WILDE.

TWO VIEWS OF HIS PRESENT POSITION.

Has he been Unfairly or Prematurely Judged by Magistrate and Public, or does His Case Illustrate the Need of Prison Reform?

TO THE EDITOR OF "THE STAR."

SIR, — After some howls of execration, the expunging of an author's name from the public playbills, and other acts of Christian charity which have lately been witnessed, it may not be out of place to enter some kind of protest against this very hasty prejudgement of a case still pending. After all, in sexual errors, as in every thing else, the real offence lies, and must always lie, in the sacrificing of another person in any way, for the sake of one's own pleasure or profit; and judged by this standard — which though not always the legal standard is certainly the only true moral standard — the accused is possibly no worse than those who so freely condemn him. Certainly it is strange that a society which is continually and habitually sacrificing women to the pleasure of men, should be so eager to cast the first stone — except that it seems to be assumed that women are always man's lawful prey, and any appropriation or sacrifice of them for sex purposes quite pardonable and "natural." – Yours, &c.,

HELVELLYN.

The Star, 23 April 1895

OSCAR WILDE.

MR. BUCHANAN PLEADS FOR A BROTHER ARTIST.

And Says That Wilde Has Already Lost Everything That Can Make Life Tolerable — Another Correspondent Holds Different Views of "Christian Charity."

TO THE EDITOR OF "THE STAR."

SIR, — Just one word before you close this discussion, in answer to your correspondent "Common Sense." What I claim for Mr. Wilde I should certainly claim for any untried prisoner, Mr. William Sikes included; and I certainly do not think that a question of the liberty of the subject should be postponed sine die, on any possible plea of inexpedience. When an outrage on liberty is committed or threatened is the right time to protest against it.

But I will even go a little further. Just in so far as a man has been respected by us, has amused us, has afforded us harmless pleasure, should he receive delicate consideration. Treatment which would not in the least trouble Mr. Sikes may break the heart of a gentleman and a scholar like Mr. Oscar Wilde; and if we who follow his calling do not speak the needful word on his behalf, who is to do so? Whatever he is, whatever he may be assumed to be, he is a man of letters, a brother artist, and no criminal prosecution whatever will be able to erase his name from the records of English literature. That I say advisedly, though we are far as the poles asunder in every artistic instinct of our lives, and though on more than one occasion I have ridiculed some of his opinions. And I say in conclusion that even if he is as guilty as some suppose him, he has already been terribly and cruelly punished; for while Mr. Sikes would lose nothing by conviction, Mr. Wilde would lose everything — has already lost everything — that can make life tolerable. I have hopes that even a British jury will perceive this, and, not for the first time, temper justice with mercy; for already, I think, the public are awakening to the fact that they have gone too far. "Alas for the rarity of Christian charity under the sun!" Now, as ever, the priests of all creeds are dumb, and it is left for an ordinary citizen to write as I have written. — Yours, &c.,

22 April.   ROBERT BUCHANAN.

Sir, — The two letters which you publish to-day appear to be specimens of the opposite views held on the Wilde case. It is a matter for regret that an epistle like that of "Helvellyn" should be produced as the views of anyone.

However, that expression carries its own mark with it, and requires no general comment. The two or three points in it will hardly bear touching. That affectation of heavy sarcasm as to Christian Charity is an example of inanity which might hardly have been surpassed by any of the correspondents whose contributions are for various reasons unpublished. To publish a letter like that is hardly charitable to the writer, and there are few who would be deceived by its contents. The writer seems unable to appreciate the fact that in the action at law now concluded, Wilde had tacitly admitted, with the ablest counsel on his side, that he was compelled to abandon the attempt to refute another man's right to address him in terms of the grossest condemnation.

When vice cannot be openly palliated the last resort is usually a sneer at Christian Charity. Perhaps "Helvellyn" will learn that Christian Charity does not mean weakness and toleration of Pagan viciousness. Moreover, virtue is something in itself, and is older than Christianity. Everyone who believes in virtue is not tied to Christianity; but everyone who disbelieves in the one is sure to oppose the other. A sneer is not always the fruit of moral or intellectual superiority.

When a man has offended the ears of all decent people, in the most ordinary sense, by openly flaunting the universal and not too exacting code of this world's morals, and by posing as the apostle of corruption, and all that is opposed to civilisation itself, it is not Christian Charity that has anything to do with it — until he has reversed his ways and rendered some satisfaction to an outraged public. The howls of execration, if they have reached "Helvellyn," are a healthy sign; and as to the erasure of a name from playbills, I say emphatic- ally that I wonder why the productions themselves have not been withdrawn. Along with broad opinions on many subjects, it is possible to have a narrow aversion to countenancing even the works of the man who has, with diffidence, been compelled to expose himself to the contempt of mankind.

There is no question as to Sir John Bridge's treatment of Wilde. Everyone is aware that but for the serious nature of the charge, and that the evidence was in Sir J. Bridge's estimation "not slight," he could have been released on bail. With this in mind is it to be supposed that the loss of cigarettes, but with the advantage of good meals — not possible to many others — renders the man a martyr? It is puerile nonsense to suggest he is not well enough treated.

On the other hand many people are asking why the indictment has been drawn under the Act involving the minor penalties. If rumour is but tinged with truth the reason is a good one — and as bad as it could be. — Yours, &c.,

Whitehall, S.W., 22 April. DIKE.

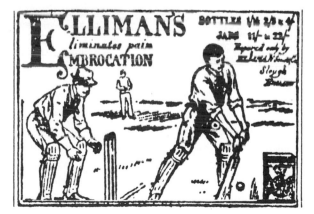

[We have received another large batch of letters on this subject, some of them from Liverpool, Middles- brough, and other far-off centres, but none expresses views different from those which have been published from other correspondents.]

... While we have a whole mob of savages clamoring ... for lynch-law and retribution, we have not one Christian clergyman to utter a sound. Be the victim either Jean Valjean or Oscar Wilde, "Bill Sikes" or the Marquess of Queensberry, no Bishop Miguel appears (save in romantic fiction), to preach and to practise forgiveness. That, I may add, is left to the "agnostic," who has most right to feel revengeful. I heard from the Marquess of Queensberry's own lips that *he* would gladly, were it possible, set the public eye an example of sympathy and magnanimity. – Yours, &c.,

23 April. ROBERT BUCHANAN

The Star, 25 April 1895

TO THE EDITOR OF "THE STAR."

Sir, — I must take exception to the word "sympathy" that is placed in my mouth. I never used it. In my time I haved helped to cut up and destroy sharks. I had no sympathy for them, but may have felt sorry, and wished to put them out of pain as soon as possible.

What I did say was that as Mr. Wilde now seemed to be on his beam ends and utterly down I did feel sorry for his awful position, and that supposing he was convicted of those loathsome charges brought against him that were I the authority that had to mete out to him his punishment, I would treat him with all possible consideration as a sexual pervert of an utterly diseased mind, and not as a sane criminal. If this is sympathy Mr. Wilde has it from me to that extent. — Yours, &c.,

24 April. QUEENSBERRY.

The Morning, 25 April

At the Central Criminal Court yesterday before
Mr. Justice Charles, Mr. Charles Mathews, who
has been retained with Sir Edward Clarke for the
defence of Oscar Wilde, asked that the trial might
be postponed until the May Sessions. The application was made on the grounds set out in an
affidavit which he would hand to his lordship,
namely, that the defence had not had proper time
to prepare their case; and further that in the
present state of popular feeling Mr. Wilde would
not get a fair and impartial trial. Mr. Grain, who
defends Taylor, said that his client was desirous of
having the charges against him brought to an
issue as early as possible. Mr. Gill, for the
prosecution, opposed the application for the postponement of the trial. Under ordinary circumstances the difficulties mentioned by Mr. Mathews
would be reasonable grounds for such an application, but he submitted they were not reasonable in
this instance. The fullest possible information was
given to Mr. Wilde as to the charges he would have
to meet. He asked that the application be not
granted. Mr. Justice Charles said that he did not
feel justified, on the material contained in the
affidavit, to accede to the application. As to the
defendants not having a fair trial, he thought that
any suggestion such as that was groundless.

The case stands accordingly in the list for trial
either for Friday or Saturday, subject to the
remaining business. The defendants were not
present in the court during the application.

SALE OF HOUSEHOLD GOODS.

Oscar Wilde's belongings at 16, Tite-street,
Chelsea, were sold by auction yesterday by order of
the sheriff, acting upon three writs representing
somewhere about £400. The creditors enforcing
the proceedings claimed principally for cigarettes
and cigarette cases. There was a great gathering
at the house at the time fixed for the commencement of the sale, many people not being in
possession of the fact that the major part of the
furniture and effects had been removed under the
right of Mrs. Wilde. Brokers were in great force,
anxious to secure the books, prints, pictures, and
Moorish china to be disposed of; but there were also
a large number of curiously-minded persons who
made their way all over the premises with a morbid
view of seeing something that belonged to a man
under trial at the Old Bailey. Oscar Wilde's
bedroom was the chief point of attraction. It is a
little apartment — dingy one might call it, with
furniture about fitted to a servant's room; but over
the entrance, on the inside, was inscribed, in
elongated type-written characters, these lines: —
"Spirit of Beauty, tarry yet awhile;
    They are not dead, thine ancient votaries;
Some few there are to whom thy radiant smile
    Is better than a thousand victories."
The curiosity of this musical inscription is that the
letter "O" in each word where it occurs is made a
very small circle. Above the inscription referred to
there were arranged a series of sunflowers in
glowing gilt; above them, in painted arrangement,
a series of flaming "Aureoles." In a chest of
drawers in this bedroom — which, by the way, was
lighted with a curious copper lamp of oriental
design — lay a choice selection of Oscar Wilde's
MSS., said to include a yet unproduced play. There
were also many letters in this drawer, and for a
time people sported with them, until restrained by

100

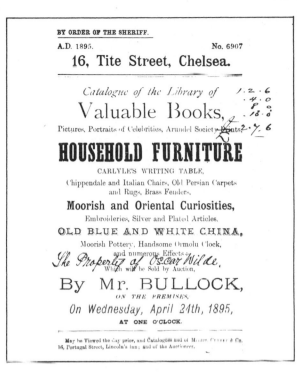

(of which only 75 copies were printed), three copies of "The Sphinx," bound in vellum, two large paper copies of "Lady Windermere's Fan," two copies of "Salome," and one of "A Woman of No Importance" — all sold in a bundle — £8 5s. was taken. Five copies of "Dorian Grey" fetched £3 3s. Thirteen volumes of the Parnell Commission were among the things found in the Wilde library. Oscar's life-length portrait went for £14; singular to say, the same sum bought Carlyle's writing desk — a wondrous piece of mechanism in furniture, which there is little doubt is destined for America. A crayon drawing of a nude female, by Whistler, fetched £21; and another portrait sketch, on brown paper, by the same artist, realised £15. The Arundel prints made fair prices, but the old blue china and Moorish pottery did not excite connoisseurs to high bidding.

the auctioneer's subordinate. Some strange information, however, had in the meantime been gathered. A singular book had been incidentally picked up — "Lo Latin Mystique" — and was being devoured by those who understood French. In a little alcove, just round by the end of Oscar's humble bedstead, was heaped a pile of correspondence, and some of the more inquisitive roaming about the premises looked into it. There were some remarkable letters in that pile. The sale took place in what was called the drawing-room — a small room, in which Oscar Wilde's full-length portrait, in gilt frame, loomed very large. The place was crowded to suffocation, buyers being largely in evidence. Books were taken first. They were a miscellaneous lot, and, it may be said, fetched more than they were worth. A parcel of "Dorian Grey" and Oscar Wilde's poems realised £2 2s.; a bundle of MSS. (really type-written) brought £5 15s.; and a parcel of books containing three copies of "Salome," bound in silk, "The Spirit Lamp," and Wilde's poems, were knocked down for £4 15s. For a copy of "The Happy Princess; and Other Tales"

Sale of Oscar Wilde's household effects at Tite Street

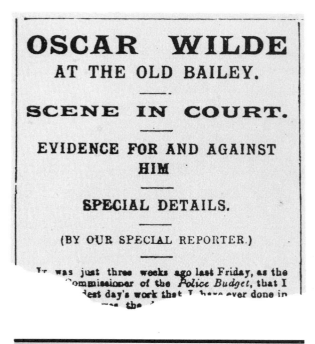

**The Illustrated Police Budget,
4 May 1895**

It was just three weeks ago last Friday [5 April], as the Special Commissioner of the *Police Budget*, that I did the hardest day's work that I have ever done in my life — that was the day on which Oscar Wilde was arrested. Last Friday was also a trying day for me, as I had to be up at Holloway prison at a very early hour to see the actual commencement of the great trial — the trial of a man who, but three short weeks ago, was prosecuting Lord Queensberry for an alleged atrocious libel. But to return to Holloway prison, and more especially to the neighbourhood of Wilde's private cell. Punctually at 8.30 a warder proceeded to Oscar's quarters, and requested him to follow him. Wilde, who was already attired in his long overcoat with the velvet cuffs, was evidently expecting the summons. In his hands he carried his suede gloves, and on his head wore the now familiar American slouch hat. He walked with brisk step before the warder down the long passage leading to the central yard of the prison. Wilde did not appear to look so troubled as

has been his wont of late, in fact his countenance seemed to have brightened up considerably since the days of the Police Court proceedings. In the centre of the yard the police van was waiting, and in one of the little, small and inconvenient compartments in this vehicle Wilde was placed. The prisoner safely locked in, the van started for Newgate Prison, where it arrived shortly after nine o'clock, and pulled up in the centre of the yard immediately behind the court. Wilde was taken from the van and placed in one of the dirty, dingy, damp and unwholesome cells immediately underneath the court, and communicating with the dock by means of a set of turret stairs. These cells are in such a disgraceful state of sanitation that it is not

Charles Willie Mathews

too much too say that they are hardly fit for a cat to live in, let alone a human being. Nevertheless a "kindly and humane law" placed Wilde in one of them, and that one not the best in the building by a very long way. About half-past nine o'clock Mr. Charles Mathews, Wilde's junior counsel, who had obtained an order from the judge, descended the stairs and entered Wilde's cell. He remained closeted with the distinguished literary prisoner for nearly three-quarters of an hour, and then returned to the Court to consult with Sir Edward Clarke. Punctually at half-past ten o'clock the judge (Mr. Justice Charles) entered the Court and took his seat at his desk, on which had been placed a bouquet of beautiful flowers. . . .

Immediately the judge had taken his seat the two prisoners, Wilde and Taylor, were brought into Court. They came up the stairs leading from the cells into the dock. All was silence when they entered, and every eye in Court was turned upon them. They bore the scrutiny well, and to all outward appearances were unmoved or cared little for the opinion of many of the motley crew who had assembled to witness this trial. Wilde, however, looked haggard and worn, and his long hair, which is usually so well kept, was dishevelled and untidy. Taylor, on the other hand, was neatly dressed, and appeared not to have suffered at all from his enforced confinement. He no longer, however, regarded the proceedings with merriment and indifference as he did at the police-court. His manner in the Old Bailey dock was becomingly grave. Both men, still wearing their overcoats and holding their hats in their hands, stood in the front of the dock and waited events. On each side of them and at the back were warders placed to guard against any possibility of escape. I could not at this point help contrasting in my mind the reverse of this picture that last scene Friday presented to me. Here was Wilde, the wit, the epicure, standing in the greatest and most renowned criminal dock in the world, to answer a grave and unwholesome charge. It was but three weeks ago I saw in his place the self-contented and unmoved form of Lord

Mr Justice Charles

Queensberry. He did not, however, enter from the cells — he was requested politely by a warder to step from the body of the Court into the dock. In that there was a difference, but, nevertheless, he was in the dock. In the witness-box was the now prisoner Wilde, replying in brilliant language, talking far above the heads of his hearers, and constantly becoming epigrammatical in his arguments with Mr. Carson, Q.C., who was cross-examining him. Yes! truly in these days the world moves apace, and even a criminal picture can be considerably altered in three weeks for either good or bad. It is not for me to say as yet whether the alteration is in the interests of public morality for good or evil. I have my own ideas, and I still contend, as I did three weeks ago, that the case ought to have been heard *in camera*.

Immediately the prisoners were placed in the front of the dock, the Clerk of the Court rose and read out the indictment. I have, however, dealt with this phase of the case lower down, so I need

103

SCENE AT THE OLD BAILEY.
THE MOST SENSATIONAL TRIAL OF THE CENTURY.

not refer to it again here. When all the preliminaries were finished, and Mr. Gill ready to make his opening speech, the two prisoners removed their overcoats, carefully folded them up, and placed them over the back of the chairs which the warders had provided for them to sit down on. This done, they both took their seats. Wilde crossed his legs, placed his left arm on his leg, and on his hand leant his head. He stared apparently into vacancy, but to anyone watching him closely it was at once perceptible that he was drinking in and listening intently to the grave charges Mr. Gill was levelling at his head. All through the speech, however, he did not move a muscle, and after a time he gave one the impression of a man who was becoming rapidly bored. In some like position Oscar sat hour after hour. He never spoke, laughed, or scowled, but stared incessantly into vacancy, and so on for two long days.

I will now describe the court. Following my usual rule, I will first sketch it empty, and then as I proceed in my narrative I will fill in the various figures and put them in their proper positions.

The Old Court of the Old Bailey is the room, for it is nothing more, in which the trial of Wilde takes place. It is approached from Newgate Street through the main entrance to the building. Ascending by a small staircase a landing is reached, and then two doors, which open outwards, are seen in front. These doors lead to the court, and make the only entrance direct from the street. But now to the court in its empty state. Right opposite to the doors in question, and on the far side of the court, is a kind of elevated platform. At the extreme end of this, to the left, is the judge's desk. On his immediate left is another desk, placed under a kind of decorated canopy, in which is hung the sword and arms of authority of the City of London. Under this canopy sits the Lord Mayor or his representative. As strange as it may seem, at all Old Bailey trials the judge is no judge at all. He is only the legal accessor to the Lord Mayor, and before he passes any sentences he consults his lordship or his representative as to the term of

imprisonment he shall pass upon the prisoner. At the present day the old custom is but a mimicry, but, nevertheless, it is still kept up with all due formality. Next to the Lord Mayor's table — as his desk is technically termed — is another desk, and this is followed to the end of the row by three more, the last one being placed at the extreme end near the door which leads to the private apartments of the court reserved for the judge. At the back of these desks runs a long continuous seat, on which Aldermen of the City of London in their gorgeous robes are wont to sit during any sensational trial. At right angles with the judge's seat and on his right hand side is the little and inconvenient witness-box. To the right of this is the jury box, and immediately below the old-fashioned windows, which give a light to the court, sit the twelve good men and true. On the right of this box is a passage leading to the door through which the witnesses enter. To the right side of this is the dock — a high old-fashioned box with glass panels at each side, and constructed to accommodate at least twenty prisoners. But yet the Old Bailey dock is historical, for have not prisoners of note, criminals of a century, and villains of the deepest die found a place in the centre of its four partitions? On the left-hand side of the dock is erected a desk at which the warder in charge — an old veteran — sits during the time of the trial of any prisoner. To the right of the dock is another passage leading to the main entrance to the court. To the right of this and working round to the extremity of the judge's bench are various kinds of boxes, which are tenanted respectively by Pressmen, jury-in-waiting, the general public, and friends of City officials. A space is left on a low level in front of the jury box for a passage leading from the witness's entrance to the court to the witness box, which is entered by the ascending of some half-dozen steps. Merging on the passage to the rear side is a table which serves as the bench for the solicitors instructing counsel. Immediately behind this is the first row of counsel benches, followed by six other like rows. Then another passage and more of the

Atkins confronted with the Constable who arrested him.

box for the accommodation of the privileged public. At a lower level but just in front of the judge's seat is erected a kind of platform. In the centre seat sits the Clerk of the Court in his wig and gown and on his right and left other officials of the Court. Above the dock is a small gallery — in which is a clock — and reserved for the accommodation of the general public. Thus is the Central Criminal Court when empty.

I will now endeavour to describe the court when full, and I will take for my illustration a scene which took place last Saturday afternoon — the denouncement of the witness Atkins by Sir Edward Clarke. The youth is for the second time in the dock. He stands leaning over the mahogany rail of the box, with clasped hands and immovable clean-shaven face, awaiting a question. On the bench sits the judge, pen in hand, and ready to take down in his notebook the answers the witness shall give. In front of the judge, and on the extreme edge of his desk, is a bouquet of fragrant flowers — flowers that to the artistic mind of Wilde must seem in this place to be a sarcasm upon their existence — flowers which come from a purity of air and existence placed in an atmosphere of all kinds of unwholesome criminality. Next to the judge, and just under the City sword, sits the

senior alderman of the City of London, who is there to represent the Lord Mayor, and on his left he has for companions other majestically-adorned aldermen. In fact, the judicial bench presents a gay and festive scene radiant in colour. The jury-box is full, each of its three tiers being occupied by a set of very intelligent-looking men. The passage leading to the witnesses' entrance is crammed by persons who have passed through the ordeal of examination, police officers, and other minor officials. Next to this is the dock in which Wilde and his companion, Taylor, sit and listen to the evidence given against them. The clock in the gallery over their heads ticks on, and seems by its mournful sounds to be ebbing away the life of the men who are compelled to sit under it. Warders are also placed in the dock, and stand like so many mutes during the hearing of the trial. The passage on the other side of the dock is filled up by a morbid crowd anxious to hear every word of the disgusting evidence, whilst the boxes reserved for the friends of the members of the Corporation are also crammed to suffocation. The table reserved for the solicitors is also full. At the end nearest the Judge sits Mr. Angus Lewis, of the Public Prosecutor's office, who is the instructing solicitor in the case. At the other end is Mr. Humphreys, the lawyer who is responsible for the defence of Wilde; next to him is Mr. Arthur Newton, the man Taylor's solicitor. The first row of the bench reserved for counsel, and immediately behind the solicitors' table is, to use an Americanism, full of brains. Sir Edward Clarke, Q.C., Wilde's leading counsel, is almost unrecognisable as he sits behind Mr. Humphreys, surrounded by briefs. Behind him, in the next bench, is Mr. Charles Mathews and Mr. Travers Humphreys, the prisoners' two other advocates. Next to Sir Edward sits Mr. Grain, and behind him Mr. Paul Taylor, the two advocates representing Taylor. Next in order on the front bench comes Mr. Horace Avory and Mr. Gill, the two counsel who are prosecuting on behalf of the Treasury. All the other vacant spaces are filled in by the general public, newspaper men, and the

Horace Avory

The actual Old Bailey proceedings commenced punctually at half-past ten o'clock last Friday morning. . . . After the indictment, which contained no less than twenty-five counts, had been read, the prisoners, Wilde and Taylor, were called upon by the clerk of the court to plead "Guilty" or "Not Guilty." At this point Sir Edward Clarke caused somewhat of a surprise by interposing before the prisoners answered the indictment. His objection, however, turned out to be nothing more than a technical one as to the manner in which the various counts had been joined, and an appeal to the judge to call upon the prosecution to elect the specific counts upon which they relied for a conviction. Both points the judge decided against Sir Edward. Wilde was first called upon to make his plea, and with perfect coolness answered, "Not Guilty." Taylor, somewhat sharply, responded to like effect. The prisoners having been accommodated with chairs, the Court settled down to listen to Mr. Gill's opening speech for the prosecution. The learned counsel had little to say that has not already been made public, either by Mr. Carson during the Queensberry trial or by counsel himself

officials of the court. This was the constitution of the court at the Old Bailey on Saturday afternoon last.

We have left the witness Atkins in the box. Suddenly Sir Edward Clarke rises from amidst his bundle of papers, and pointing with his index finger towards the witness, gives him a warning to speak the truth. The witness, however, hums and hars, and Sir Edward calls into court a policeman, and confronts him with Atkins. The scene is dramatic in the extreme, and it has the desired effect. The witness tells the truth. This scene was one of the most sensational during the whole trial, and I have given details of it in another column. Thus was the court "made," thus were its soundings on the day that will for ever be marked down in history as an historical one — the day on which the trial of the greatest wit and one of the cleverest men of the nineteenth century stood his trial at the Old Bailey for the alleged perpetration of a fearful crime.

Sir Edward Clarke

at the police court. In referring to the prisoners by name Mr. Gill made the delicate distinction of mentioning Wilde as "the prisoner Wilde," and Taylor as "the man Taylor." Mr. Gill's speech was very impatiently received. Wilde, in common with everybody in court, looked terribly bored.

Proceeding, Mr. Gill described Taylor's rooms, with their heavily draped windows, their candles burning on through the day, and the languorous atmosphere, heavy with perfumes. Here, he said, men met together, and here Wilde was introduced by Taylor to youths who would give evidence in the case. Analysing the indictment, Mr. Gill said the first nine counts referred to misconduct with the lads named Parker, the next three to Frederick Atkins, the next five to Alfred Wood, two more to incidents at the Savoy Hotel, two to the young man named Mavor, three to charges of conspiracy, and the last to Wilde's conduct in regard to the lad Shelley. Taking these in their order he roundly accused Taylor of corrupting the first-named lads, and inducing them to meet Wilde by assuring them that he was liberal in his payments. In regard to Taylor the most serious counts of the indictment charge him with attempting the actual felony with both the lads named Parker, whose evidence was abundantly corroborated. Mr. Gill then went over the facts already published in connection with the Queensberry suit and the police-court proceedings as to Wilde's relations with the Parkers, Atkins, Mavor, and Wood, and with the latter's alleged attempt to extort blackmail. There was a difference about Wilde's acquaintanceship with Shelley, whom he met in the shop of his publishers, where he was employed. It was an acquaintance with a literary side, but it went through the same stages. Tamely concluding, when he seemed to be only in *medias res*, with an assurance that the evidence which he would call would justify the jury in finding the prisoners guilty on all counts of the indictment, Mr. Gill called his first witness.

Charles Parker. He is a good-looking young man of twenty-one years, and was dressed well, though quietly, in a serge suit, with a high white collar and

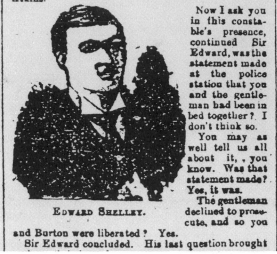

Who did? I did not hear anybody. You were taken to Rochester Row, and the gentleman went with you? Yes.

P.C. 396A was here called into court in sight of Atkins.

Now I ask you in this constable's presence, continued Sir Edward, was the statement made at the police station that you and the gentleman had been in bed together? I don't think so.

You may as well tell us all about it, you know. Was that statement made? Yes, it was.

The gentleman declined to prosecute, and so you

EDWARD SHELLEY.

and Burton were liberated? Yes.

Sir Edward concluded. His last question brought

neat black bow. His hair was carefully parted down the centre and greased into shape on a low receding forehead. He cultivates neither whiskers nor moustache. In his left hand he carried a hard felt hat. His manner in the witness-box was subdued and respectful, and all his answers were given in monosyllables, uttered in a low tone, so low, indeed, that the judge had often to ask him to speak a little louder. During the time he was under examination and cross-examination Wilde intently watched him, with his head resting on his hand. What the effect of the evidence was upon Wilde it is impossible to say. His features betrayed no sign of emotion. In striking contrast was the manner of Taylor, who fidgeted about on his chair, and was obviously ill at ease. The cross-examination of the witness was chiefly directed to showing that Wilde in all his meetings with the witness made no attempt at secrecy. Mr. Grain, cross-examining on behalf of Taylor, established a serious discrepancy in the witness's statements. At Bow Street he had said that no misconduct had taken place between himself and Taylor at Camera Square, while yesterday he told Mr. Gill that there had been misconduct. An admission by the witness that six months after his first meeting with Taylor he had gone to Paris with an operatic composer caused much speculation as to the identity of the unknown. Parker further admitted, in re-examination, that he was introduced to Taylor by Lord Alfred Douglas.

Charles Parker was succeeded in the witness-box by his brother William. There is a striking likeness between the two youths. William, like his brother, was well dressed. He is just one year older. Beyond corroborating his brother, his evidence was of no moment, and he gave place to a string of female witnesses, who were either landladies or lodgers in the house where the parties lodged.

The last witness of the day was the notorious Alfred Wood. He is slightly taller than either of the Parkers, and though the most intellectual looking and best educated, has the worst record. He was living with Taylor when he received a telegram from Lord Alfred Douglas asking him to introduce himself to Wilde at the Café Royal. The old story of his negotiations with Wilde for the sale to him of letters written to Lord Alfred Douglas was again told. Then the Court adjourned for the day, Sir Edward Clarke postponing for the nonce the cross-examination of Woods.

SECOND DAY

On the resumption of the trial on Saturday the lad, Alfred Wood, again entered the box, and after giving serious evidence against Wilde, was cross-examined by Sir Edward Clarke, when he admitted that he received £175 out of over £300, which was alleged to have been extorted from a gentle-man. The witness did not desire to disclose the name of his last employer in England, before he went to America, where he was in honest employment. It was not true that he had got money from other gentlemen in the same way that the £175 was obtained.

At what date did you come into possession of Mr. Wilde's letters? Between January and March, 1893. They were only a few days in my possession.

Did you leave them on the table or give them to Mr. Wilde? I left them on the table.

He knew that there was one letter which he was not giving back. It was in the possession of Allen, who had taken it out of his pocket with his knowledge. He did not want it back from Allen, and it never came back into his possession. He did not know whether Allen kept it or not — he heard nothing more of it. He did not ask Wilde to give him money to help him go away. Wilde offered to do so. He went to America about the end of March. He had said at the police court that he was under the influence of drink when he first went with Wilde to Tite Street, and that was perfectly true. Wilde's house was near the corner of Tite Street, and on the occasion Wilde met him at the corner the second time he went there. He said nothing at the police court about Wilde having given him shirts and collars, because he was not asked.

Thomas Price, employed at a private hotel in St. James's Place, gave evidence as to Wilde having rooms there from October, 1893, to April, 1894. He had seen Taylor, Parker, Atkin, and Scarfe there.

Cross-examined by Sir E. Clarke: Wilde usually came in the morning, did writing there, and left, as a rule, about six in the evening.

Frederick Atkins, examined by Mr. Horace Avory, said he became acquainted with Taylor in 1892. In November of the same year he was introduced to Wilde at a dinner at a café. There were present Wilde and Lord Alfred Douglas. During the dinner Wilde kissed the waiter. He asked witness to go to Paris as his private secretary. Witness two days afterwards met Wilde by appointment at Victoria Station, and went with him to Paris. On returning to London Wilde gave him £3 before he left him at Victoria Station.

Cross-examined by Sir Edward Clarke, he said he could not remember the date on which Wilde came to his lodgings. Wilde had visited him there twice, about the same time. On the second occasion he was ill with small-pox, and the day after Wilde's visit he was moved to the hospital ship. He had not seen Wilde since except before the curtain at the St. James's Theatre on a first night.

In reply to further questions, witness said he had known a man called Burton all his life, and lived in the same house with him for three years. Burton was a bookmaker, and witness was his clerk. They attended race meetings.

Have you been engaged in the business of blackmailing? I do not remember it.

What names have you gone by? Frederick Atkins and Denny. Will you swear that you have never gone in the streets in woman's dress? I will. Sir Edward then wrote the name of a person on a slip of paper, which he handed to witness. Do you know that name? I never saw it before. Did a Birmingham gentleman go with you to your rooms, and did Burton go into the room shortly afterwards, and did you and Burton between you get a large sum of money from the gentleman? No. Do you swear that nothing of the kind ever took place? I swear. Didn't Burton come into the room where you and the gentleman were and demand money, and threaten to lock him up? No. Did the gentleman give Burton a cheque for £200? Not to my knowledge. Do you swear that it did not happen? I do not know that it happened. Did you not take the gentleman's watch and chain, and give them to Burton? No. Were you not both taken to Rochester Row the next night, and did you not then give up the watch and chain? No. Sir Edward Clarke pursued the matter, but the witness sullenly replied "No" and "No" to every question.

Sir E. Clarke questioned witness as to an hotel in Northumberland Avenue, to which witness said he had never been.

Witness last heard from Burton about a week ago. He wrote from Monte Carlo. Burton used to go in the betting ring under the name of Watson. There was no blackmailing of a gentleman at Nice, and no dispute between Burton and himself about it. They might have had a little row.

Cross-examined by Mr. Grain: He admitted that he had been to Scarborough with Burton about a year ago. He went to fulfil an engagement at the Aquarium there. He did not make the acquaintance of a foreign nobleman there (Mr. Grain handed up the name), but he had heard his name mentioned by young fellows whom he got to know at Scarborough. It was for pleasure that Burton went there with him. He heard this nobleman's name by asking who was the owner of a big yacht that he saw in the bay. That man did not give Burton or him £500 or any other sum.

Mary Applegate, residing in Osnaburg Street, proved that Wilde called twice on Atkins. There was an interval of about three days between the two visits.

Sidney Mavor was next examined with reference to his relationship with Taylor and other persons, but he gave an emphatic denial to any suggestions as regarded his conduct with Wilde.

Edward Shelley, formerly in the employ of a firm of publishers in 1891, with whom Mr. Wilde had business, spoke to his knowledge of the latter. The witness was subjected to a very close cross-examination with a view of testing the truth of certain grave allegations.

Sir Edward Clarke read a number of letters written by the witness in a pleading and religious strain to Wilde, in which he said that he had had a horrible interview with his father, who had told him to leave the house, and that he was in the direst poverty, but would accept it as part of a Christian's life, although he was "sick, body, and soul, of his harsh existence." He addressed the letters, "Dear Oscar," and in one missive he said, "I can never forget your kindness, and I am conscious that I can never sufficiently express my thankfulness to you." This was after the alleged misconduct.

At this point the witness Atkins was re-called into the box. Everyone in court became on the *qui vive* of expectation, and every man asked his neighbour what the *dénouement* would be?

Sir Edward Clarke, addressing the witness Atkins, said: —

Now, I warn you. I'm going to ask you a question. Think before you reply.

Just you be careful now, put in the judge. And Wilde leant forward in his chair and seemed to drink in every word his advocate uttered.

Sir Edward went on: On June 10, 1891, you were living at Tachbrook Street, Pimlico? Yes. Was James Dennis Burton living there with you? Yes. Were you both taken by two constables, 396A and 500A — you've probably forgotten the numbers — to Rochester Row Police Station and charged with demanding money from a gentleman with menaces? I was not charged with that, murmured the young fellow in a husky voice. Were you taken to the police station? Yes. You and Burton? Yes. What were you charged with? With hitting a gentleman. In what place was it alleged you had hit him? At the card table. In your room at Tachbrook Street? Yes.

What was the gentleman's name? continued Sir Edward, after consultation with his junior, Mr. Charles Mathews. I don't know. How long had you known him? That night, and I met him at the Alhambra. Had you seen him before that time? Not to speak to. Meeting him at the Alhambra, did he go with you to Tachbrook Street? Yes, to play cards. Was Burton at home? Yes. Anyone else there? I don't think so. Was the gentleman sober? Yes. What room did you go into? Sitting-room. Who called the police? I don't know. I believe the landlady. Did the landlady give you and Burton into custody? Nobody did. Who did? I did not hear anybody. You were taken to Rochester Row, and the gentleman went with you? Yes.

P.C. 396A was here called into court in sight of Atkins.

Now I ask you in this constable's presence, continued Sir Edward, was the statement made at the police station that you and the gentleman had been in bed together? I don't think so.

You may as well tell us all about it, you know. Was that statement made? Yes, it was.

The gentleman declined to prosecute, and so you and Burton were liberated? Yes.

Sir Edward concluded. His last question brought a characteristic reply.

About two hours ago, Atkins, I asked you these very questions, and you swore upon your oath that you had not been in custody at all and had never been taken to Rochester Row. How came you to tell me those lies? I did not remember it.

Atkins looked very abashed, and yet some of his former impudence still gleamed upon his now scarlet face.

Leave the Court, said the judge, and pointed to the doorway with his pencil.

After some formal evidence the hearing was adjourned till Monday morning.

THIRD DAY

Punctually at eleven o'clock on Monday morning the trial was resumed at the Old Bailey. The two prisoners, Wilde and Taylor, were in the dock some minutes before the arrival of the judge. The counsel arrived early, and consultations were held amongst the various factions. Wilde sent two notes by the usher to Sir Edward Clarke, who read them and nodded a kind of assent to the prisoner, which seemed to greatly please him. The first witnesses of the day were:

Two shorthand writers, who produced the notes of the Queensberry trial, and the Savoy masseur, Anton Migge, went into the box and repeated the evidence he gave at Bow Street Police Court. Next followed Jane Cottar, the Savoy chambermaid. She spoke to Wilde staying at the hotel in March, 1893. At that time Wilde had two bedrooms, 361 and 362; he occupied the one and Lord Alfred Douglas the other. Wm. Harris, a police sergeant, spoke to visiting Taylor's rooms in Little College Street. The rooms were darkened, muslin across the windows, and the walls and ceiling were draped with muslin, and hung with fans and ornaments. There was no bedstead; the bed was on the floor. He, the officer, arrested Taylor, who replied, in answer to the charge, "I expected you last night."

The evidence of the prosecution at this point appeared to be drawing to a close. Inspector Richards proved the arrest of Wilde in the evening of April 5 at the Cadogan Hotel. The next day witness went and searched Taylor's rooms, and found a brooch, and seven pairs of trousers of curious make.

Inspector Brockwell proved the granting of the warrant, and Wilde being brought to Scotland Yard. Wilde wished to read the warrant, but was refused, and then asked the dates mentioned, and was told them.

When Taylor was arrested, and the warrant read to him, he said, "Is that the only charge?"

The documents found in Taylor's hat-box were then put in and read — a note from Wood in America, a few returned cheques, and some telegrams to Taylor: "Could you call at six o'clock? — OSCAR, Savoy." "Cannot manage dinner to-morrow. — OSCAR." "Obliged to see —, cannot come. What about the friend? — OSCAR." Also a New Year's card from Mavor, which ran: —

> Always a bob in you pocket to spend,
> Always a bob to lend to a friend,
> Wishing you these I add one wish more,
> A happy and prosperous '94.
> SYDNEY MAVOR.

Then followed the reading of the examination and cross-examination of Wilde in the Queensberry trial by Mr. Gill and Mr. Horace Avory. This was dreary work, and the event quickly cleared off many of the crowd which had assembled to see the concluding scenes of the famous trial. The reading was done from the shorthand notes taken during the trial, and was dry work indeed.

WILDE-TAYLOR CASE.
EVIDENCE OF THE PRISONERS.

On Mr. Justice Charles taking his seat on the bench, Mr. Gill said: My lord, I have had an opportunity of considering the indictment since the case for the prosecution was closed, and, in consultation with my friends Mr. Avory and Mr. Gill, I have come to the determination not to ask for a verdict on the counts of the indictment charging conspiracy. Of course I do that having in my mind that no evidence has been given here at all which was not directly material to the other charges.

Sir E. Clarke: Of course, if this had been done in the first instance, I should have applied that the prisoners be tried separately. My learned friend, I agree, is entitled to tell your lordship that he does not suggest that there is evidence of conspiracy. That is all he can do.

His Lordship: After the evidence was given it occurred to my own mind that the counts of conspiracy were really unnecessary.

Mr. Gill: That was the conclusion arrived at on going through the evidence.

Sir E. Clarke: It is not a matter upon which I have anything to say at the moment. Mr. Gill is entitled at any part of the case to say that he does not intend to ask the jury to say there is evidence before them on the charge of conspiracy, and I understand that to be the position?

Mr. Gill: That is not exactly the position.

Sir E. Clarke: I don't want to be pertinacious, but I wish to know what is the position, and whether he asks your lordship now to strike out these counts from the indictment.

Mr. Gill: I am taking the course of not asking for a verdict on those counts because it has been suggested that there would be a difficulty with regard to calling the prisoners by reason of these counts being in the indictment, and that I might take advantage of these counts to cross-examine upon matters outside the specific charges in the indictment. For that reason I desired to take this course to avoid any difficulty being placed in the way of either of the prisoners, Wilde or Taylor, giving evidence.

His Lordship: You are entitled to take that course, Mr. Gill, and I understand, therefore, that you do not ask the jury to give a verdict of guilty upon the counts of conspiracy.

Sir E. Clarke: Then I shall ask that the verdict of the jury of not guilty on these counts shall be at once taken.

His Lordship: I cannot assent to that course.

Sir E. Clarke: Of course, my lord, I am entitled to a verdict at some time hereafter, because the prisoners have been given in charge—

His Lordship: I think at the present stage of the trial all I can do is to say that I felt it my duty to accede to Mr. Gill's application.

Sir E. Clarke: All I say at this moment is that, at some time of the case, I shall claim that a verdict of not guilty be entered on these counts.

Sir E. Clarke, having addressed the jury, called out the name of Oscar Wilde, and the defendant stepped lightly from the dock and entered the witness-box, where his presence soon led to the overcrowding of the court.

Sir E. Clarke: Was the evidence you gave upon the libel action absolutely and in all respects true evidence? — Entirely true evidence.

You have heard the evidence given in this case. Is there any truth in any one of the allegations against you? — There is no truth whatsoever in any one of these allegations — no truth whatsoever.

Cross-examined by Mr. Gill: You said in cross-examination at the last trial that Lord Alfred Douglas had contributed two poems to the "Chameleon"; that you had read these poems, and that they were beautiful poems? — Yes.

The first was one "In Praise of Shame"?

Sir E. Clarke: I do not want to make any difficulty again, but I understood my learned friend to say that he was going to confine his cross-examination to the specific charges made here.

Mr. Gill: This is cross-examination to credit.

Mr. Justice Charles: I don't see how I can interfere. Questions which the learned counsel thinks should go to credit he is entitled to put.

Mr. Gill: Listen, Mr. Wilde. I shall only keep you a very short time in the witness-box. (Counsel proceeded to read an extract from one of the poems spoken of, and, having done so, asked:) Is that one of the beautiful poems?

Sir E. Clarke, again interposing, said: That is not Mr. Wilde's.

Mr. Gill: I am not aware that I said it was.

Sir E. Clarke: I thought you would be glad to say it was not.

The learned Judge: I understand that was a poem by Lord Alfred Douglas.

Mr. Gill: Yes, my lord, and one which the witness describes as a beautiful poem. The other beautiful poem is one that follows immediately, and precedes "The Priest and the Acolyte."

Witness: Might I be allowed—

Mr. Gill: Kindly listen to me.

Mr. Justice Charles (to the witness): You are at liberty to make any explanation you like afterwards.

Witness: I will merely say this, my lord. It is not for me to explain the work of anybody else. It does not belong to me. But the word "shame" used in that work is a word used in the sense of modesty. I mean I was anxious to point out that "shame that burns cold lips" — I forget the line exactly — "to fire" is a quickened sense of modesty.

Mr. Gill: Your view, Mr. Wilde, is that the shame mentioned there is that shame which is a sense of modesty?

Witness: That was the explanation given to me by the person who wrote it. The sonnet seems to me obscure.

During 1893 and 1894 you were a good deal in the company of Lord Alfred Douglas? — Oh, yes. He read that poem to me.

The next poem is one described as "Two Loves." Was that poem explained to you? — I think that is clear.

There is no question as to what it means? — Most certainly not.

Then what is the love described?

Witness: The "Love that dare not speak its name in this century" is such a great affection of an elder for a younger man as there was between David and Jonathan, such as Plato made the very basis of his philosophy, and such as you find in the sonnets of Michael Angelo and Shakespeare — that deep, spiritual affection that is as pure as it is perfect, and dictates great works of art like those of Shakespeare and Michael Angelo and these two letters of mine, such as they are, and which is in this century misunderstood — so misunderstood that on account of it I am placed where I am now. It is beautiful, it is fine, it is the noblest form of affection. It is intellectual, and it repeatedly exists between an elder and a younger man when the elder man has intellect and the younger man has all the joy, hope, and glamour of life. That it should be so the world does not understand. It mocks at it, and sometimes puts one into the pillory for it.

At this stage there was loud applause in the gallery of the court, and the learned judge at once said, speaking very sternly, "I shall have this court cleared if there is the slightest manifestation of feeling. There must be complete silence preserved."

Cross-examination continued: You were staying at the Savoy Hotel with Lord Alfred Douglas at the beginning of March 1893? — Yes.

And after that he went into rooms? — Yes.

I understand you to say that the evidence given in this case by the witnesses called in support of the prosecution is absolutely untrue? — Entirely.

Entirely untrue? — Yes.

Did you hear the evidence of the servant from the Savoy? — It is absolutely untrue.

Had you a little quarrel with Lord Alfred Douglas in that week? — No; we never did quarrel — perhaps a little difference. Sometimes he said things that pained me, and sometimes I said things that pained him.

Had he that week said unkind things? — I always make a point of forgetting when he ever says anything unkind.

Mr. Gill then read the letter written by the witness to Lord Alfred Douglas which was produced in the Queensberry case. Asked whether he considered it a perfectly harmless letter, Wilde replied that there was nothing in it of which he was ashamed. It was full of deep feeling and sentiment. With regard to the other letter quoted, it was more of a prose poem — a literary answer to a sonnet sent by Lord A. Douglas.

Questioned with regard to a particular part of the evidence adduced, he replied hotly: How can I answer the statements of servants two years after I left the hotel? It is childish. I have stayed at the hotel and been there constantly since.

You had the opportunity of seeing the plea of justification in the Queensberry case, and you saw the different names? — Yes.

At the hearing of that case before Mr. Justice Collins, except the hall porter of your club and yourself, no other witness was called? — No.

You had seen Taylor within a few days of the trial? — Yes.

He was not called? — No, he was subpoenaed by the other side. I knew that he was here.

And you know that while the counsel for Lord Queensberry was addressing the jury, the case was interrupted, a verdict of "Not Guilty" was agreed to, and the jury found that the justification was proved and the libel published for the public benefit? — I was not in court.

But you knew it? — No, I did not. I knew my counsel had considered it would be impossible to get a verdict on the question as far as the literature went, and it was not for me to dispute their superior wisdom. I was not in court, nor have I ever read any account of that trial.

What is there untrue in the evidence of Shelley? — I say his account of what happened is entirely untrue. It is true that he came to the Independent

Theatre with me, but it was in a box with some friends. Witness added that Shelley was in the habit of writing him morbid letters, which he tore up, and in which he said he was a great sinner and anxious to be in closer communion with religion. Proceeding, he denied emphatically that Parker had ever been to the Savoy with him. Atkins had never tried to blackmail him. He found him bright and amusing, and invited him to go to Paris because he (witness) did not care to travel alone. Atkins had given a grotesque and monstrous account of the dinner-party at the London restaurant. It was also entirely untrue that Wood ever went to Tite-street. Wood was introduced to him by Lord Alfred Douglas, and Taylor by Mr. Schwabe. He went to Taylor's rooms because he there met actors and singers of many kinds.

Mr. Gill: A curious establishment, was it not?

Sir E. Clarke: Is this on the conspiracy, my lord?

Mr. Gill: Those counts were withdrawn. This is evidence to credit.

The Judge: This evidence is relevant upon the points that remain?

Mr. Gill: Certainly, my lord. (To the witness): Did it strike you that this place was at all peculiar? — Not at all. I thought it Bohemian.

Not a sort of street you would usually visit in. You had no other friends there? — No. This was merely a bachelor's place.

Rather a rough neighbourhood? — That I don't know. I know it was near the Houses of Parliament. I went there to amuse myself by smoking cigarettes, singing, chatting, and nonsense of that kind.

Did you see a boy named Tankard at Calais? — Oh, no.

Think? Do you mean after the plea of justification was issued?

You were at Calais about that time? — Yes. I remember that I saw Tankard. That was before the plea was put in.

Tankard was employed at the Calais Hotel, and you were going abroad with Lord Alfred Douglas? — Yes.

Did you know last year of Taylor's arrest? — Oh, yes; I read it in the papers.

You know the circumstances? — Yes. I saw that the charge was dismissed by the magistrate.

That satisfied you? — What satisfied me was that I did not see on what grounds the police went there at all.

I may take it, Mr. Wilde, that you see no reason why the police should keep observation at Little College-street? — No.

With regard to your friendship towards the persons I have mentioned, may I take it, Mr. Wilde, that it was as you describe, the deep affection of an elder man to a younger? — Certainly not. One feels that once in one's life, and once only, towards anybody.

In re-examination by Sir E. Clarke, Wilde said he became aware at one time that Wood had some letters, and he communicated with Sir George Lewis.

Wood returned them? — He gave me three letters back. They were not what I would call matters of great consequence, but no one likes their private letters read. They contained some slighting allusions to other people which I should not have liked made public.

Wilde then left the witness-box, and his place was taken by the prisoner Taylor.

Examined by Mr. Grain, he stated that his father was formerly in a large way of business, which was now a limited company. He had been educated at Marlborough, and after that he went to a private tutor at Preston, near Brighton. He afterwards served in the militia, with the view of entering the army. In 1883, on attaining his majority, he came into the sum of about £45,000. He absolutely denied the allegations made against him. They were entirely untrue.

Cross-examined: When he was living at Chapel street he had been adjudicated a bankrupt. He had introduced Charles Parker to Mr. Wilde because he thought the latter might use his influence to obtain for him some work on the stage.

After the luncheon adjournment, Sir E. Clarke

addressed the jury on behalf of Wilde, and again referred to the tardy withdrawal of the charge of conspiracy.

An outburst of applause followed the conclusion of the learned counsel's speech, which had occupied two hours, but the demonstration was at once silenced.

Mr. Grain then addressed the court in the defence of Taylor. He reviewed the evidence given against him, and observed that it was a remarkable fact that with all the resources at their command and with the means of employing police and detectives, neither during the progress of the Queensberry trial nor in the period subsequent to it had the prosecution been able to obtain from any one of the numerous lodgings Taylor had occupied any evidence substantiating that which had been adduced by the principal witnesses against him. It was also a significant fact, as showing that the prisoner had no desire to avert a public investigation, that he was in attendance during the three days of the Queensberry trial, in response to the subpoena with which he had been served. As to the character of the testimony brought against him, Parker was an admitted blackmailer, and one of the most significant and remarkable incidents in this trial was that which on Saturday revealed the witness Atkins as an unscrupulous perjurer.

At considerable length Mr. Gill then replied on behalf of the Crown, and with regard to what had been said by counsel for the defence concerning the withdrawal that day of the counts alleging conspiracy against the prisoners, he maintained that the evidence which had been called was relevant to the other charges as well. He went on to deal in detail with the statements made by the witnesses on behalf of the prosecution, remarking that there was nothing to support the suggestion of Sir E. Clarke that Shelley, who had shown himself to be an absolutely respectable and trustworthy witness, was in a disordered state of mind, while as for those witnesses who had been described as blackmailers they could have had no conceivable object in bringing the accusations against the accused unless they were true in substance and fact.

The learned counsel had not concluded his address till seven o'clock, at which hour the Court adjourned until this morning, when Mr. Justice Charles will commence his summing up.

The Daily Graphic, 2 May 1895

THE CHARGES AGAINST WILDE AND TAYLOR.

DISAGREEMENT OF THE JURY.

At the Central Criminal Court, yesterday, the trial of Wilde and Taylor was resumed before Mr. Justice Charles.

The judge having summed up, the jury retired at 1.35. At three o'clock a communication was conveyed by the Clerk of Arraigns to the judge, and shortly afterwards the jury had luncheon taken into them. At 4.15 the judge sent for the Clerk of Arraigns, Mr. Avory, who proceeded to his lordship's private room. Subsequently Mr. Avory went to the jury, apparently with a communication from the judge, and returned in a few minutes to the judge's private room.

Eventually the jury returned into court at a quarter past five o'clock.

The Judge: I have received a communication from you to the effect that you are unable to arrive at an agreement. Now, is there anything you desire to ask me in reference to the case?

The Foreman: I have put that question to my fellow jurymen, my lord, and I do not think there is any doubt that we cannot agree upon three of the questions. . . .

The Judge: Is there no prospect of agreement if you retire to your room? You have not been inconvenienced; I ordered what you required, and is there no prospect that with a little more deliberation you may come to some agreement as to some of them?

The Foreman: My fellow-jurymen say there is no possibility.

The Judge: I am very unwilling to prejudice your deliberations, and I have no doubt that you have done your best to arrive at an agreement. On the other hand, I would point out to you that the inconveniences of a new trial are very great. If you thought that by deliberating for a time you could arrive at a conclusion upon any of the questions I have asked you, I would ask you to do so.

The Foreman: We considered the matter before coming into court, and I do not think there is any chance of an agreement. We have considered it again and again.

The Judge: If you tell me that I do not think I am justified in detaining you any longer.

Sir E. Clarke asked that a verdict should be given on the conspiracy counts.

Mr. Gill opposed this, but the judge said he directed the acquittal of the prisoners on the conspiracy counts that morning. He thought that was the best course to adopt; and the same remark might be made with regard to the two counts in which Taylor was charged with improper conduct towards Wood and Parker. It was unfortunate that the real and material matters which had occupied the attention of the jury for so many days were matters upon which the jury were unable to agree. Upon these matters, and upon the counts which were concerned with them, he must discharge the jury.

Sir E. Clarke thereupon applied for bail for Wilde.

Mr. Hall made the same application for Taylor.

The Judge: I don't feel able to accede to the application.

Sir E. Clarke intimated that he might renew the application.

The Judge: That should be done to the Judge in Chambers.

Mr. Gill said the case would certainly be tried again, and probably it would go to the next Sessions.

The prisoners were then taken from the dock.

The Morning, 2 May 1895

THE WILDE CASE.

It is on all grounds unfortunate that the jury should have failed to arrive at a decision upon the charges brought against Oscar Wilde and his fellow prisoner. The gravest stigma continues to attach to the two men who for five days have stood in the dock; society feels that a gross public scandal has not yet been probed to its depths; and that a great mass of loathsome evidence must once more be heard in open court. Nobody can be satisfied with such a result. Charges of the kind here involved cannot be left hanging in the air; they must be proved or disproved. That the public are entitled to ask. The truth, it is quite certain, is not yet before us; for as between the guilt and the innocence of the accused men there is no middle course such as the jury have taken. As the case stands at present either the prisoners are the victims of a terrible injustice or society has failed to obtain the satisfaction which is its due. To say that the ordeal through which these wretched men have passed is punishment enough for whatever they may have done is to assume that they are guilty, since no innocent acts, however ill-advised, can deserve the opprobrium that rests upon the objects of this abortive prosecution. We trust, therefore, that Mr. Gill speaks the mind of the Treasury in declaring that the case will be pushed to some definite issue.

Ought the prosecution to stop there? That is a very grave question. Whatever may be the truth as regards Wilde and Taylor, the evidence given at

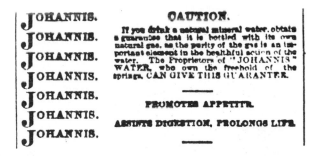

WEATHER FORECAST FOR TO-DAY

ISSUED BY THE METEOROLOGICAL OFFICE

Scotland, N.	North-westerly and westerly
Scotland, E.	breezes; fair, cold at first.
Scotland, W.	
England, N.E.	North-westerly breezes, light; fine,
England, E.	cold in early morning, milder
Midland Counties.	later.
England, S. (London and Channel).	
England, N.W. and N. Wales).	
England, S.W. (and S. Wales).	Westerly to south-westerly breezes,
Ireland, N.	light; fair, but hazy or foggy in
Ireland, S.	places.

The Morning

THURSDAY, MAY 2, 1895.

THE WILDE CASE.

It is on all grounds unfortunate that the jury should have failed to arrive at a decision upon the charges brought against Oscar Wilde and his fellow prisoner. The gravest stigma continues to attach to the two men who for five days have stood in the dock; society feels that a gross public scandal has not yet been probed to its depths; and that a great mass of loathsome evidence must once more be heard in open court. Nobody can be satisfied with such a result. Charges of the kind here involved cannot be left hanging in the air; they must be proved or disproved. That the public are entitled to ask. The truth, it is quite certain, is not yet before us; for as between the guilt and the innocence of the accused men there is no middle course such as the jury have taken. As the case stands at present either the prisoners are the victims of a terrible injustice or society has failed to obtain the satisfaction which is its due. To say that the ordeal through which these wretched men have passed is punishment enough for whatever they may have done is to assume that they are guilty, since no innocent acts, however ill-advised, can deserve the opprobrium that rests upon the objects of this abortive prosecution. We trust, therefore, that Mr. Gill speaks the mind of the Treasury in declaring that the case will be pushed to some definite issue.

Ought the prosecution to stop there? That is a very grave question. Whatever may be the truth as regards Wilde and Taylor, the evidence given at the Old Bailey seems to affect more reputations than those that have been openly impugned. What are these mysterious names written on slips of paper and passed between counsels' table, the witness-box, and the Bench? If there is a widespread canker in our midst, as the authorities seem to believe, it cannot too soon be thoroughly cauterised.

THE WALWORTH VACANCY.

Against East Leeds the Conservatives ought to be able to set off Walworth, now vacated by the death of Mr. William Saunders. The late

---

the Old Bailey seems to affect more reputations than those that have been openly impugned. What are these mysterious names written on slips of paper and passed between counsels' table, the witness-box, and the Bench? If there is a widespread canker in our midst, as the authorities seem to believe, it cannot too soon be thoroughly cauterised.

BAIL FOR OSCAR WILDE.

The question of bail for Oscar Wilde in connection with the charges still pending against him was tentatively settled yesterday. An application was made before Mr. Baron Pollock on the previous day, when his lordship expressed his willingness to accept bail, but declined at the time to fix the amount, although Mr. Charles Mathews, who appeared for Wilde, suggested that two sureties in £1,000 each would be forthcoming. Yesterday the legal representatives of both sides were present in Mr. Baron Pollock's private room, and his lordship announced that he had decided to fix the amount of bail at £5,000. The prisoner would have to give his personal security for £2,500, and two other sureties in £1,250 each. Mr. Mathews, on hearing this, intimated that there might be some difficulty in finding two sureties for the amount fixed, but said that he should have no difficulty in finding one surety for a very much larger sum. Mr. Baron Pollock replied that, in that event, another application had better be made on Monday. Detective-inspector Brockwell was present in chambers, and Mr. Humphreys, Wilde's solicitor, informed him who the sureties would in all probability be, but formal notice of this fact will have to be given at Bow-street in order that the police may make the usual inquiries. At present no application has been made on behalf of Taylor. It is said that Oscar Wilde's liberation is not likely to take place before Tuesday.

The Marquis of Queensberry met with an accident on Monday while cycling, and is now confined to his room.

THE ILLUSTRATED Police News
LAW COURTS AND WEEKLY RECORD
ESTABLISHED 1864.

No. 1628. [REGISTERED FOR CIRCULATION IN THE UNITED KINGDOM AND ABROAD.] SATURDAY, MAY 4, 1895. Price One Penny.

Closing Scene at the Old Bailey. Trial of Oscar Wilde

Oscar Wilde as a Lecturer 1882 America.

Oscar Wilde as a Prisoner 1895 Bow Street

CENTRAL CRIMINAL COURT.

The May Sessions of this Court began yesterday at the Old Bailey.

[Before Mr. JUSTICE WILLS.)

THE WILDE CASE. — The second trial of Oscar Wilde and Alfred Taylor for offences under the Criminal Law Amendment Act was proceeded with. — Sir. F. Lockwood (Solicitor-General), Mr. Sutton, Mr. Gill and Mr. Avory prosecuted; and Sir. E. Clarke, Q.C., Mr. Mathews, and Mr. Travers Humphreys defended Wilde, who surrendered to his bail; and Mr. G. P. Grain and Mr. Clarke Hall appeared for Taylor. — On the application of Sir E. Clarke the judge directed that the defendants should be tried separately, but he declined to interfere with the discretion of the prosecution by ordering Wilde to be tried first. — Sir E. Clarke intimated that at the conclusion of the case against Taylor he should apply for a postponement of the trial of Wilde until next Sessions. — Sir F. Lockwood opened the case against Taylor, and evidence having been called,

Mr. Justice Wills

Mr. Grain, in defence, said he should place his client in the witness-box, and he would give an emphatic denial of the evidence given in support of the case for the prosecution. — The case was then adjourned.

CENTRAL CRIMINAL COURT.

[Before Mr. JUSTICE WILLS.]

THE WILDE AND TAYLOR CASE. — Alfred Taylor was again placed on his trial for offences under the Criminal Law Amendment Act. — The jury, after an absence of three-quarters of an hour, returned into court with a verdict of guilty on certain of the counts as concerned the two Parkers, but said they failed to understand the counts as they affected Wilde. — By direction of Mr. Justice Wills, a verdict of not guilty was entered with regard to the latter counts, the Judge explaining that it was hardly necessary to trouble them upon questions as to which they were in doubt. The ends of justice, he remarked, would be satisfied by the verdict

Sir Frank Lockwood

Edward Clarke, May 1895

given, and sentence on Taylor would be postponed. — Sir E. Clarke, on behalf of Wilde, said the jury having for the second time disagreed with regard to this matter — Sir F. Lockwood (interposing) objected to the remarks of his learned friend, and Mr. Justice Wills said they could hardly look upon it as a disagreement, as if he had thought the matter material he should not have discharged the jury from giving a verdict. — Sir F. Lockwood said he had hesitated from assenting to the course suggested in the expectation of the use which might be made of it. — The jury were then discharged, the Judge stating that the case of Wilde would be taken to-day.

QUEENSBERRY

Has a Maul With His Son in Piccadilly.

BOTH ARRESTED

And Will Appear in a Small Ring at Marlborough-street.

The Marquis of Queensberry and his son, Lord Douglas of Hawick, met in Piccadilly yesterday evening, and fought, creating a scene which cannot be regarded otherwise than as one of the most disgraceful episodes of the unsavoury history surrounding the lamentable changes for which Oscar Wilde enters on his trial again at the the Old Bailey to-day.

The marquis was returning to his hotel in Albemarle-street from the Old Bailey, where he had sat all the afternoon waiting the verdict of Guilty declared against Wilde's ex-associate, Taylor. At the bottom of Old Bond-street, in Piccadilly, Lord Douglas of Hawick, who, with the Rev. Stewart Headlam, is a bailee for Wilde, met the marquis and accosted him with a remark which was afterwards repeated to the crowding spectators of the quarrel as follows:

"Ever since I became bail for Mr. Wilde, that man (the marquis) has persisted in sending letters to my wife. I wrote to him and told him to desist, but he has continued his persecution. I had no option but to thrash him as soon as I met him."

The father is said to have cried out that he would "Fight his son for £10,000 in any part of the country, but not in Piccadilly." Fight they did, however, and the people round, making the mistake of imagining the young man to be Lord Alfred Douglas, cheered and applauded the marquis. In the struggle the father had

HIS HAT SMASHED,

and the son one of his eyes blackened. Onlookers cheered and cried out to incite the combatants in their hateful attacks on each other, and the whole business was treated as a great joke.

It is impossible, however, to speak of the scene with levity. The noble marquis and his son were taken by the police to Vine-street Police-station, followed by a howling mob. On the way to the police-station Lord Douglas is reported to have said, "I'm Lord Douglas of Hawick, son of the Marquis of Queensberry, and that's my father."

To which the marquis replied, "That's my son, Lord Douglas of Hawick, and I'll fight him anywhere in the three kingdoms for £10,000."

Father and son were charged before the police inspector on duty with "disorderly conduct and fighting in Piccadilly, in the parish of St. George's." They were released on their own bail, to surrender for trial at the Marlborough-street Police-station this morning.

The communication sent to Lady Douglas of Hawick, which gave rise to the quarrel, is said to be a cutting from one of the weekly illustrated newspapers containing a picture of the antediluvian reptile "the Iguanodon," with the words written beneath the picture, "This is Oscar Wilde's ancestor." The marquis seems to have thought this was a good joke.

LORD QUEENSBERRY AND HIS SON.

THE AFFRAY IN PICCADILLY.

PROCEEDINGS AT THE POLICE COURT.

BOTH BOUND OVER TO KEEP THE PEACE.

When Mr. Hannay entered his court at Marlborough-street this morning the Marquis of Queensberry, with a big white old-fashioned cravat, was sitting in the counsel's pew ; and the Marquis's son, Lord Douglas of Hawick, in a fancy waistcoat, was at the solicitors' table. The Marquis immediately rose and, with the easy air of one to whom legal practice has become familiar, said he wished to make an application. " Eh ? What ? " said Mr. Hannay. " In my case," said Lord Queensberry, " and, I am sorry to say, my son, I appeal to you to take this case first, as I am extremely anxious to get down to hear another case." Mr. Hannay said, " Certainly," and the Marquis walked into the dock, where the one gleam of sunshine that got into court with the crowd lighted on his face and on the big yellow rose in his button-hole, making a fine splash of colour. Lord Douglas of Hawick walked after him, and the two carefully edged as far away from one another as the limits of their common habitation allowed. The charge against them was of fighting together and causing a disturbance in Piccadilly. Police-constable Morrow was called, and told in regulation style how at 5.10 yesterday he observed the prisoners fighting together at the corner of Old Bond-street, to the enjoyment of a large crowd. They were separated, but began fighting again ; were again separated, but once more commenced. Eventually the witness arrested the Marquis, while another constable took the son. Lord Queensberry,

DISDAINING THE ARTS OF LAWYING,

or feeling his case so strong, had no counsel. " I am defending myself," he said, and he put one or two very effective questions in cross-examination. The officer readily admitted that, as far as he saw, the son was the agressor, and that on each occasion when the fighting was recommenced, it was the son who followed the father and not the father who attacked the son. In reply to Lord Douglas of Hawick's counsel, the officer said that at Vine-street the Marquis declared his readiness to fight his son for £10,000, anywhere in the country whenever he liked. The constable, who arrested the son, told practically the same story as to the fighting and who began it. On the way to the station Lord Douglas said that his father had been writing offensive letters to his wife, and refused to desist, so that this was the only remedy he had. " Do you wish to put any questions ? " asked Mr. Hannay of Lord Queensberry. " No—no—no," said the Marquis, in fine airy Old Bailey style. Lord Douglas's counsel did, however. He did not appear so familiar with practice in the criminal courts as the Marquis—and he asked as to the challenge to fight issued at the station. The officer's version of it was that the Marquis said he was willing to fight his son for £10,000 at any place, but he did not wish to make a scene in Piccadilly. According to the inspector who took the charge, the Marquis said at the station that it was the fault of his son, who had hailed Oscar Wilde, and to-day had followed the Marquis about, and struck him in Piccadilly. The son said it was all through his father writing letters of a most improper character to his wife. Then

LORD QUEENSBERRY OPENED HIS DEFENCE.

He had come away from the Old Bailey in a cab he said, and had walked up St. James's-street into Piccadilly when he saw his son and a gentleman walking along at some little distance. The son came straight at him and struck him, knocking his hat off. " I struck him, I certainly struck him then,' said the Marquis with conviction, " but it was in self-defence." Lord Douglas's counsel next found his opening, and contrived to introduce some extraneous matter. Lord Queensberry, he said, had been writing letters of an improper character and had that very afternoon sent a telegram to Lady Douglas of Hawick upon the Taylor verdict, as follows : " Must congratulate you on verdict ; cannot do so on Percy's appearance. He looked like a dug-up corpse. Shall have Wilde to-morrow." Lord Queensberry had pursued a system of letter writing of an offensive character to both his sons, to his late wife, to Lady Douglas, and to her ladyship's family. He had been to his son's house with the object of creating a disturbance, and some time ago the annoyance had become so great that counsel had laid the letters before his worship asking for the court's interference, which was refused. All Lord Douglas did

yesterday was to ask his father to cease writing letters to his wife, whereupon his father hit him in the eye, and an assurance to that effect was all that Lord Douglas wished. Then came the witnesses. For the Marquis two shop assistants from a neighbouring establishment said the son was the aggressor. After this the Marquis wanted to make a statement about the letters to show that they were not of an improper character. Mr. Hannay, however, strongly recommended him not to. So the son's witness was called. This was Mr. Frederick Wisdom, of Harley Lodge, South Hampstead. The interesting part of his testimony was the answer he gave to the question who struck the first blow.

"IT WAS A VERY NEAR THING,"

said Mr. Wisdom, " but I should say the Marquis was just a shade the quicker "—an observation that made most people in court laugh. To the Marquis it seemed to give an added sense of dignity and virtue. Eventually the policeman arrested them both, " and that,' said the impartial Mr. Wisdom, " struck me as the best thing the policeman could do." The Marquis then made another little scene in his anxiety to repel the charge of writing improper letters to his daughter-in-law. He heard ten days ago he said that Oscar Wilde was staying in Lord Douglas's house, and for the sake of his other son he went to see that Lord Alfred was not there too. There was a scene, and it became necessary to explain to his daughter-in-law why he did not wish Wilde and Lord Alfred to be in the same house. But he never wrote any improper letters. Mr. Hannay was very judicious as usual. Nothing mattered that either side said. They were fighting in the street, and although there was a policeman at hand neither invoked him. They were, therefore, equally responsible, whichever began it, and he should bind them both over in their own bonds of £500 to keep the peace for six months. The Marquis went off gaily in a hansom amid cheers.

The Daily Graphic, 23 May 1895

CENTRAL CRIMINAL COURT.

(Before Mr. JUSTICE WILLS.)

OSCAR WILDE'S CASE. — The second trial of Oscar Wilde for offences against the Criminal Law Amendment Act was continued. — The Solicitor-General (Sir F. Lockwood, Q.C.,), Mr. Gill, and Mr. Avory prosecuted; and Sir E. Clarke, Q.C., Mr. Mathews, and Mr. Travers Humphreys defended. — A number of witnesses were called in support of the case, which was adjourned at the rising of the Court. — The Marquis of Queensberry was present in court during a part of the day.

The Daily Telegraph, 24 May 1895

CENTRAL CRIMINAL COURT — May 23.

(Before Mr. Justice Wills.)

PROSECUTION OF OSCAR WILDE.

The trial was continued for the third day of Oscar F. O'Flahertie Wills Wilde, who again surrendered to his bail to answer certain grave charges under the Criminal Law Amendment Act. The court was crowded, amongst those present being the Marquis of Queensberry and Lord Douglas of Hawick. . . .

Further evidence was called for the prosecution, with reference to the accused's proceedings at the Savoy Hotel, and in Park-Walk, Chelsea, but no new facts were disclosed. At the close of the evidence of the witnesses the Solicitor-General said he proposed to put in parts of the cross-examination of the accused in the Queensberry trial.

Sir Edward Clarke, Q.C., said he should ask leave to read the examination in chief.

His Lordship: It won't be necessary to read the whole, I hope. (Laughter.)

Sir Edward Clarke replied in the negative, and said he proposed to also put in the evidence given by the accused in the present case.

The Solicitor-General dissented.

His Lordship said he did not think the learned Solicitor-General was bound to do that.

Sir Edward Clarke: I do not say he is bound to.

After some further discussion, Sir Edward Clarke proceeded to read portions of the evidence of the accused in the Queensberry case, and this was followed by the reading by the prosecution of part of the cross-examination. This closed the case for the Crown.

Sir Edward Clarke submitted that there was no case to go to the jury upon the general counts.

In the course of a discussion as to the character of the evidence,

Mr. Justice Wills said a number of things had been put together to prove something else, which was a process which he should do his best to point out to the jury ought not to be applied to anybody. He could not help thinking, if the evidence from the hotel were true, it was very strange that nothing was done at the time.

Sir E. Clarke: That being so, I hope your lordship will relieve me from the necessity of dealing with it.

The Solicitor-General submitted that the question was entirely one of the amount of evidence, and that was a matter which must be left to the jury. There were grave reasons why the persons interested in the hotel would hesitate to create a scandal. He could not, of course, say whether that was or was not a high motive, but it was one which would evidently operate in such a matter.

Mr. Justice Wills said this matter was one of those which was just upon the line, and so nearly upon it that he thought his safer and wiser course would be to leave it to the jury; but he felt it to be so completely on the line or near the line that, if it should become necessary, he should certainly reserve the question for the Court of Criminal Appeal. The view he was inclined to take was that he should express a strong opinion to the jury that the evidence was of the slenderest kind; but he thought the responsibility must be theirs. He could not say that it was a case which he should withdraw from them. He should be only too glad if he could, but his sense of duty led him the other way.

Sir E. Clarke then submitted that, similarly, the cases of Shelley, Woods, and Parker also failed on the grounds of absence of corroboration.

Mr. Justice Wills said in the case of Shelley there was an important difference from the others. In his case there were traces of disturbed intellect and actual delusions. His manner in the box conveyed to him that the man was stamped with a peculiar exaltation, which was a common accompaniment of mental disturbance. There was mental derangement in his family, his brother being incapable for that reason of doing anything. He did not stand on the same footing as the other men, however. No one who had read his letters could say they were written for money. He did not, however, see any corroboration of Shelley's statements.

The Solicitor-General submitted, with regard to Shelley, that he was not to be treated as an accomplice; but that again was a question for the jury. That being so, however, no corroboration was necessary in order that the case might go to the jury.

Mr. Justice Wills asked what facts there were, apart from those which were uncorroborated in this case, which were not consistent with innocent conduct. It would be terrible to society at large if the asking of a young man to dine at a club or his own house was to be pressed into service as evidence of guilt.

The Solicitor-General called attention to the evidence, and submitted that there was ample corroboration. He had to impress upon his lordship, in view of the very grave importance of the case to the defendant as well as to the public at large, and having regard to the enormous difficulty which existed as to the production of direct corroboration, that although Shelley was not in the position of an accomplice, yet that his story was corroborated, and that the case ought to be left to the jury.

Sir E. Clarke said he intended not to follow his learned friend, but to keep strictly to the legal points. According to Shelley's own evidence he was an accomplice. It had been laid down over and over again that the corroboration must be as to some facts the truth or falsehood of which went to prove or disprove the offence, and this was entirely absent. The corroboration stopped at the very point where the innocence stopped.

Mr. Justice Wills said he entertained a very clear view with regard to this case, and he had arrived at the decision without hesitation. In the first place, Shelley must be treated as an accomplice. It was a rule of law that when an offence was proved by the evidence of an accomplice, there was no case to go to the jury unless the evidence of the accomplice was corroborated in some particular which rendered it highly probable that the offence was committed. He could see nothing — apart from what Shelley had himself said — in the admitted facts which was inconsistent with a perfectly honourable relationship, and the letters put in by Shelley were immensely against the notion that there was anything dishonourable between them.

Wilde in the Dock

He entertained a perfectly clear view, therefore, that it was his duty to withdraw the case of Shelley from the jury.

Sir E. Clarke next asked his lordship to take the same view in the case of Wood.

The Solicitor-General said he must enter his protest against this case, which involved the question of the consideration of the evidence being decided other than by the tribunal which had to deal with the facts, and that there was no rule of law which took from the jury the right to consider the evidence submitted. It had never yet been laid down that it was absolutely and entirely within the province of the judge. The decision upon the evidence was for the jury, subject to the direction of the judge. He submitted that in this instance there was ample corroboration.

Mr. Justice Wills said there was no doubt that the rule of practice fixedly required corroboration of the evidence of an accomplice. There could be no doubt about it. He thought the present instance was, however, one which should be left to the jury, and when he came to sum up the case he would explain why he thought so. He would rather not say more at this stage.

Sir E. Clarke: I presume your lordship will not ask me to go on now?

Mr. Justice Wills: No; to-morrow morning.

The case was again adjourned, the accused being admitted to bail.

CENTRAL CRIMINAL COURT, May 24.

(Before MR. JUSTICE WILLS.)

The trial of OSCAR WILDE, 40, author, upon an indictment charging him with unlawfully committing certain acts with Charles Parker and Alfred Wood, and with certain persons whose names were unknown, was resumed.

The Solicitor-General (Sir F. Lockwood, Q.C.), Mr. C. F. Gill, and Mr. Horace Avory appeared for the prosecution on the part of the Director of Public Prosecutions ; Sir Edward Clarke, Q.C., Mr. Charles Mathews, and Mr. Travers Humphreys defended.

SIR EDWARD CLARKE now opened the case for the defence. He said it became his duty to make some observations to the jury on what remained of the case which was deliberately launched against Mr. Wilde. He should not detain the jury long now, and he did not think it would be necessary to detain them long when he came to address them hereafter on the subject of the evidence on which the jury were asked to rely, as the area of the case was very limited. He should not discuss in detail now the evidence which had been given in the case, because that evidence was not complete. He should call Mr. Wilde into the witness-box again to state on his oath for the third time in this Court that there was no truth whatever in the accusations which were made against him, and to face for the third time in this Court, now with a new assailant, the cross-examination which might be administered to him with regard to the matters which were contained in these accusations. When he had given his evidence and had been cross-examined the evidence would be complete, and he should then have to address the jury on the evidence with which they were asked to deal. He had to deal with the remains of a case. Some weeks ago the indictment contained 25 counts, some of which were counts for conspiracy, and on which indictment there was a point reserved which could be argued if necessary. Suddenly the counts for conspiracy were withdrawn, and as to the other counts the jury were discharged because they could not agree upon a verdict. Then came this trial. When the case was more important than it was now it was not thought necessary to have a law officer of the Crown to conduct the prosecution, but it was left to the practised and competent hands of Mr. Gill. He had not to remonstrate with Mr. Gill at any point of his address. But now came down a law officer. There was a strange and an invidious distinction belonging to the law officers of the Crown—why they enjoyed it he did not know—he never availed himself of it when he was a law officer, and would not do so if it was his fate to fill that position again. It was the privilege of the Attorney-General and the Solicitor-General when they came down to prosecute that if the defendant called no witnesses at all the law officer had the last word. That was an important change. Mr. Wilde had twice given a denial to these charges, but he was kept in prison without bail contrary to practice and, as he believed, contrary to law. Broken in health as Mr. Wilde was by the anxiety of these successive trials, he might have spared him the indignity and the pain of having again to go into the witness-box, but if he did not call him he knew what the reply of the Solicitor-General would be. A further hardship was inflicted on Mr. Wilde. He (Sir Edward Clarke) made an application that these persons should be tried separately, and it was decided that they should be tried separately. He was here representing Mr. Wilde, who was the first person mentioned in the indictment, and he claimed that he should be tried first. He could not imagine any reason of logic or fairness which could be suggested for the course which was adopted of trying the other defendant first. In Taylor's case the jury were unable to agree as to the issue referring to Mr. Wilde, and were discharged without giving a verdict as to that issue. Practically this was the third time that this issue had been placed before a jury. There could be no cause for complaint against him if he felt a little soreness at the treatment which Mr. Wilde had sustained. He asked the jury to remember that it was Mr. Wilde's own action in preferring the charge of libel against the Marquis of Queensberry that had brought about this inquiry. He could not leave one observation unmade, that in the evidence given by Mr. Wilde at the hearing of the charge of libel against the Marquis of Queensberry there was only one statement which was contradicted by an independent witness, that Mr. Wilde had never been to Park-walk, and a woman had been called on the part of the prosecution who stated that she had seen a gentleman who, she said, was Mr. Wilde drive away in a hansom cab from Park-walk, and she was the only independent witness who contradicted any statement made by Mr. Wilde. He asked the jury to remember that in relation to the question with which they had to deal. What he had to say as to the character of the witnesses on whose evidence they were asked to rely were observations which he would make hereafter. He submitted that on the evidence before them the jury could not come to any other conclusion than that it was their duty to acquit Mr. Oscar Wilde.

Wilde was then called and examined by SIR EDWARD CLARKE. He said that every one of the statements which he made in his evidence given at the hearing at this Court of the charge of libel preferred by him against the Marquis of Queensberry was entirely true, and he had no qualification or alteration to make with regard to any of them. He had rooms in St. James's-place from October, 1893, to April, 1894. He took the rooms to write in, because his house was small for literary purposes, and at that time he was writing a play. He took the rooms for the purpose of writing there—entirely for the purposes of literary work. Most literary men liked to write out of their own houses. There was no truth whatsoever in the accusations made against him in the indictment.

In cross-examination by the SOLICITOR-GENERAL Wilde repeated his denial of the accusations.

Wilde was then re-examined by SIR EDWARD CLARKE.

SIR EDWARD CLARKE then addressed the jury for the defence. He commented in severe terms upon the witnesses Charles Parker and Alfred Wood. It was upon the evidence of these two men that the jury were asked to condemn Mr. Wilde. He reminded the jury that Wood and Charles Parker had shared in a sum of £400 or £500 which he contended was obtained by a man named Allen from a gentleman by blackmail. It seemed to him that if these blackmailers were to be listened to, or their word accepted before the word of Mr. Wilde, who gave a denial to their story, the profession of blackmailing might become more deadly and more dangerous than it had ever been before. Mr. Wilde knew nothing of the men's character. They were introduced to him, and it was his love of admiration that caused him to like to be in their society. The positions should be changed—it was these men who ought to be the accused and not the accusers. It was true that Charles Parker and Wood never made any charge against Mr. Wilde before the plea of justification in the libel case; but what a powerful piece of evidence that was in favour of Mr. Wilde, for if Charles Parker and Wood thought they had material for making a charge against Mr. Wilde, did the jury think they would not have made it? Did the jury think they would have remained year after year without trying to get something from him? Charles Parker and Wood made no charge against Mr. Wilde, and did not attempt to get money from him, and that circumstance was one among other cogent proofs to be found in the case that there was no truth whatever in the accusation against Mr. Wilde. He contended that there was no corroboration of the evidence of Charles Parker and Wood and that their evidence could not be relied upon, and he also urged that there was nothing to support the counts charging Mr. Wilde with committing the acts alleged with persons whose names were unknown. The jury must not act upon suspicion or prejudice, but upon an examination of the facts, and he respectfully urged that he was entitled to claim for Mr. Wilde a verdict of acquittal. If on an examination of the evidence they felt it their duty to say that the charge had not been proved, he was sure they would be glad that the brilliant promise which had been clouded by these accusations and the bright reputation which was so nearly quenched by the prejudice which a few weeks ago swept through the Press had been saved by their verdict from absolute ruin and that it had left him the distinguished man of letters and the brilliant Irishman to live among us with honour and repute, to give, in the maturity of his genius, gifts to our literature of which he had given the promise in his early youth.

There was loud applause in Court at the conclusion of Sir Edward Clarke's address.

The SOLICITOR-GENERAL then replied on the part of the prosecution and denied that the prosecution had behaved with any unfairness towards Wilde. He thought that those conducting the prosecution were quite right in thinking that a law officer should be instructed to appear for the prosecution. With regard to the right of reply which belonged to the law officers and with reference to Sir Edward Clarke's observation that he had never availed himself of that right when he was a law officer, the Solicitor-General said that his learned friend had no right to lay down a rule which could not affect others who filled that office.

The Solicitor-General had not concluded his speech when the Court rose.

The hearing of the case was adjourned until to-morrow, Wilde being admitted to the same bail.

guilty with a person unknown at another room in the same hotel.

During the recital of the verdict by the foreman, Wilde remained standing, and when the first "Guilty" was uttered, he clutched convulsively at the front rail of the dock. His face became paler than before — if that was possible — his eyes glared and twitched from an unseen excitement within, and his body practically shook with nervous protestation, whilst a soft tear found a place in his eye. At this point there is no doubt whatever that the man felt his position keenly, and his whole demeanour spoke volumes to any casual observer of human nature. Yes, Wilde was indeed affected, and at the last seemed to realise that he was in great danger of not seeing the light of freedom for some time to come.

Whilst all eyes were turned on the man in the dock, a deep silence prevailed in the court. During this silence Taylor was brought up the stairs leading from the cells into the dock. He took up his

After the trial. Scene outside the Old Bailey

position to the right of Wilde, and, folding his arms behind him, looked defiantly at the spectators and counsel in court. He did not even deem it necessary to recognise Wilde, and during the whole time Mr. Justice Wills was passing sentence he stood with folded arms in the dock, and never moved a muscle of his face. Wilde, however, placed one hand — his right — on the front of the dock, and shed many a tear down his face as the judge proceeded to utter his remorseless words. Yes, Wilde at this point was, as far as any hope for a reprieve went, "dead to all hope."

The severity of the judge's comments, together with the punishment awarded, produced a painful sensation in court. Wilde appeared to be totally unable to realise what had happened. He leaned upon the rail of the dock, and made a feeble attempt to say something, but checked himself on the touch of the warder by his side. Wilde gave one last despairing glance round the court, and submissively descended the steps leading to the cells. Among those who witnessed the final scene of the trial were the Marquis of Queensberry and Lord Alfred Douglas of Hawick, and the Rev. Stewart Headlam (Wilde's bail).

And thus passed from the light of freedom one of the most brilliant wits, epicures, and epigrammatists we have seen in England for years. That the sentence was deserved I have not the slightest doubt; but yet I cannot help feeling a kind of sorrow that a man I have admired for his cleverness has, so to speak, gone down to the grave.

Immediately after the passing of sentence, Oscar Wilde and Taylor were removed to the cells in Newgate Prison, adjoining the Central Criminal Court, pending the preparation of legal warrants authorising their detention for two years. Both men were suffering from nervousness, and betrayed their mental anxiety. From the first the two were separated, but were conveyed in the same van to Pentonville Prison, where they will serve the preliminary portion of their sentence, a period to be eventually decided by the officials of the gaol. When handed over to the governor of Pentonville the prisoners were taken separately into the reception ward. Each had to give details of his identity and religion, and submit to a medical examination, after which they passed through the hands of the prison bath-room attendant and barber. Wilde was taken first into the barber's room, which is a little compartment having at one end a washing basin with a glass about it. To the left of the basin is a rack of razors and another small glass. At the back of the room near the door is a wooden bench upon which is a hat rack used for hanging up the convicts' clothes whilst they are undergoing the operation at the hand of the prison barber, who, by the way, is, at Pentonville, a tall fine man with a beard and moustache which would be the envy of any French banker. But to return to Wilde. On Saturday he was taken to this room, and sat in a chair opposite to the basin and the glass, and a towel placed round his neck. The prison barber, who is a man well used to his work, at once commenced to crop off with a pair of scissors Oscar's renowned and ever admired — at least by Society — locks. It must have taken Mr. Wilde years to train and grow his hair as it stood early on Saturday; it took the prison barber just two minutes to cut all the locks off. When the hair was reduced to an ordinary length by the aid of a pair of scissors, the barber got to work with his cropping machine, and in less than fifteen minutes had reduced Mr. Wilde's hair to so fine a point that even a man with long nails could not get hold of it. Oscar looked a poor picture when all his locks were gone. Probably when his whiskers grow he may present a better appearance; but at the present moment he looks an awful sight, more like a well-to-do butcher who has served a sentence for fraud than the great dramatic genius of the 19th century. Once the hair was cut, Wilde was ordered to put on his arrow-marked coat, which had remained hanging on the peg by the door, and then was conducted to the bath-room, where the last vestige of his days of freedom, his cotton shirt and trousers, were removed.

Emerging from the water he found a full suit of prison clothes ready for him, from the under linen to the loose shoes and hideous Scottish cap. The clothes are of the well-known dirty drab colour, plentifully adorned with broad arrows.

On Monday morning Wilde was examined by the doctor, and if he is passed as sound and well and fit for first-class hard labour, he will be compelled to take his first month's exercise on the treadwheel; six hours daily; making an ascent of 6,000 ft; twenty minutes continuously and then five minutes' rest. The necessity for close medical examination is obvious before a man is subjected to this labour, and Wilde will be ascuited and tapped and thoroughly overhauled before the decision is made.

During the first month, while on the wheel, Wilde will sleep on the plank bed, a bare board raised a few inches above the floor and supplied with sheets — clean sheets are given to each prisoner — two rugs and a coverlet, but no mattress. His diet will be —

Cocoa and bread for breakfast at 7.30.

Dinner, at noon, one day bacon and beans, another soup, another cold Australian meat, and another brown flour suet puddings, with the last three repeated twice a week, potatoes with every meal. And —

Tea at 5.30.

After he has finished his spell on the wheel he will be put to some industrial employment, not play-writing, although it might be the most profitable to the prison department, but probably post bag making, tailoring, or merely picking of oakum. He will exercise in the open air daily for an hour, walking with the rest of his ward in Indian file, no talking being allowed.

Thus has ended a brilliant life — a life that at one time might have become as great as a Shakespeare or a Bacon, but yet a life ruined by the evil indulgence in a sphere of immorality. If the moral to be drawn from Wilde's downfall and fate only deters others from following in the same line, the law will at least be revenged and the public satisfied.

NEWS OF THE WORLD

LONDON, SUNDAY, MAY 26, 1895.

AMUSEMENTS.

HAYMARKET MR. TREE,
THEATRE. Sole Lessee and Manager.
FEDORA
EVERY EVENING, at 8.15.
Loris Ipanoff ... ... Mr. TREE.
Princess Fedora Romazoff... Mrs. PATRICK
CAMPBELL.
Countess Olga Soukareff ... Mrs. BANCROFT
(who has been specially engaged to act her original
part).

FIRST MATINEE, SATURDAY NEXT, at 2.30.
Box-office (Mr. Leverton), 10 to 5.

LYCEUM. — At 9.10 o'clock, for a
limited number of nights, A STORY OF
WATERLOO, by A. Conan Doyle, Corporal Brewster,
Mr. Irving, followed by DON QUIXOTE, by the late
W. G. Wills; Don Quixote, Mr. Irving. Preceded at
8.15 by BYGONES, by A. W. Pinero. MATINEES of
KING ARTHUR, by J. Comyns Carr, Thursday, May
30; Saturdays, June 1 and 8 (100th performance), and
Wednesday, June 5, at 2 o'clock. Mr. Irving, Miss
Genevieve Ward, and Miss Ellen Terry. NANCE
OLDFIELD, Miss Ellen Terry; and THE BELLS,
Mr. Irving, evenings of June 3, 4, 6, 7. Box-office (Mr.
J. Hurst) open 10 till 5, and during the perform-
ance. Seats also booked by letter or telegram.—
LYCEUM. 4584

ST. JAMES'S. — MR. GEORGE
ALEXANDER, Sole Lessee and Manager,
EVERY EVENING, at 9 Punctually, will be pre-
sented THE TRIUMPH OF THE PHILISTINES,
An Original Comedy in three acts, by HENRY
ARTHUR JONES. Mr. George Alexander, Messrs.
Herbert Waring, H. V. Esmond, E. M. Robson,
Ernest Hendrie, H. H. Vincent, James Welch, Arthur
Royston, Mark Paton, Duncan Tovey, Master Frank
Baker, Lady Monckton, Miss Elliott Page, Miss
Blanche Wilmot, and Miss Juliette Nesville. Pre-
ceded, at 8.15, by TOO HAPPY BY HALF, by Julian
Field. Miss Evelyn Millard, Mr. H. V. Esmond, Mr.
Arthur Royston. Doors open 8, commence 8.15;
curtain 10.45. MATINEE EVERY SATURDAY, at
3. Box-office (Mr. Arnold) open daily 10 till 5. Seats
may be booked one month in advance by letter, tele-
gram, telephone (3586). ST. JAMES'S THEATRE.

COMEDY THEATRE.— Lessee and
Manager, Mr. J. Comyns Carr.
Every Evening, at 8.30 precisely, a Comedy in
3 Acts, entitled
THE PRUDES PROGRESS,
By Jerome K. Jerome and Eden Phillpotts. Mr. Cyril
Maude, Mr. W. T. Lovell, Mr. Ernest Leicester, Mr.
Arthur Playfair, and Mr. Edward Righton; Miss Lena
Ashwell, Miss Ettie Williams, Miss Alice Mansfield,
and Miss Fanny Brough. Box-office open 10 to 5.
Special Matinee Thursday, May 30th, at 2.30.—
Manager, Mr. E. F. Bradley. 4405

News of The World, 26 May 1895

The Wilde case is over, and at last the curtain has fallen on the most horrible scandal which has disturbed social life in London for many years. The cries of "Shame!" with which the sentence pronounced by Mr. Justice Wills was received, indicate that a certain section of the public in court regarded the verdict with disfavour, and that feeling will very possibly be shared by a section of the public outside. But it is well to remember, that the jury are in a position to form the best and honest opinion. They have heard all the evidence and seen the witnesses in the box, while outsiders have only newspaper reports — necessarily containing the barest suggestion of the facts — to guide them. Yet even those who have read the reports and have taken the trouble to understand what lies between the lines, cannot but feel that Wilde and his associate — no whit more outcast and disreputable than the erstwhile apostle of aestheticism himself — have got off lightly. Society is well rid of these ghouls and their hideous practices. Wilde practically confessed his guilt at the outset, and the unclean creatures with whom he chose to herd specifically owned that the charges were true. It is at a terrible cost that society has purged itself of these loathsome importers of exotic vice, but the gain is worth the price, and it is refreshing to feel that for once, at least, justice has been done.

Translation of the end of a news item in *Le Figaro* (Paris), 26 May:

Thus ends this scandalous affair. One may be permitted a certain regret that others will not endure the same fate and that it has not been possible to carry out the big wash of dirty linen that this case has shown to be necessary.

It is difficult, however, not to feel deep sympathy for the wife and children of Wilde, who is ending his literary career in such a wretched fashion.

No sterner rebuke could well have been inflicted on some of the artistic tendencies of the time than the condemnation on Saturday of OSCAR WILDE at the Central Criminal Court. We have not the slightest intention of reviewing once more all the sordid incidents of a case which has done enough, and more than enough, to shock the conscience and outrage the moral instincts of the community. The man has now suffered the penalties of his career, and may well be allowed to pass from that platform of publicity which he loved into that limbo of disrepute and forgetfulness which is his due. The grave of contemptuous oblivion may rest on his foolish ostentation, his empty paradoxes, his insufferable posturing, his incurable vanity. Nevertheless, when we remember that he enjoyed a certain popularity among some sections of society, and, above all, when we reflect that what was smiled at as insolent braggadocio was the cover for, or at all events ended in, flagrant immorality, it is well, perhaps, that the lesson of his life should not be passed over without some insistence on the terrible warning of his fate. Young men at the Universities, clever sixth form boys at public schools, silly women who lend an ear to any chatter which is petulant and vivacious, novelists who have sought to imitate the style of paradox and unreality, poets who have lisped the language of nerveless and effeminate libertinage — these are the persons who should ponder with themselves the doctrines and the career of the man who has now to undergo the righteous sentence of the law. We speak sometimes of a school of Decadents and Aesthetes in England, although it may well be doubted whether at any time its prominent members could not have been counted on the fingers of one hand; but, quite apart from any fixed organisation or body such as may or may not exist in Paris, there has lately shown itself in London a contemporary bias of thought, an affected manner of expression and style, and a few loudly vaunted ideas which have had a limited but evil influence on all the better tendencies of art and literature. Of these the prisoner of Saturday constituted himself a representative. He set an example, so far as in him lay, to the weaker and the younger brethren; and, just because he possessed considerable intellectual powers and unbounded assurance, his fugitive success served to dazzle and bewilder those who had neither experience nor knowledge of the principles which he travestied, or of that true temple of art of which he was so unworthy an acolyte. Let us hope that his removal will serve to clear the poisoned air, and make it cleaner for all healthy and unvitiated lungs.

"Art for art's sake" — that is the original catch-word of half the folly which is talked in our midst. A falser or more foolish sentiment could not be imagined: it is demonstrably an error both on historical and psychological grounds. At the beginning of recorded annals art was clearly imitation, at the apogee of its glory it is the necessary expression of the inner moods of the personality, and in neither case can be divorced from the common life of us all. If it cannot be divorced from life, it must be subject to the same judgements, it must be related to the same ends as all our human existence; in other words it, too, must be justified by its bearing on our civilisation, and therefore cannot be exempted from ordinary moral standards. But because art is held to be an independent thing, with its own laws, its own rights, and its own sanctions, we advance to that fatal separation between it and morality which has done so much to degrade and vilify its best work and its choicest aims. Art is, of course, not the same thing as morality — for if so, a religious tract would be its characteristic product — nor yet should it be its business to be directly didactic and educational; but from life and nature, in the true sense of those words, it cannot be disjoined without lowering the one and travestying the other. Observe, however, how the mournful chain of deductions is drawn, ring by ring and link by link, from this misconceived and parodied first principle. Because KANT and LESSING and SCHILLER talked sometimes as if "l'art pour l'art" were the right axiom or postulate of aesthetics — a doctrine, by the way, which was repudiated by FICHTE and HEGEL, to say nothing of our own English RUSKIN — the modern disciple proceeds to urge that art, being non-moral, has no ethical bearing whatever, and therefore may deal frankly with the immoral. Hence has come upon us the detestable invasion of the foul and the squalid and the ugly, in what is called Realism; hence, too, in other writers, the marked preference for the unnatural, the sensual, the erotic — the suggestion of unhealthy passion, the poison of a sentimental dalliance with vice. We shall never get rid of the products unless we understand the cause; we shall never wash our hands clean of these stains unless we recognise how the waters of art have been fouled at their very source. Art, as existing solely in and for itself, art as separated from life, art as independent of moral standards, art as a cloistered thing apart dwelling in a godless temple, which we can only enter by divesting ourselves of all that has hitherto guided and civilised and elevated us, all that up till now kept us clothed and in our right minds — these are the primal errors which have to be detected and disavowed and spurned, before our literary and artistic sanity can return. And if such a reaction towards simpler ideas be called Philistinism, then let us all be Philistines, for fear of national contamination and decay.

It is the young men and maidens, the students whose zeal outruns their sobriety, the writers who yearn to show themselves unconventional and daring, who may be especially urged to review the principles on which they work and think. To be cultured is not necessarily to be in perpetual revolt; to be of "the elect" does not imperatively require one to be naked and unashamed. A man can think deeply and yet live cleanly; a woman can be free and happy and yet recognise the obligations of law. It would be absurd to insist on such elementary truths if so much pernicious nonsense from the mouths of self-elected prophets had not found its way into our current literature and our common speech. We are told that Art is the supreme object of activity, which it is not and cannot be so long as the progress of human civilisation depends on knowledge rather than emotion; we are informed that life and nature imitate Art — the modern painters, for instance, having taught the Thames to wreathe itself in mists and fogs — which would be more midsummer madness if it were not also indicative of a deep-seated perversion of the artistic instincts. Above all, we are bidden in our aesthetic judgment to worship the form alone without any regard for the content — an attitude which is just possible in sculpture and painting, and, perhaps, some kinds of poetry, but which is wholly out of the question in reference to literature as a whole. Will it be said that we take this modern "movement" too seriously, and apply to the fashion of the hour a criticism which misunderstands its essential emptiness and frivolity? In the first place, opinions and principles like those we have been examining have from time to time manifested themselves all down the course of history, generally in over-ripe civilisations wavering on the brink of decay. In the next place, they are found side by side with great intellectual brilliance, and to the youthful and inexperienced judgment they are clothed in glamour which hides the hollowness within. In our Universities there are certain sections of the undergraduate world, and sometimes even of the young tutorial world, which are captivated by the apish genius of paradox, and seem to believe that Art is eccentricity. It is to these and such as these that the story of Saturday ought to be the handwriting on the wall. Rejoice — the wise moralist would say — O young man, in thy youth; know all the wisest things that have been thought in past ages; do all the best things that can be done on the river, on the running-path, and in the cricket-field. But remember that it is far better to overtax the brain by reading, and to strain the muscles of the heart by excessive athletics, than to worship false ideals of art and life, and seek to shift the unalterable standards of right and wrong.

SPECIAL EDITION

The  Star

THE "CRICKET EXTRA" STAR IS A COMPLETE PAPER.

No. 2,264. [REGISTERED AT THE G.P.O. AS A NEWSPAPER.] LONDON, MONDAY, 27 MAY, 1895. ONE HALFPENNY.

THE WILDE CASE.

Beyond an expression of deep regret that a brilliant career should have come to so terrible an end, we have two, and only two, comments to make upon the Wilde case. The first is that if this trial had not resulted in a conviction the law relating to such offences might as well have been erased from the Statute-book. Judge and jury alike are to be congratulated upon the unflinching discharge of a grave responsibility. Our second comment is that the lesson of the trial ought not to be lost upon the headmasters, and all others who are responsible for the morals of public schools. It rests with them, more probably than with anybody else, to exorcise this pestilence.

THE FRENCH SUNDAY REST LEAGUE.

Paris, Thursday.—The French Sunday Rest League held its fifth general meeting yesterday evening. M. Léon Say, who was to have presided, was prevented from attending by a sudden indisposition. Letters were read from a number of high personages who had joined the league, and from others expressing sympathy with its objects. These included a letter from Mr. Gladstone declaring Sunday rest to be a social necessity. The Pope also sent an encouraging letter praising the objects of the league, which since its formation has made perceptible progress. At the end of the first year of its existence, 1890, its members numbered 960, in November last they had reached 3,764, and more than two hundred new members have joined during the last three months.—*Reuter.*

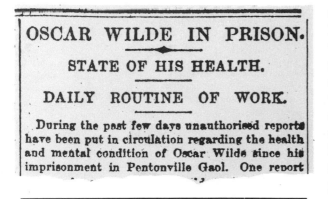

OSCAR WILDE IN PRISON.

STATE OF HIS HEALTH.

DAILY ROUTINE OF WORK.

During the past few days unauthorised reports have been put in circulation regarding the health and mental condition of Oscar Wilde since his imprisonment in Pentonville Gaol. One report

The Morning, 6 June 1895

During the past few days unauthorised reports have been put in circulation regarding the health and mental condition of Oscar Wilde since his imprisonment in Pentonville Gaol. One report went so far as to state that Wilde had been placed in a padded room on account of his having developed violent insanity. From inquiries made in official quarters by a MORNING reporter yesterday, it appears that the facts of the case are as follows:—

On the Monday morning following his conviction Wilde was conveyed to Pentonville, and, after passing through various preliminary ordeals, was handed over to the prison doctor for examination. This medical inspection is rather a long process in the case of persons condemned to hard labour. The doctor was apparently satisfied with the condition of Wilde, and passed him as "fit" for first-class hard labour — which means six hours on the tread-mill daily for the first month, and the performance of other arduous duties.

When the doctor had "passed" Wilde he was given his first dose of prison medicine. This consisted of a certain quantity of bromide of potassium, which is administered to all prisoners at stipulated intervals. In the case of a new prisoner, such as Wilde, this drug is given more frequently than to those who have served some time. For three days Wilde took his medicine without complaint, and performed his allotted task on the tread-mill. At the end of this period, however, the changed conditions of life began to tell on him, and he was suddenly taken ill. His illness commenced on the fourth day after his admittance. It was an attack of diarrhoea. This was followed by mental prostration and melancholy. For a time little was thought of his condition, as it was put down to what is known as "a prison head" — a complaint most new prisoners suffer from owing to the preliminary dose of bromide of potassium. This drug is said to produce in some people extreme melancholia. As soon as Wilde's case was diagnosed, the doctor discontinued the use of the drug, but his condition did not improve, and he was thought to be in such a bad state that he was removed to the infirmary, where he was placed in a bed surrounded by screens, and watched night and day.

The melancholia, however, continued. The doctor again examined him, and ordered him to be placed on second-class work. He gets up at six in the morning, and proceeds to clean and wash out his cell. At seven, breakfast, consisting of cocoa and bread, is served. After the meal the prisoner is given an hour's exercise, and then returns to his cell to pick oakum until 12 o'clock. Then dinner, consisting sometimes of bacon and beans, sometimes of soup, and one day a week of cold meat, is brought to him. At half-past 12 he resumes the work of oakum picking, and continues thus engaged until six o'clock, when tea is served. At seven o'clock he goes to bed.

This is now the daily routine of Wilde's life. He is compelled to pick a certain quantity of oakum per day, is not allowed to converse with any one, and, with the exception of his hour's exercise, is kept in solitary confinement in his cell. He is still suffering from a form of depression, but is said to be improving daily, although for a time his mental state gave the prison officials — who have treated him with the greatest kindness and consideration — some anxiety. With the exception of the melancholia, he has enjoyed fairly good health since his removal to Pentonville.

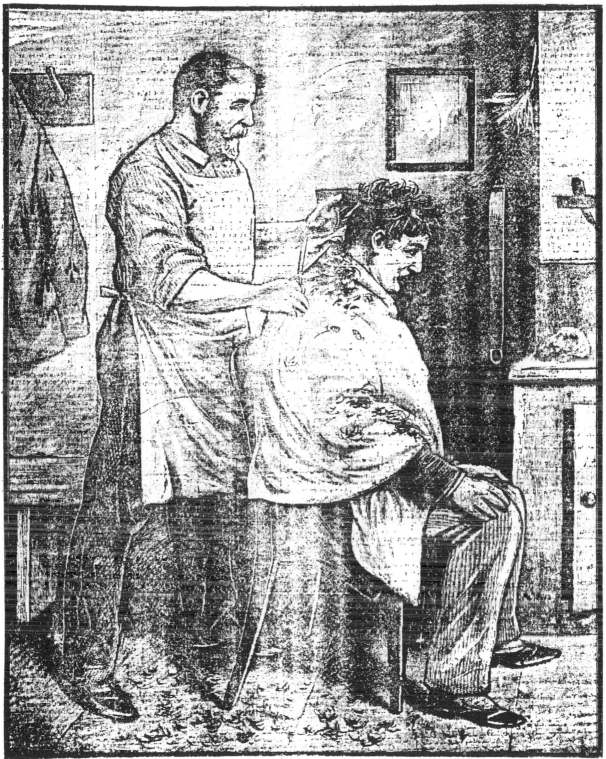

OSCAR WILDE.
THE LOCKS THAT HAVE BEEN ADMIRED AND ADMIRED BY SOCIETY, ALAS! HOW THEY HAVE FALLEN.

Extract from a letter, with enclosure, of 30 July 1895 from Lord Alfred Douglas (at 66 Boulevard François, Le Havre, France) to the Home Secretary, Sir Matthew White Ridley, Bart.:

. . . I beg you to inform me, sir, whether it is a fact, as stated in this article [in Echo de Paris], that permission was given to a gang of filthy journalists to go and gape at Mr Oscar Wilde in his prison dress while exercising in the prison yard. If it is true that permission was granted, allow me to express the opinion that whoever was responsible for the granting of that permission was guilty of an outrage against humanity and common decency, the outrage of exhibiting to a gang of sightseers the spectacle of a great poet and man of incomparable genius in the shameful dress and under the revolting conditions to which a nation of cowards and hypocrites has condemned him. If you, sir, are the person responsible for this disgusting outrage pray have no hesitation in accepting my remarks as addressed to yourself, or in requiring from me any satisfaction or explanation you may deem due to you. . . .

I have the honour to be sir

Your most obedient servant

Alfred Douglas

(Many other persons addressed letters to the Home Secretary, pleading that Wilde should be treated more humanely than were the generality of convicts, and that his sentence should be reduced; a large proportion of these missives were from women, most of whom wrote anonymously, signing themselves as, for instance, 'A Lover of Fair Play', 'An Ideal Wife', 'A Woman of No Importance'.)

On 21 June (by which time Wilde had been transferred to Wandsworth Gaol), the Marquis of Queensberry presented a bankruptcy petition against him, claiming £677 'in respect of law costs in connexion with legal proceedings instituted by the debtor'. A receiving order was made on the 25th, and four days later the Home Department granted permission to a representative of Day, Russell & Co., the Marquis's solicitors, 'to visit the Gaol, for the purpose of serving Mr Wilde with the Petition in question'. A meeting of creditors took place before the Official Receiver on 26 August. The public examination of the debtor was fixed for 24 September, then adjourned till 12 November.

The Times, 13 November 1895

The receiving order was made on July 25 last, upon the petition of the Marquis of Queensberry, who claims £677 in respect of costs in connexion with legal proceedings instituted by the debtor. The statement of affairs shows liabilities of £3,591, of which £2,514 is for money lent and £233 for tobacco, wine, jewelry, flowers, &c., while the value of the assets, which consist of royalties on published literary works and plays and a life policy, is not given. It appears that the debtor's income has averaged about £2,000 per year, which, he states, has been derived chiefly, if not entirely, from royalties on plays and literary works written by him. These include the plays, *Lady Windermere's Fan, An Ideal Husband, A Woman of No Importance, The Importance of Being Earnest*, a novel entitled "Dorian Gray," and a book of poems called "The Sphinx." The debtor ascribed his insolvency to the failure of legal proceedings taken by him against the Marquis of Queensberry, and to his conviction in the prosecution of "Regina *v*. Wilde."

The day after the public examination, Wilde was transferred to Reading Gaol.

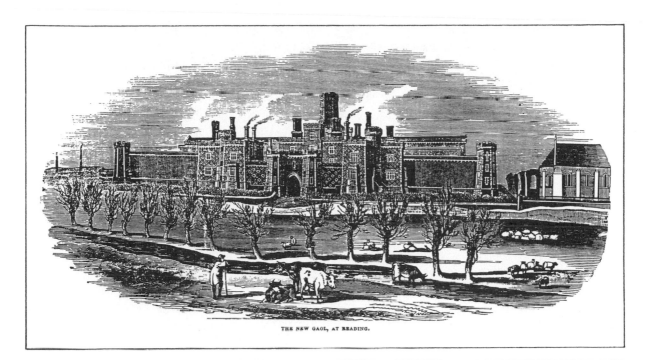

THE NEW GAOL, AT READING.

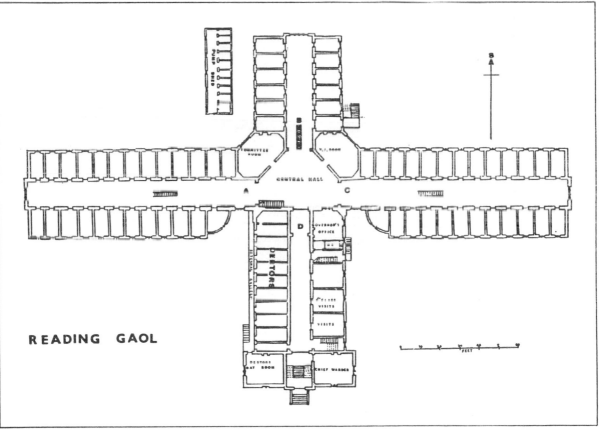

READING GAOL

Shortly after Wilde's conviction, his wife — calling herself Constance Holland — had travelled, with their sons, to the Continent. Early in September 1895, the Governor of Wandsworth Gaol rejected her written request to visit Wilde, adding that 'the prison rules will not admit of a visit for some considerable time'. On 13 September, she wrote to the Prison Commissioners, begging for relaxation of the rules: 'My husband, I have reason to know, is apprehensive of my obtaining a divorce from him within a short time. As my mind is not however definitely made up to this step but is dependent on questions which can only properly be discussed between him and me personally, I am most anxious to talk over matters with him and discuss the arrangements, business and others of an intimate nature, by which so extreme a step might be avoided.' The Commissioners allowed a visit — during which Wilde agreed to sign a deed of separation, giving Constance custody of the children, on the understanding that, following his release, she would pay him £150 a year from her private money so long as he did not live with Lord Alfred Douglas.

When, on 3 February 1896, Wilde's mother died, Constance was permitted to visit him to break the news.

Constance afterwards wrote to her brother: 'I went to Reading on Wednesday and saw poor O. They say he is quite well, but he is an absolute wreck compared with what he was.'

During his time in Wandsworth Gaol, Wilde had lost 22 pounds in weight (a fact that *The Daily Chronicle* saw as 'one among many illustrations of the way in which our prison system destroys the mind and enfeebles the body of its victims'), but by January 1896 most of the lost weight had been regained, and the Medical Officer at Reading reported that he was 'in good health both bodily and mentally, the only complaint he makes being that he has restless nights'. Seven months later, however, it was decided that there were medical grounds for allowing him writing materials in addition to those doled out to him for a rationed number of letters and for petitions to the Home Secretary, pleading for remission of sentence.

From January till March, 1897, he used most of the medicinal paper for an incredibly long and vitriolic letter to Lord Alfred Douglas, who had neither written to him nor visited him since the trial. The letter was subsequently published — eventually entire — as *De Profundis*, a title suggested by E. V. Lucas.

Lady Wilde

A well-known artist and friend of Oscar Wilde has received from that person a letter written from Paris, informing him of his release, which took place some six weeks ago, making an inquiry as to the illustrating of one of his works. The matter has been kept very secret and is known only to a few individuals. It is understood that Wilde's release some three months before his sentence of two years' imprisonment with hard labour had expired, was made on medical grounds. The secret of his freedom has, says *Reynolds's*, been well kept, and the fact that he was at large has been known only to a very few individuals.

To these, however, it caused little or no surprise, and, indeed, it has been almost expected by them for some months past. Despite the facts stated at his two trials, Wilde still retains the friendship of many persons of importance. All the influence that these —and their influence was very considerable—could bring to bear on the Home Secretary to release Wilde has been brought.

In scarcely any other case have such determined efforts been made to attain the freedom of a prisoner, and had it not been that some of Wilde's less discreet friends endeavoured to start a Press campaign in his favour, it is believed that the Home Office, whose officials were afraid of appearing to yield to popular clamour, would have thrown open the prison door to him earlier. As for Wilde's future plans, a representative of my contemporary had an interview with an intimate friend and relative of Wilde at the time of the rumour of the release last year, and is, therefore, in a position to give special information.

The person in question, who knew the brilliant Irish man of letters long before his name was sullied and his liberty taken from him, said, " Oscar Wilde's career is by no means at an end. Before his second trial, and while he was out on bail, Wilde had decided on his future plans, should he be convicted, and I may say that convicted he expected to be. These plans were decided on only after consultation and discussion with the many powerful friends on whose support the man could count, for whatever may have been his faults, that he had the gift of attracting others to him and retaining their affection and regard there can be no doubt whatever.

"According to what was settled then, it was decided that on his release he should seek an asylum that had been provided for him out of this country and live there in retirement, but only till his health and strength had been regained. So soon as that is done he will come back again and take up his residence in London. He will go on writing plays even if they are not performed, and will make such contributions as he can to periodical literature. This, I know, sounds a very bold resolve, but remember that he formed it when London was ringing with his name,

and remember, too, whatever else he may be, he is a man of plenty of courage, and one of the most remarkable personalities and greatest men of letters of the day.

"It would be useless," continued this gentleman, "for me to discuss what I have always regarded as the madness of the man. But I think the chief cause lay in the fact that he was so flattered, caressed, petted, and made much of by all he came in contact, that at last he could brook no interference whatever with his desires, and, as he said to me himself when he knew his fate was on him, ' I thought I could do what I liked.' "

It is a remarkable and striking proof of the courage it is claimed by Wilde's friends he possessed that, at the time he was out on bail awaiting his second trial, opportunities for escape were offered him which he stedfastly refused to avail himself of, despite assurance that the person who had stood bail for him would be reimbursed to that amount, and that the police would offer no objection, and although, as has been said, his mind was made up as to the result of the trial.

Were it not that the matter is one of real seriousness there is much that is supremely ludicrous in the decision come to in the Appeal Court in the action of Hawke v. Dunn. By the finding of the Court it will henceforth be an illegal thing to bet in ready money on a race course. Of course, we may still bet as much as we like " on the nod," but the passing of actual money is henceforth a heinous and punishable matter. Could anything be much more preposterous?

The publisher of the *Sun* has sent me a singularly well got-up and useful little racing and cricket-fixture guide. Its price is one penny, and it is certainly worth several.

On Saturday afternoon Mr. Ernest Pertwee will give a recital in the French Saloon, St. James's Hall. The recital begins at 3 o'clock. Tickets may be had at the usual agents, or from Mr. Ernest Pertwee, 19, Cheyne-court, Chelsea.

For the ninth season, Mr. F. R. Benson has undertaken the Shakespearian Birthday Celebration performances at Stratford-on-Avon, which will commence this year on Easter Monday, April 19, and continue for the remainder of the week.

The subject of the bestowal of honours on dramatic celebrities during the Jubilee is really attaining absurd limits. It has been suggested—and seriously, too—that a special Order should be created for rewarding histrionic merit. I do not see any necessity for this. The Order of the Push is always with us.

Contrary to the report in *Reynold's Newspaper,* and *The Pelican's* embroidery on it, Wilde was still in gaol.

On 22 April, he petitioned the Home Secretary to cut a few days from his sentence, as he was 'extremely anxious to avoid the notoriety and annoyance of newspaper interviews and descriptions on the occasion of his release, the date of which is of course well known'. The petition was refused.

RELEASE OF MR. WILDE.

REMOVED SECRETLY FROM READING TO HOLLOWAY.

HE WILL BE A FREE MAN AGAIN THIS MORNING.

The Morning, 19 May 1895

READING, Tuesday night. — Oscar Wilde is no longer an inmate of Reading Prison. Late tonight he was secretly removed to London, and will be released from Holloway Prison at 6.30 to-morrow morning. The prison commissioners were most anxious that his release should take place without any demonstration, and their precautions to prevent the press knowing the movements of Mr. Wilde seemed, on the surface, somewhat absurd. The information I gathered leads me, however, to agree with them. It seems from this that the fact that his two long years of imprisonment were at an end had had a great effect on the mind of Oscar Wilde. He is said to be perfectly rational, but yet requiring rest to rehabilitate his mental powers. Through a channel, which I need not here explain, I became acquainted with the exact plans those in authority deemed expedient to take for the secret departure from Reading of this distinguished prisoner. No one in Reading, not even the head warder, knew when Wilde would depart. Only one man was in the secret of the Commissioners — the governor — and he was as the sphinx.
Wilde, in total ignorance of his imminent removal,

retired to bed at an early hour. At 8.30 he was aroused and ordered to dress in the clothes in which he was sentenced. He did as he was bid, and, although he frequently asked of the warder, who stood by his side, the meaning of the strange order on the night before his legal release was due, he received no definite reply. When Mr. Wilde was dressed in the clothes of fashion — including the frock coat, silk hat, and patent leather boots — he was requested by his warder to come down to the main entrance to the prison. Here Mr. Wilde found a cab awaiting him, and he was received by the governor and deputy governor of the prison, and several warders. Mr. Wilde, on instruction, entered the cab and was followed by the deputy governor and one warder, both of whom were in private clothes. When the cab came out of the prison gates there was nothing to distinguish the party except the familiar face of Mr. Wilde.

Only two men outside the prison gates witnessed the transaction, the representative of an American journal and myself. The cab, on leaving the prison, proceeded to Twyford, a local station. The prison party had nearly 15 minutes to await their train, and, to avoid recognition, they retired to the waiting room. The deputy-governor, to prevent any display, left Mr. Wilde in charge of the warder in private clothes, and went to negotiate terms with the station master for a reserved second-class compartment to London. By the time this was arranged the train arrived, and Mr. Wilde was hurried to his compartment, and locked in with the deputy-governor and the warder.

I had an opportunity of observing Mr. Wilde while he was in the waiting room at Twyford. He looked very well. His build and general appearance were — as of old — distinguished and attractive. In short, Oscar Wilde of to-day is the Oscar Wilde, so far as appearance goes.

The train conveying Mr. Wilde arrived at Westbourne Park at 10.40 p.m. He was at once hurried to a cab and driven to Holloway Prison. Last night, of course, he slept there, but at 6.30 this morning he will be a free man.

Actually, Wilde was released from Pentonville Gaol (in accordance with a rule that sentences had to be ended where they began). He was met by his friend William More Adey and the Reverend Stewart Headlam (who, though he hardly knew Wilde, had gone bail for him in 1895 because he believed that the case was being prejudged), and was taken by cab to Headlam's house, 31, Upper Bedford Place, Bloomsbury. Soon after his arrival there, he was visited by his friends Ernest and Ada Leverson. Mrs Leverson, who contributed witty pieces to *Punch* and other periodicals, and who was known to Wilde as The Sphinx, afterwards recalled:

He came in, and at once he put us at our ease. He came in with the dignity of a king returning from exile. He came in talking, laughing, smoking a cigarette, with waved hair and a flower in his buttonhole, and he looked markedly better, slighter, and younger than he had two years previously. His first words were, "Sphinx, how marvellous of you to know exactly the right hat to wear at seven o'clock in the morning to meet a friend who has been away! You can't have got up, you must have sat up." He talked on lightly for some time, then wrote a letter, and sent it in a cab to a Roman Catholic Retreat, asking if he might retire there for six months. . . .

"Do you know one of the punishments that happen to people who have been 'away'? They are not allowed to read *The Daily Chronicle*! Coming along I begged to be allowed to read it in the train. 'No!' Then I suggested I might be allowed to read it upside down. This they consented to allow, and I read all the way *The Daily Chronicle* upside down, and never enjoyed it so much. It's really the only way to read newspapers."

The man returned with the letter. We all looked away while Oscar read it. They replied that they could not accept him in the Retreat at his impulse of the moment. It must be thought over for at least a year. In fact they refused him.

Then he broke down and sobbed bitterly.

That night, Wilde crossed to Dieppe, where his friends Robert Ross and Reginald Turner were awaiting him, having booked rooms for him at the Hôtel Sandwich. His luggage, a coming-out present from Turner, was marked S. M., as he had decided to adopt the alias of Sebastian Melmoth. Sir Rupert Hart-Davis has explained that Melmoth is 'the "Wandering Jew" hero of *Melmoth the Wanderer* (1820) by the Irish writer Charles Robert Maturin (1782-1824), who was Wilde's great-uncle. Robert Ross and More Adey had collaborated in an anonymous biographical introduction to a new edition of the novel in 1892, and Ross suggested this alias to Wilde. The Christian name Sebastian was probably in memory of the martyred saint.'

The hostility of English residents of Dieppe — and the suspicion of the sub-prefect of the district, who warned Wilde that any 'irregularity of conduct' would result in his expulsion, not only from the town, but also from the country — caused Wilde to move to Berneval-sur-Mer, where, after staying for a week or so at the Hôtel de la Plage, he rented a chalet.

Hôtel de la Plage

The Newbury Express, 1 July 1897

MR. OSCAR WILDE WRITES TO
A FORMER PRISONER AT READING GAOL.

We have had the opportunity of perusing the following letter written by Mr. Oscar Wilde, the poet and dramatist, to one of his former companions in Reading Prison. We append a copy of the letter, feeling sure that such a communication will prove of great interest to Reading people, showing as it does one of the commendable traits in the character of this *fin de siecle* society exponent of aestheticism:—

c/o Stoko and Hansell,
14, Gray's Inn Square, W.C.

My Dear Friend, — I send you a line to show you that I haven't forgotten you. We were old friends in gallery C3, were we not? I hope you are getting on well and in employment.

Don't, like a good little chap, get into trouble again. You would get a terrible sentence. I send you £2 just for luck. I am quite poor myself now, but I know you will accept it just as a remembrance. There is also 10s. which I wish you would give to a little dark-eyed chap who had a month in, I think, C4–14. He was in from February 6th to March 6th — a little chap from Wantage, I think, and a jolly little fellow. We were great friends. If you know him give it to him from C33.

I am in France, by the sea, and I suppose I am getting happy again. I hope so. It was a bad time for me, but there were many good fellows in Reading. Send me a line *c/o* my solicitors to my own name.

Your friend,
C33.

This letter was written to a Reading man at his home, and steps are being taken to find the former Wantage prisoner.

Wilde began writing *The Ballad of Reading Gaol* within ten days of his release, and had the uncorrected manuscript typed during the last week of August. The poem was published (as by 'C.3.3.' — Wilde's prison number) on 13 February 1898, in an edition of 800 copies at half a crown, plus thirty numbered copies printed on vellum at a guinea, by the London bookseller and publisher Leonard Smithers — described by Wilde (in a letter of 10 August 1897 to Reginald Turner) as 'usually in a large straw hat, has a blue tie delicately fastened with a diamond brooch of the impurest water — or perhaps wine, as he never touches water: it goes to his head at once. His face, clean-shaven as befits a priest who serves at the altar whose God is Literature, is wasted and pale — not with poetry, but with poets, who, he says, have wrecked his life by insisting on publishing with him. He loves first editions, especially of women: little girls are his passion. He is the most learned erotomaniac in Europe. He is also a delightful companion, and a dear friend, very kind to me.'

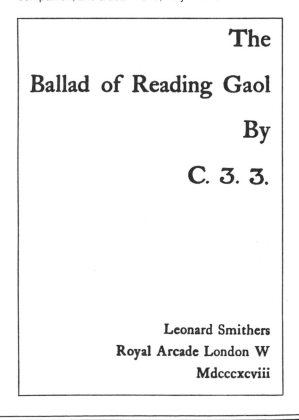

The
Ballad of Reading Gaol
By
C. 3. 3.

Leonard Smithers
Royal Arcade London W
Mdcccxcviii

From *Who He? Goodman's Dictionary of the Unknown Famous*

Oscar Wilde's poem 'The Ballad of Reading Gaol' has the following dedication:

In memoriam C.T.W.,
sometime Trooper of the Royal Horse Guards,
obit H.M. prison, Reading, Berkshire, July 7, 1896.

C.T.W. were the initials of Charles Thomas Wooldridge, who, believing his wife Ellen to be unfaithful, travelled from his barracks in Regent's Park, London, to the cottage in Arthur Road, Windsor, where Ellen was living under her maiden name, and when she tried to run away, murdered her by cutting her throat; he then gave himself up to a constable, saying, 'Take me. I have killed my wife.' The trial judge, Mr Justice Hawkins, ignored defence counsel's argument that a *crime passionel* could be treated as manslaughter rather than murder, and summed up strongly against Wooldridge. After an absence of just a couple of minutes, the jury returned a verdict of 'guilty', but asked the judge to recommend mercy. Hawkins simply pronounced the death sentence, and Wooldridge was taken to Reading Gaol, where, in the three weeks before his execution, he was seen by Oscar Wilde (prisoner C3.3):

A cricket cap was on his head,
    And his step seemed light and gay;
But I never saw a man who looked
    So wistfully at the day.

HORRIBLE TRAGEDY AT WINDSOR.
A YOUNG WOMAN'S THROAT CUT—AS ALLEGED—BY HER SOLDIER HUSBAND, AND WHO IS NOW IN CUSTODY.

Front page of 'The Illustrated Police Budget' 4 May 1896

Forgetful of his bitter comments about Lord Alfred Douglas in *De Profundis*, Wilde began corresponding with him again, calling him 'my dear boy', at the start of June 1897 — though by the 6th of that month he was telling Douglas, 'I must give up this *absurd* habit of writing to you every day.'

Late in August, they met at Rouen. A day or so later, Wilde wrote:

My own Darling Boy,

I got your telegram half an hour ago, and just send you a line to say that I feel that my only hope of again doing beautiful work in art is being with you. It was not so in the old days, but now it is different, and you can really recreate in me that energy and sense of joyous power on which art depends. Everyone is furious with me for going back to you, but they don't understand us. I feel that it is only with you that I can do anything at all. Do remake my ruined life for me, and then our friendship and love will have a different meaning to the world.

I wish that when we met at Rouen we had not parted at all. There are such wide abysses now of space and land between us. But we love each other. Goodnight, dear. Ever yours

OSCAR

In September, he and Douglas travelled to Italy: first to Naples, then to Posilippo, where Douglas had rented a villa. Learning that they were living together, Constance threatened to cut off her husband's allowance. But the intimate relationship was ended by Douglas, who decided that he had 'lost that supreme desire for his [Wilde's] society which I had before, and which made a sort of aching void when he was not with me'. He accepted his mother's offer to pay the rental of the villa, and to give Wilde £300 as the Queensberry family's share of his court costs, on condition that he, Douglas, departed for Rome. Wilde remained at the villa till the end of the year, then pottered around Italy before travelling to Paris — arriving there towards the end of February 1898, at about the time that *The Ballad of Reading Gaol* was published by Smithers. He stayed for a while at the Hôtel de Nice, then moved down the Rue des Beaux-Arts to the cheaper Hôtel d'Alsace.

Hôtel d'Alsace

Letter from Wilde to the Editor of *The Daily Chronicle*, published on 24 March under the heading

DON'T READ THIS IF YOU WANT TO BE HAPPY TODAY

Sir, I understand that the Home Secretary's Prison Reform Bill is to be read this week for the first or second time, and as your journal has been the one paper in England that has taken a real and vital interest in this important question, I hope you will allow me, as one who has had long personal experience of life in an English gaol, to point out what reforms in our present stupid and barbarous system are urgently necessary.

From a leading article that appeared in your columns about a week ago, I learn that the chief reform proposed is an increase in the number of inspectors and official visitors that are to have access to our English prisons.

Such a reform as this is entirely useless. The reason is extremely simple. The inspectors and justices of the peace that visit prisons come there for the purpose of seeing that the prison regulations are duly carried out. They come for no other purpose, nor have they any power, even if they had the desire, to alter a single clause in the regulations. No prisoner has ever had the smallest relief, or attention, or care from any of the official visitors. The visitors arrive not to help the prisoners, but to see that the rules are carried out. Their object in coming is to ensure the enforcement of a foolish and inhuman code. And, as they must have some occupation, they take very good care to do it. A prisoner who has been allowed the smallest privilege dreads the arrival of the inspectors. And on the day of any prison inspection the prison officials are more than usually brutal to the prisoners. Their object is, of course, to show the splendid discipline they maintain.

The necessary reforms are very simple. They concern the needs of the body and the needs of the mind of each unfortunate prisoner. With regard to the first, there are three permanent punishments authorised by law in English prisons:

1. Hunger.
2. Insomnia.
3. Disease.

The food supplied to prisoners is entirely inadequate. Most of it is revolting in character. All of it is insufficient. Every prisoner suffers day and night from hunger. A certain amount of food is carefully weighed out ounce by ounce for each prisoner. It is just enough to sustain, not life exactly, but existence. But one is always racked by the pain and sickness of hunger.

The result of the food — which in most cases consists of weak gruel, badly-baked bread, suet, and water — is disease in the form of incessant diarrhoea. This malady, which ultimately with most prisoners becomes a permanent disease, is a recognised institution in every prison. At Wandsworth Prison, for instance — where I was confined for two months, till I had to be carried into hospital, where I remained for another two months — the warders go round twice or three times a day with astringent medicines, which they serve out to the prisoners as a matter of course. After about a week of such treatment it is unnecessary to say the medicine produces no effect at all. The wretched prisoner is then left a prey to the most weakening, depressing, and humiliating malady that can be conceived; and if, as often happens, he fails, from physical weakness, to complete his required revolutions at the crank or the mill he is reported for idleness, and punished with the greatest severity and brutality. Nor is this all.

Nothing can be worse than the sanitary arrangements of English prisons. In old days each cell was provided with a form of latrine. These latrines have now been suppressed. They exist no longer. A small tin vessel is supplied to each prisoner instead. Three times a day a prisoner is allowed to empty his slops. But he is not allowed to have access to the prison lavatories, except during the one hour when he is at exercise. And after five o'clock in the evening he is not allowed to leave his cell under any pretence, or for any reason. A man suffering from diarrhoea is consequently placed in a position so loathsome that it is unnecessary to dwell on it, that it would be unseemly to dwell on it. The misery and tortures that prisoners go through in consequence of the revolting sanitary arrangements are quite indescribable. And the foul air of the prison cells, increased by a system of ventilation that is utterly ineffective, is so sickening and unwholesome that it is no uncommon thing for warders, when they come in the morning out of the fresh air and open and inspect each cell, to be violently sick. I have seen this myself on more than three occasions, and several of the warders have mentioned it to me as one of the disgusting things that their office entails on them.

The food supplied to prisoners should be adequate and wholesome. It should not be of such a character as to produce the incessant diarrhoea that, at first a malady, becomes a permanent disease.

The sanitary arrangements in English prisons should be entirely altered. Every prisoner should be allowed to have access to the lavatories when necessary, and to empty his slops when necessary. The present system of ventilation in each cell is utterly useless. The air comes through choked-up gratings, and through a small ventilator in the tiny barred window, which is far too small, and too badly constructed, to admit any adequate amount of fresh air. One is only allowed out of one's cell for one hour out of the twenty-four that compose the long day, and so for twenty-three hours one is breathing the foulest possible air.

With regard to the punishment of insomnia, it only exists in Chinese and English prisons. In China it is inflicted by placing the prisoner in a small bamboo cage; in England by means of a plank bed. The object of the plank bed is to produce insomnia. There is no other object in it, and it invariably succeeds. And even when one is subsequently allowed a hard mattress, as happens in the course of imprisonment, one still suffers from insomnia. For sleep, like all wholesome things, is a habit. Every prisoner who has been on a plank bed suffers from insomnia. It is a revolting and ignorant punishment.

With regard to the needs of the mind, I beg that you will allow me to say something.

The present prison system seems almost to have for its aim the wrecking and the destruction of the mental faculties. The production of insanity is, if not its object, certainly its result. That is a well ascertained fact. Its causes are obvious. Deprived of books, of all human intercourse, isolated from every humane and humanising influence, condemned to eternal silence, robbed of all intercourse with the external world, treated like an unintelligent animal, brutalised below the level of any of the brute-creation, the wretched man who is confined in an English prison can hardly escape becoming insane. I do not wish to dwell on these horrors; still less to excite any momentary sentimental interest in these matters. So I will merely, with your permission, point out what should be done.

Every prisoner should have an adequate supply of good books. At present, during the first three months of imprisonment, one is allowed no books at all, except a Bible, prayer-book, and hymn-book. After that, one is allowed one book a week. That is not merely inadequate, but the books that compose an ordinary prison library are perfectly useless. They consist chiefly of third-rate, badly-written, religious books, so-called, written apparently for children, and utterly unsuitable for children or for anyone else. Prisoners should be encouraged to read, and should have whatever books they want, and the books should be well chosen. At present the selection of books is made by the prison chaplain.

Under the present system a prisoner is only allowed to see his friends four times a year, for twenty minutes each time. This is quite wrong. A prisoner should be allowed to see his friends once a month, and for a reasonable time. The mode at present in vogue of exhibiting a prisoner to his friends should be altered. Under the present system the prisoner is either locked up in a large iron cage or in a large wooden box, with a small aperture, covered with wire netting, through which he is allowed to peer. His friends are placed in a similar cage, some three or four feet distant, and two warders stand between, to listen to, and, if they wish, stop or interrupt the conversation such as it may be. I propose that a prisoner should be allowed to see his relatives or friends in a room. The present regulations are inexpressibly revolting and harassing. A visit from our relatives or friends is to every prisoner an intensification of humiliation and mental distress. Many prisoners, rather than support such an ordeal, refuse to see their friends at all. And I cannot say I am surprised. When one sees one's solicitor, one sees him in a room with a glass door, on the other side of which stands the warder. When a man sees his wife and children, or his parents, or his friends, he should be allowed the same privilege. To be exhibited, like an ape in a cage, to people who are fond of one, and of whom one is fond, is a needless and horrible degradation.

Every prisoner should be allowed to write and receive a letter at least once a month. At present one is allowed to write only four times a year. This is quite inadequate. One of the tragedies of prison life is that it turns a man's heart to stone. The feelings of natural affection, like all other feelings, require to be fed. They die easily of inanition. A brief letter, four times a year, is not enough to keep alive the gentler and more humane affections by which ultimately the nature is kept sensitive to any fine or beautiful influences that may heal a wrecked and ruined life.

The habit of mutilating and expurgating prisoners' letters should be stopped. At present, if a prisoner in a letter makes any complaint of the prison system, that portion of his letter is cut out with a pair of scissors. If, upon the other hand, he makes any complaint when he speaks to his friends through the bars of the cage, or the aperture of the wooden box, he is brutalised by the warders, and reported for punishment every week till his next visit comes round, by which time he is expected to have learned, not wisdom, but cunning, and one always learns that. It is one of the few things that one does learn in prison. Fortunately, the other things are, in some instances, of higher import.

If I may trespass on your space for a little longer, may I say this? You suggested in your leading article that no prison chaplain should be allowed to have any care or employment outside the prison itself. But this is a matter of no moment. The prison chaplains are entirely useless. They are, as a class, well-meaning, but foolish, indeed silly, men. They are of no help to any prisoner. Once every six weeks or so a key turns in the lock of one's cell door, and the chaplain enters. One stands, of course, at attention. He asks one whether one has been reading the Bible. One answers "Yes" or "No," as the case may be. He then quotes a few texts, and goes out and locks the door. Sometimes he leaves a tract.

The officials who should not be allowed to hold any employment outside the prison, or to have any private practice, are the prison doctors. At present the prison doctors have usually, if not always, a large private practice, and hold appointments in other institutions. The consequence is that the health of the prisoners is entirely neglected, and the sanitary condition of the prison entirely overlooked. As a class I regard, and have always from my earliest youth regarded, doctors as by far the most humane profession in the community. But I must make an exception for prison doctors. They are, as far as I came across them, and from what I saw of them in hospital and elsewhere, brutal in manner, coarse in temperament, and utterly indifferent to the health of the prisoners or their comfort. If prison doctors were prohibited from private practice they would be compelled to take some interest in the health and sanitary condition of the people under their charge.

I have tried to indicate in my letter a few of the reforms necessary to our English prison system. They are simple, practical, and humane. They are, of course, only a beginning. But it is time that a beginning should be made, and it can only be started by a strong pressure of public opinion formularised in your powerful paper, and fostered by it.

But to make even these reforms effectual, much has to be done. And the first, and perhaps the most difficult task is to humanise the governors of prisons, to civilise the warders and to Christianise the chaplains. Yours etc.

AUTHOR OF "THE BALLAD OF READING GAOL"

On 7 April 1898, Constance died in Genoa, and was buried in the Protestant cemetery there.

From shortly before Christmas, Wilde travelled about Europe, most of his expenses being paid by friends. On his way from the Riviera (where he had been subsidised by the author, editor and rascal, Frank Harris) to Gland, in Switzerland (where he would stay with a neurotic young man named Harold Mellor who had been left wealthy by the death of his father, a Bolton mill-owner), he stopped at Genoa to see Constance's grave:

It is very pretty — a marble cross with dark ivy-leaves inlaid in a good pattern. The cemetery is a garden at the foot of the lovely hills that climb into the mountains that girdle Genoa. It was very tragic seeing her name carved on a tomb — her surname, my name, not mentioned of course — just 'Constance Mary, daughter of Horace Lloyd, QC' and a verse from *Revelations*. I bought some flowers. I was deeply affected — with a sense, also, of the uselessness of all regrets. Nothing could have been otherwise, and Life is a very terrible thing.

Returning to Paris in the late spring of 1899, he spoke of literary intentions, but never fulfilled them. them.

The Times, 1 February 1900

OBITUARY.

The death of Lord Queensberry, which occurred last night in London, removes a curious figure from the social world. The late peer represented a type of aristocracy which is less common in our time than it was a century ago—the type which is associated in the public mind with a life of idleness and indulgence rather than with the useful aims which such a man as the late Duke of Westminster set steadfastly before him. The eighth Marquis of Queensberry was in many ways a man of strong character, but unfortunately also of ill-balanced mind, and he never turned to any account either his talents or the powers which his position gave him. For his failure to do so he was perhaps not altogether to blame. The title he bore still has associations clinging to it from the days of the fourth Duke of Queensberry, whose personality is preserved to us in the memoirs of the 18th and early 19th centuries. For more than half a century "Old Q.," as he was called,

was notorious for his follies and wildness. He began to be noted for his escapades before he left school. At 70 he was still a "polished, sin-worn fragment," and the picture of him that lives in the mind of posterity is that of a worn-out *roué*,

"Ogling and hobbling down St. James's-street."

It cannot be said that the eighth marquis, his kinsman, did anything to bring the title into better repute. Born in 1844, he succeeded his father at the age of 14. The seventh marquis was killed by an accidental discharge of his gun while he was shooting, and by a sad coincidence the same manner of death befell the late peer's heir, Lord Drumlanrig, a popular young nobleman, who had been a Lord-in-Waiting to the Queen and had acted as assistant private secretary to Lord Rosebery when he was Foreign Secretary in Mr. Gladstone's 1892 Ministry. Shortly before his death, Lord Drumlanrig had been created, for purposes of official convenience, Lord Kelhead, so that he was able to sit in the House of Lords with his chief. A curious feature of the situation thus brought about was that the son became a peer of the United Kingdom with a seat in the Upper House, while the father was only a Scottish peer and had no seat. He had sat from 1872 until 1880 as a representative peer for Scotland, but in the latter year he was not re-elected.

Lord Queensberry was an undoubted authority on one thing, and that one thing was boxing. The Queensberry rules, which govern the contests of the prize-ring, will keep his fame alive at any rate amongst pugilists and amateurs of the "noble art." Of his career there is little to be said. He served in the Navy for a time, and he held a commission in the Dumfriesshire Volunteers. Except in these capacities he came little before the public, save when his eccentricities were subjects of nine-day wonder for all the gossips of the town. As an instance may be mentioned his demonstration at a performance of Tennyson's drama, *The Promise of May*, at the Globe Theatre in 1882. At a certain point in the play Lord Queensberry rose in the stalls and protested, in the name of Free Thought, against the manner in which the poet had drawn the character of a freethinker, denouncing it as "an abominable caricature." He was at this time a strong supporter of Mr. Bradlaugh and other militant apostles of Atheism. Lord Queensberry's intervention in a scandalous case which disturbed society some years ago will probably be within most people's recollection. The action he then took was dictated by the fact that the name of his son, Lord Alfred Douglas, was connected with the proceedings, which eventually brought the affair into a criminal Court.

Lord Douglas of Hawick, who now becomes marquis, was born in 1868. He is married to a daughter of the Rev. Thomas Walters, vicar of Boyton, Launceston, and has two sons and a daughter.

Wilde, in a letter to Robert Ross, 22 February 1900:

Bosie is over here with his brother. They are in deep mourning and the highest spirits.

In October, Wilde underwent an operation on his ear, which seems to have been injured while he was in prison. Before he left the hospital, the doctors warned him that he would not live more than a few months unless he gave up drinking absinthe

---

The Times, 1 December 1900

OBITUARY.

A Reuter telegram from Paris states that OSCAR WILDE died there yesterday afternoon from meningitis. The melancholy end to a career which once promised so well is stated to have come in an obscure hotel of the Latin Quarter. Here the once brilliant man of letters was living, exiled from his country and from the society of his countrymen. The verdict that a jury passed upon his conduct at the Old Bailey in May, 1895, destroyed for ever his reputation, and condemned him to ignoble obscurity for the remainder of his days. When he had served his sentence of two years' imprisonment, he was broken in health as well as bankrupt in fame and fortune. Death has soon ended what must have been a life of wretchedness and unavailing regret. Wilde was the son of the late Sir William Wilde, an eminent Irish surgeon. His mother was a graceful writer, both in prose and verse. He had a brilliant career at Oxford, where he took a first-class both in classical moderations and in *Lit. Hum.*, and also won the Newdigate Prize for English verse for a poem on Ravenna. Even before he left the University in 1878 Wilde had become known as one of the most affected of the professors of the æsthetic craze and for several years it was as the typical æsthete that he kept himself before the notice of the public. At the same time he was a man of far greater originality and power of mind than many of the apostles of æstheticism. As his Oxford career showed, he had undoubted talents in many directions, talents which might have been brought to fruition had it not been for his craving after notoriety. He was known as a poet of graceful diction ; as an essayist of wit and distinction ; later on as a playwright of skill and subtle humour. A novel of his, " The Picture of Dorian Gray," attracted much attention, and his sayings passed from mouth to mouth as those of one of the professed wits of the age. When he became a dramatist his plays had all the characteristics of his conversation. His first piece, *Lady Windermere's Fan*, was produced in 1892. *A Woman of no Importance* followed in 1893. *An Ideal Husband* and *The Importance of Being Earnest* were both running at the time of their author's disappearance from English life. All these pieces had the same qualities—a paradoxical humour and a perverted outlook on life being the most prominent. They were packed with witty sayings, and the author's cleverness gave him at once a position in the dramatic world. The revelations of the criminal trial in 1895 naturally made them impossible for some years. Recently, however, one of them was revived, though not at a West-end theatre. After his release in 1897, Wilde published " The Ballad of Reading Gaol," a poem of considerable but unequal power. He also appeared in print as a critic of our prison system, against the results of which he entered a passionate protest. For the last three years he has lived abroad. It is stated on the authority of the *Dublin Evening Mail* that he was recently received into the Roman Catholic Church. Mrs. Oscar Wilde died not long ago, leaving two children.

Wilde's death was ascribed to an intercranial complication of middle-ear disease. Naturally, he left a selection of Last Words: among them, 'It's the wallpaper or me — one of us has to go.' Lord Alfred Douglas was among the mourners at the funeral in the cemetery at Bagneux.

Oscar and Bosie

151

AFTERWORDS

Charles Brookfield died, aged 56, on 20 October 1913. *The Times* obituarist, while making no reference to Brookfield's role in bringing about the downfall of Oscar Wilde, noted that 'he was the author of a skit on *I Pagliacci*, which he entitled *A Pal o' Archie's*, of the libretto of *The Grand Duchess*, of *The Cuckoo*, and of other plays, in which Mr. Charles Hawtrey appeared. Among these plays was one which achieved an unenviable reputation. *Dear Old Charlie*, an adaptation from the French, was mentioned more than once before the Royal Commission on Stage Plays (Censorship) of 1909 as a play which ought not to have been licensed for performance. Surprise was expressed, therefore, when in November, 1911, it was announced that one of Lord Spencer's last acts as Lord Chamberlain was the appointment of his old Cambridge friend, the author of *Dear Old Charlie*, to the post of Examiner of Plays, to act in conjunction with the holder of the office, Mr. G. A. Redford. Protests were raised in various quarters against the selection for the office of the author of a play which was itself open to criticism on the ground of impropriety, but they were unavailing. . . . When the new Examiner took up his duties at the beginning of 1912 (Mr. Redford having meanwhile resigned) his activity in protecting the public from contamination was quickly and sharply felt. By a curious coincidence, for which Mr. Brookfield was not, of course, responsible, his play *Dear Old Charlie* was revived within a few weeks of his taking up his duties.'

The Times, 21 March 1945

LORD ALFRED DOUGLAS

A POET OF DISTINCTION

Lord Alfred Douglas, who died at Old Monks Farm, Lancing, Sussex, early yesterday morning, was a poet of much more than ordinary merit.

A formalist of the most rigid kind, who would allow himself no liberties of form or expression, he sought through the restrictions he imposed upon himself to create the beauty for which he sought. Only in his satirical vein did he attempt poems of any length, but in both his sonnets and his lyrics he showed himself capable of excellent and sometimes exquisite verse. His poetic writing was, however, one of the few brilliant gleams in a life which continued to be overcast by the storms of his own temperament and the shadow of a distant episode which he suffered to darken almost the whole of it.

Lord Alfred Bruce Douglas was born on October 22, 1870, the third son of the eighth Marquess of Queensberry by his marriage with Sybil, younger daughter of the late Alfred Montgomery. He went to school at Winchester, where, as he once wrote, he found "an earthly paradise," and to Magdalen College, Oxford. In his younger days he was as much interested in sport, and particularly in racing, as he was in letters. Well born, handsome and brilliant, he might well have looked forward to a great career in the London of the early 1890s. There, however, he became known as the close friend of Oscar Wilde, and a member of his circle. Douglas was captivated by Wilde's wit, audacity, and power of finding "under the common thing the hidden grace," though he has himself explained that one of Wilde's attractions for him was that he was "a supreme consoler."

In 1895 Wilde was proved to have transgressed the criminal law and was sent for two years to gaol. To have been identified with the fallen playwright was naturally a misfortune for a young man on the threshold of life; but the world would doubtless have forgotten soon enough if Douglas had permitted it to do so. Unhappily for himself, however, he persisted in believing that his fellow-men bore enmity against him, and therefore fell to arguing, quite unnecessarily, that pictures drawn of him in the insignificant writings of certain friends of Wilde's did not resemble him. Thus in his autobiography which he published in 1929 he wasted a notable talent upon an episode which by then was scarcely known except by historical reference to the younger generation and was remembered with but little interest by the great majority of his own contemporaries. In his " Without Apology " of 1938 and in his " Oscar Wilde; A Summing Up " of 1940, although in the latter book particularly he wrote with candour and generosity, he returned to the subject of his former friend as if unable to escape the hauntings of the past.

The Wilde scandal not only embittered Douglas's life but may well have helped to warp his nature. Thus he became quarrelsome and almost fiercely litigious. His invocation of the law of libel, and collisions with it; his imprisonment for a libel on Mr. Churchill in 1923; his domestic and financial troubles; and the newspaper controversies in which he indulged from time to time may now, however, be left without injustice to him in an undisturbed oblivion.

Douglas's first book of poetry was " The City of the Soul," published when he was 29 years old. In his schooldays he had shown in light and comic verse the sense of nicety of form that gives durability to his nonsense poems, in " Tales with a Twist." " The Placid Pug," and the others. It was natural, and no occasion for complaint, that the serious poems of his young manhood should show the influence of his models, among whom Rossetti and Dowson were the most easy to detect. In " The City of the Soul " there is less soul than city—and a dainty and gracious city it is. A quarter of a century later the sonnet-sequence, " In Excelsis " (1924), shows the soul full grown, and the poet secure in the sincerity that was the second of his two tests for poetry. In prison Oscar Wilde had written " De Profundis." In prison Alfred Douglas wrote " In Excelsis." The contrast was intentional, no doubt; but the sincerity of the poems is proved by the innocent outbursts of the old Adam in flashes of arrogance, anti-Semitic and the like. He may have been over-sanguine, but it is abundantly evident that he had set his feet on the highway of self-surrender and had travelled far along it towards spiritual maturity. The minutely elaborated execution does not always strike the full chord of the meaning. A graver cause for disappointment lies not in these sonnets but in the poetry that followed them. Never again did Douglas fill his mould so richly with the fruits of his highest and most arduous thought. For delicate and subtle moods and feelings he always had the perfect word. " In Excelsis " suggests that great poetry was within his reach, and he did not take and master it.

For all that, he has left much more than elegant fancies and fragrance. His conversion to the Church of Rome in 1911 gave his mind stability and substance. With that background and support he could relax his distrust of " art for art's sake," a distrust always rather moral than intellectual, the dread of disorder and licence in life and conduct. It was not, he came to think, a fatal complaint. Oscar Wilde was infected with it, yet he wrote " one really great and sincere poem, ' The Ballad of Reading Gaol,' which is an answer to, and an implicit repudiation of, his own heresy." Thus Douglas, addressing the Royal Society of Literature in 1943, disclaimed some of his earlier strictness. But there must be no relaxation of the rules of poetic form. To take him literally would be to condemn half the lines in English poetry as irregular; and he intended to be taken literally. This impossible correctness he not only prescribed, he also practised it. He was happiest within the most rigid limits that he could impose upon the most strict of forms—the Petrarchan sonnet; and the power of his poetic faculty can best be measured by the variety and vitality of the beauty that he breathed into each frame. Thus he kept his poetry too small in volume for his powers, but as pure in form as he could have desired. His sonnets are too far from the modern development—or decay, as he believed it—of poetry to be in many hands and heads in this age; but they have won and will go on winning ardent admiration from a few.

In 1902 Lord Alfred Douglas married Olive Eleanor, daughter of Colonel F. H. Custance, C.B., late Grenadier Guards, a marriage chequered, as the public came to know, by the unhappiness which dogged him. By it he had one son. Lady Alfred Douglas died in February, 1944.

153

CHANCERY DIVISION
NO INTERLOCUTORY RELIEF
WARWICK FILM PRODUCTIONS LTD. AND ANOTHER v. EISINGER AND OTHERS

Before Mr. Justice Danckwerts

His Lordship refused to grant an interim injunction on the application of Warwick Film Productions Ltd. and William Hodge & Co. Ltd. to restrain Joseph Eisinger, script writer, of Belgrave Square, Robert Goldstein, of Soho Square, Gregory Ratoff, producer, of the May Fair Hotel, Berkeley Street, and Vantage Films Ltd. from infringing the plaintiffs' copyright in a literary work entitled *The Trials of Oscar Wilde* and written by H. Montgomery Hyde, and the first plantiffs' copyright in a literary work entitled *Oscar Wilde: Three Times Tried* and written by Christopher Millard.

Mr. Guy Aldous, Q.C., and Mr. Douglas Falconer appeared for the plantiffs; Sir Andrew Clark, Q.C., Mr. Michael Stranders, Q.C., Mr. J. N. B. Penny, and Mr. Patrick Neill for the defendants.

JUDGMENT

His Lordship said that both film companies were producing films based on the misfortunes of Oscar Wilde, and the object of the application was to prevent the defendants from exhibiting their film, entitled *The Story of Oscar Wilde*, until after the hearing of the action. Both films were produced from the book published in 1948 by Mr. Montgomery Hyde, the second plaintiff company having granted a licence of the copyright in it to the first plaintiff company. It appeared that a large part of this book was made up, with permission, from a book published in 1912 entitled *Oscar Wilde: Three Times Tried*, which contained verbatim notes of the trials. It appeared that there was no verbatim note of the trials in existence. It was admitted that the defendants had copied some 30 pages of Mr. Hyde's book. The earlier book had been published by the Ferrystone Press and had been anonymous, but it was now said that it was written by a Mr. Christopher Millard who died in 1927. Thus the copyright in the 30 pages would belong to the person who owned the copyright in the earlier book. At a later stage, in April, 1960, the plaintiffs had obtained an assignment of the copyright from the surviving executor of Mr. Millard. It was not clearly established that Mr. Millard was the actual author or the owner of the copyright. The position under the law of copyright was very complicated and was impossible to resolve until the facts were fully known. There was not much to choose between the moral conduct of the parties in a matter of cut-throat competition. Great damage would be caused to Vantage Films, Ltd. if they were prevented from showing their film. If Warwick Film Productions, Ltd. succeeded in their action heavy damages would follow. Having regard to these considerations this was not a case in which to grant interlocutory relief.

Solicitors.—Messrs. Hall, Brydon; Messrs. Goodman, Derrick & Co.

ROBERT MORLEY'S OSCAR WILDE

FILM OF COMPASSION

FROM OUR FILM CRITIC

A critic the other day classed Oscar Wilde with T. E. Lawrence. the Emperor Tiberius, Mary Tudor and Mr. Gladstone as belonging to that fascinating category of the human race " of which the chief characteristic is that what is popularly said about them is almost always false ". Certainly Wilde's features, good-looking in their heavy kind of way, have been blown out to grotesque and horrifying proportions by legend and the Wilde who wrote the fairy stories and the Wilde who was an enchanting conversationalist, not least

because of his consideration to others, are often totally obscured.

For many reasons, some more creditable than others, Wilde is an obvious subject for a film, and, with that astonishing perverseness which sometimes bedevils the film industry—did it not once produce two *Anastasias* on the same day—two companies took it into their heads to make films of him at the same time—poor Wilde, the subject of tragic litigation in his life, has not escaped it in death. The *Oscar Wilde*, which was shown privately yesterday and which goes to the Carlton Cinema on Sunday, is directed by Mr. Gregory Ratoff. It has Mr. Robert Morley as the central figure and so, rightaway, the outlines of the portrait are there and some of the colour is off the brush and on to the canvas. This Wilde should not lack a florid orotundity of voice and manner, and in the event he does not, but Mr. Morley is not concerned with superficial exaggerations. This Oscar Wilde certainly speaks at times with theatrical relish, but only so far as it is in character. Here is a man who was a poet, in whom the teller of fairy tales and the talker of genius are allowed their parts, who was capable of suffering and so suffered, and whose rise, decline and fall have the classic line of destiny.

Wilde is here presented as one who finds himself used as a weapon in a fanatically bitter family feud and who, worn down with exhaustion and disillusion, finds himself at the most critical moment of his life bereft of free will and initiative, as incapable of evading consequences as a character in one of his own plays.

There may be a hint of sentimentality here, but at least Wilde's pathetic condition is seen as deriving directly from his ordeal in the witness-box. It is here that the film is at its most impressive, with Mr. Morley wilting and seeming actually to change physical shape as Sir Ralph Richardson, as Carson, presses him to the point where he, Wilde, makes his slip, his unconscious, frivolous, and disastrous mistake. Sir Ralph may not resemble Carson, but he gives a remarkable performance, a matter of brain and intellect, in which every move is thought out, each gesture weighted with significance. Mr. Alexander Knox endows Sir Edward Clarke with the right shades of doubt and anxiety, but Mr. Dennis Price is somewhat too sympathetic as Ross. Mr. John Neville, in contrast to the general flow of the film, seems unhappy as Lord Alfred Douglas, and the part, difficult enough in all conscience, is one that never comes to life. Mr. Edward Chapman has another thankless task, that of presenting the Marquess of Queensberry, and here again nature seems to much for art. An over pedantic finger could point to an occasional lapse in historic fact, but the spirit of the film as a whole is compassionate—and that, perhaps, is what matters most.

Twenty-four years before, Robert Morley had appeared as Wilde in an unlicensed production of a play, *Oscar Wilde*, by Leslie and Sewell Stokes, at the Gate Theatre, London.

ANOTHER FILM ABOUT WILDE

MR. PETER FINCH'S TURN

FROM OUR FILM CRITIC

Comparisons may be odious, but they are on occasions unavoidable, and it is impossible to discuss *The Trials of Oscar Wilde*, which was shown privately yesterday at Studio One, without reference to the *Oscar Wilde* which is now at the Carlton Cinema and which was reviewed in these columns on Friday.

It is not necessary to see the films as contestants in a boxing match, to award points or to proclaim a knock-out. There need not be either a triumphant victor or a pathetic loser, but, between the black-and-white of the Carlton representative and the Technirama and Technicolor of the film seen yesterday there are contrasts that insist on investigation.

In *Wilde* Mr. Robert Morley had a part made to his style and physical presence; Mr. Peter Finch, on the other hand, has artificially to create, to go about a work of conscious and, it may be guessed, exacting adjustments. He gets a surprising amount of force and muscle into the role; this is a Wilde who dominates the screen in a manner that convincingly suggests he may likewise have dominated his particular territory in late Victorian society. He has the advantage of having in the Lord Alfred Douglas of Mr. John Fraser a partner who gives more than he gets—in the relationship between them there is an hysteria which rings true because of its very exaggerations. Lord Alfred is insatiable in his demands on Wilde as on life, and Mr. Finch is at his most imposing when he shows Wilde's tired resignation in the face of an imperious personality which proves too much for him. Mr. Lionel Jeffries joins in these scenes with a rendering of the Marquess of Queensberry compounded of baleful egotism and unreason, and altogether this part of the tragic story is put over by the cast, the script and the director, Mr. Ken Hughes, with power and success.

Mr. James Mason, as Carson, assumes an Irish accent, but his performance is not the equal of that of Sir Ralph Richardson and so the court sequences lose something of the dramatic force they had in the

smaller, shorter film. They are, nevertheless, impressive enough in their own right, and perhaps the time has come to put an end to comparisons. *The Trials of Oscar Wilde* reaches out in colour to catch the atmosphere of the period and on occasions, as in the Café Royal scenes, it does so admirably. The extensions it allows itself serve another purpose, that of giving Mr. Finch elbow-room, but it was a mistake to introduce that momentary glimpse of Bernard Shaw. It lasts for only a fraction of time, but it throws the film off balance and raises doubts which otherwise might not have intruded. Mr. Finch, however, and the film survive, and credit must go to a tactful and restrained performance by Miss Yvonne Mitchell as Constance.

John Fraser as Lord Alfred Douglas

Top: Robert Morley in the Gate Theatre production of *Oscar Wilde,* September 1936
Above: Micheál Mac Liammóir in *The Importance of Being Oscar*

Wilde's remains were taken to the cemetery of Père Lachaise, Paris, in 1909, and subsequently covered by a monument by Epstein.

The monument bears Wilde's own words:

> *And alien tears will fill for him*
> *Pity's long-broken urn*
> *For his mourners will be outcast men,*
> *And outcasts always mourn.*